Heart of the Cross

Heart of the Cross

A Postcolonial Christology

Wonhee Anne Joh

Westminster John Knox Press
LOUISVILLE • LONDON

© 2006 Wonhee Anne Joh

Book design by Sharon Adams
Cover design by Night and Day Design

First edition
Published by Westminster John Knox Press
Louisville, Kentucky

This book is printed on acid-free paper that meets the American National Standards Institute Z39.48 standard. ♾

PRINTED IN THE UNITED STATES OF AMERICA

06 07 08 09 10 11 12 13 14 15—10 9 8 7 6 5 4 3 2 1

Library of Congress Cataloging-in-Publication Data is on file at the Library of Congress, Washington, D.C.

ISBN-13: 978-0-664-23063-0
ISBN-10: 0-664-23063-6

For my parents, Charles and Young . . .
and always for Joshua and Alex

Contents

Acknowledgments

It is always difficult to discern exactly where and when one began one's theological journey. Mapping my own journey seems daunting because the routes I traveled have been convoluted and nonlinear. But, I do know that my thoughts did not generate *ex nihilo*! My theological reflections in these pages benefited from numerous conversations and multiple contexts over the years. Some I am able to recollect clearly, and some have become hazy in my memory. Nonetheless, I am aware that the complex layers of different constellations of mentors, friends, colleagues, and family have all contributed to my theological reflection. So, taking a deep breath, I would like to offer my appreciation to the following people.

My deepest respect, admiration, and gratitude to my mentor, sister, friend, and teacher, Catherine Keller, for making this project possible in so many ways that only my heart knows but balks at using inadequate words to express them. It has been and always will be my honor and privilege to have learned so much from you.

My abiding respect and gratitude to pioneer Asian American feminist theologian Rita Nakashima Brock, for her groundbreaking work in feminist Christology, which was an impetus for beginning my "formal" theological journey. Thank you.

I could not have made it this far without the mentorship, support, and encouragement of many other scholars. They have at one time or another heard or read various versions of my work and offered the gift of their critical readings. They have challenged and stretched the limits of my critical theopolitical reflection and imagination in significant ways. They have also provided me with food, music, and poetry for the soul and the body on many occasions. Here I want to specifically thank Kwok Pui-lan, Fumitaka Matsuoka, Andrew Sung

Park, Aristotle Papanikolaou, Seung-Ai Yang, Letty Russell, Otto Maduro, David Kwang-sun Suh, Jung Ha Kim, Su Yon Pak, Henry Rietz, Frank Yamada, Kathy Talvacchia, Hyun Ju Bae, Jane Iwamura, Marion Grau, Mayra Rivera, Jean Hee Kim, Sigridur Gottmarsdottir, Grace Kim, Nami Kim, Trish Sheffield, and Michael Nausner. I have benefited tremendously from their passionate and keen theological insights, but most importantly their friendship and collegiality continue to sustain and nurture my work. I have come to recognize that theological reflection is always and cannot help but be a communal process. Thank you.

I'd like also to thank my sisters who walked the journey with me through the valleys of both bitterness and sweetness at different times. From the bottom of my heart, for holding me up through thick and thin, I offer deep appreciation to Korean American women of NYC: Constance Pak, Eun Joo Kim, Mari Kim, Hannah Chon, Jeanne Jang, and Nichole Yim. Thank you for being living witnesses to the power of *jeong*. Our stickiness held me together and lifted me up many times.

Special thanks to KPCOW women. Their burgeoning hybrid feminist sensibility and commitment to being critical and faithful practitioners of their faith tradition have been a tremendous source of hope and strength. Their *jeong* for one another and for the world is impressively palpable.

I send thankful vibrations to Tallman State Park in Palisades, New York. It was my haven during the most turbulent yet exciting times of my life and writing. Thank you for life-giving and healing energies through the miles of your path I was privileged to run while theological imagination ran wild. It was while running along the Hudson River and through the trails that I saw the seasons of my life with the seasons in nature.

I offer sincere appreciation to my editor, Jon Berquist. His insights and suggestions were invaluable for the improvement of this text. He, Julie Tonini, and many other members of the editorial and production staff made this process very friendly to navigate. They have done a marvelous and superb job of making this work what it is. I only wish I had provided them with a better raw material. Thank you for believing in this project and for shepherding it through the entire process.

I want to thank Don Pittman, my Dean, and members of the faculty, administration, staff, and especially the students of Phillips Theological Seminary for welcoming this latte-slurping New Yorker into their midst. Deep appreciation and gratitude to the participants in my first Feminist Theology course for their creative and powerful presence to make that course so very rich. For pouring themselves out for each other, for finding ways to honor and hold up each other's differences and commitment to solidarity and resistance, I want to say thank you for your efforts to give birth to a person on her way to becoming a better teacher. The patience, humor, challenges, faithfulness, and love embodied by each person provided strength for the beginning of a new journey for me as a scholar and as a teacher. My deepest appreciation to Bethany Albrecht, Emily Bowen, Jacalyn Carter, Karen Clewell, Tanja Edwards, Victoria Fishel, Brenda Fletchall, Angie Gage, Debra Garfinkel, Noe Godoy, Ruthi Jacobs, Tracy Lemons, Barry Loving, Matthew Morgan, Nathan Smith, Sharyn Cosby-Willis, and Scott Taylor.

My profound appreciation and love to my family—all witnesses to the power of *jeong*. My mother, Young, my father, Charles Chul Kyu, my brothers and sisters, Sunggoo, Sungbin, Wongee, Ben, Chuck, and Helen. And to our amazing little ones so full of love, hope, and power—Chuckie, Christina, Joshua, Alex, Elizabeth, Samantha, and now Hannah Rae. I learned the complexity of compassion, love, commitment, vulnerability, and strength from them. Their indomitable and tenacious hope in all people and in life continue to give me strength to "live the talk."

I hope this is a beginning of more reflections among and with many others. It is my hope that in a time fraught with ecological, economical, biological destructions, a time beset with war, fear, death, and out-of-control imperialist impulses and delusions, we must recognize we cannot live without one another and we cannot afford not to look to *jeong* to "stick" us together and carry us into the present and the future. I am reminded of those who bear the scar of living in the interstice yet continue to live out their hopes in the fullness of *jeong*. With that in mind, this is *for the sake of all our children everywhere.*

Introduction

Philosophy thought that it had done with the problem of origins.
It was no longer a question of starting or finishing. The question
was, what happens "in between"?

Gilles Deleuze, *Difference and Repetition*

A POSTCOLONIAL PREAMBLE

The primary theological reflection of this book centers on the cross from a
particular postcolonial context. The book examines Korean Americans' experience of *han* from a postcolonial theorical perspective and is thus an invitation for constructive theological reflection and for imagining an Asian/Korean
American theopolitical aesthetic of *jeong*.[1]

Using such postcolonial conceptual tools as hybridity, mimicry, and negotiation, this book aims to introduce a Korean concept into conversation with
the traditional reflections on Christology, relationality, and the construction
of the self and the other. It thus invites the reader into a new understanding
of the meaning of the cross. While mindful of feminist critiques of state-
sanctioned violence and innocent suffering in classical atonement theories, I
propose that the power of the cross also points simultaneously to the possibility of a radical form of love that can be linked with the Korean concept of *jeong*.
Jeong saturates daily living and all forms of relationships. As a concept, *jeong*
encompasses but is not limited to notions of compassion, affection, solidarity,
relationality, vulnerability, and forgiveness. The word for *jeong*, when written
using Chinese characters, is composed primarily of words for heart, vulnerability, and something "arising." Many Koreans have a common understanding

that *jeong* is even more powerful, lasting, and transformative than love. Despite *jeong's* pervasiveness in the everyday life of Koreans and in their view of reality, the concept has not been analytically conceptualized, even by Koreans themselves. *Jeong* makes relationships "sticky" but also recognizes the complex nature of all relationalism.

This book will examine Korean concepts of *jeong* (right-relation) and *han* (suffering) in connection with Julia Kristeva's notion of the abject as a way to reconstruct Christology. Kristeva's idea of the abject is helpful for unpacking the psychodynamics of oppression and will be further discussed in later chapters. Kristeva defines the abject in this way:

> It is something rejected from which one does not part, from which one does not protect one's self as from an object . . . [abject] is what disturbs identity, system, order. What does not respect borders, positions, rules. The in-between, the ambiguous, the composite.[2]

Abjection could be loosely defined as an operation of the psyche through which the identity of the individual or the collective is shaped by *exclusion* or *expulsion* of that which threatens the borders of that particular individual subject or the collective. Kristeva's notion of the stranger/foreigner in relation to both individual psychic processes of abjection is brought to bear on my contention that our long history of politics of white supremacy in the United States might be better understood by examining the national identity with ongoing inclusion and exclusion of those deemed as other, foreign, alien, and abject. Because this process of identifying the foreigner as the other with its attending abjection, violence such as racism is maintained at an institutional level and thus enforced through national domestic policies. This argument is being developed more fully in my current work in progress.[3] Abjection is the improper, the unclean, and the "disorderly" that is required to be expelled in order for subjectivity to find its proper acceptance into the symbolic world. The abject "attests to the impossibility of clear borders, lines of demarcation or division between the proper and the improper, the clean and the unclean, order and disorder as required by the Symbolic."[4] The crucial theological thesis of my project is that the cross works symbolically to embody both the horror of *han* and the power of *jeong*.

This book will undertake three theological tasks named by Korean American theologian Anselm Min. The first task will be to examine, excavate, and retrieve life-affirming traditions from both Asia and America. This task allows us to acknowledge that Asian experiences in Asia are very different from Asian American experiences in North America. It also recognizes the powerful, creative, yet also painful position of identity that has been transformed into hybridity. The second task will be to *do* theology with Asian American lived experience as the starting point for constructive theological reflection.[5] Min points to four dimensions that must be kept in mind: ambiguity, separation, diversity, and love of the stranger. As for the third task, I take to heart his call for an Asian American political theology. Min is correct to point out that as citizens of this nation we are responsible and accountable for what our government does in both the domestic and international arenas. In short, there is an urgent need for prophetic criticism. Min notes that "as citizens of a country with historic burdens of colonialism, slavery and imperialism" Asian Americans must respond. It is imperative for our theologies to foster and speak with and out of a prophetic theopolitical imagination. This is even more so as we are part of an empire that does not admit its current problem of deadly runaway patriotism.[6]

Poststructuralism and postcolonial theory have argued foremost that any and all knowledge is situated, historicized, limited, fractured, and always under change. Our epistemic process is always partial and, most important, connected to our understanding of our positionality. If all ways of knowing are situated, historicized, fractured, and under constant and rapid change, then Asian American immigrant experience embodies ways of knowing that emerge from lived experiences within the interstitial space. Neither fully Asian nor American, the heterogeneity of Asian American experience and identity defy all attempts to homogenize it into an inscrutable yet colonized monolithic "Asian" self.

Given "situated knowledge," theology is inevitably autobiographical. While we may not dwell extensively on our situation, our theologizing is always and inescapably intertwined with our limited, particular, and fractured epistemology, even if it is a "cramped episteme." Even as we are critical of epistemologies that claim "views from everywhere," we are also mindful that our knowing is always a "view from somewhere." Whether this "somewhere" be in the center, on the boundaries, or in the interstices, it seems constantly necessary to remind ourselves of this point.

It is thus important, in the beginning, to acknowledge the inevitable interjections of autobiography that will appear within this project.[7]

SEARCHING FOR ROOTS

> If theology is contextual, it must certainly be at root autobiographical.
>
> Jung Young Lee, *Journeys at the Margin*

I have frequently wondered why I felt displaced and/or out of place while growing up in North America. Memory of my life before North America is simultaneously a nostalgic blur of colors, scents, and dreamlike images that often appear to be conflictual. Portions of these memories are also so sharply in focus that they seem inscribed into the skin of my body. This sense of feeling out of place seems, in hindsight, to be closely linked to the complex roots and routes that comprise the memory and history of my family's often traumatic yet hope-filled immigrant experience in North America. The complexity of our memory of the past, our present context, and our hope in the future have all been and continue to be sustained by the centrality of how we continue to live with *heart*. We continue to journey, to live, to resist, sometimes with wisdom and sometimes without, to navigate the complex layers of being in relationships and to have mighty and fierce hope in the future—all done with, by, and through the heart. I have witnessed this nowhere as intimately as I have in the lives of both my parents, whose lives were deeply shaped by experiences of *han*. Their lived experiences of *han* had much to do with class, politics, gender, race, and immigration. Despite this profound sense of *han*, however, their lives were lived with a powerful presence of *jeong*, which consistently gave them indomitable hope in wholeness. The rest of my family has embraced their epistemological embodiment of *jeong* as a way of life. Through them I have inherited the wisest of all the wisdom: to live with heart in spite of brokenheartedness and never to give up on our human capacity to find, gift, participate, and share in redemption. More than anything else, my lived, Korean American, immigrant experience has taught me, despite the suffering and trauma, that our profound sense of collective interconnectedness and the relational empowerment of *jeong* (the ultimate concern of this book) promote communal healing and sustaining and make way for the presence of a deep, life-affirming power.

When I backtrack through the various routes my parents have traveled, I arrive at a village outside of Kwang-Ju, Korea, known as Ock-Chun, Hae-Nam. It is in many ways like the Galilee of Jesus' time. It is the place where insurgents were exiled and the place from which insurgents emerged. It is the geographical and spiritual place that became a home for many Koreans marginalized by the dominant powers of Korean society. My father's family was heavily involved in the resistance movement against Japanese colonialism in Korea. At nine years of age, my father witnessed the capture, torture, and public execution of his oldest brother at the hands of the Japanese colonialists. His brother's crime was treason against the imperial powers of Japan for participating in the underground liberation movement. This part of our family history, which was deeply steeped in an intimate and brutal experience of suffering, has become an unresolved *han* in our family history.

Even after our immigration to North America, my father was always extensively involved both emotionally and politically with the democratic movement in Korea. Because of his political commitment, my siblings and I grew

up with an acute awareness of Korean people's collective sense of *han* as well
as their passion for resistance against oppression, which amazingly was and is
always undergirded by their deeply rooted sense of hope and flourishing of life
for the entire collectivity. I remember coming home from school one day and
for the first time witnessing my father openly weeping and lamenting the government's brutal suppression of the student uprisings in Kwang-Ju. Sometime
later, I recall helping my father construct posters and signs of protest against
the military regime of President Chun Doo Hwan. It was exciting for me at
the time to be with the grown-ups, marching and shouting in downtown
Chicago, carrying placards and watching these solemn adults tearing the military stripes off an effigy before setting it on fire. Today, my father is still deeply
occupied with democratic movements in Korea through his efforts within
immigrant communities to raise consciousness and funds for peace and reunification of Korea. I have come to recognize, despite my postmodern North
American feminist consciousness, that my roots are deep even as my routes are
circuitous.

"RESIDENT ALIEN": DISPLACEMENT(S)

"Go back to where you came from!" is one of the most recurring and painful
chants I recall hearing as a third-grade Korean immigrant. I have heard this
same demand recently from people, including those who identify themselves as
"loving Christians," who justify it with a zealous brand of American patriotism.
When I was attacked on the streets, this exclamation flew into my face once
again shortly after the terrorist attack in New York City on September 11.[8]
While I was growing up, the chant was also sometimes a benign question of
"Where are you from?" "Are you Chinese or Japanese?" Although it should not
be surprising, it still manages to throw me off guard when my children share
with me their own similar experiences. With all the cultural and institutional
talk on diversity and many people's self-congratulatory stance that racism is a
thing of the past, it is ironic that the same xenophobia that I faced three decades
ago still echoes, word for word, from elementary school playgrounds and in the
streets of such diverse places as New York City. Lest we fool ourselves, racism
is still alive and even more sinister today than in the past, for it has lodged itself
into institutions, into our cultural ethos, and into our democratic process in
ways that make it more difficult to name due to the sophisticated veneer of
diversity talk.

Recently I was told I was not American enough because of my critique of
the "War on Terrorism." The strong implication was that I was not white
enough. Being white and being American is still understood as one and the

same. This question of my origin, with its underlying implication that somehow I am a stranger, wholly unmeltable in this context, always leaves me floundering to find an adequate and yet satisfying answer to such criticisms while keeping my sense of dignity intact. Interrogation of one's origin functions as a marker of one's foreignness/otherness. In effect it functions as a process of challenge, exposure, and expulsion. As Edward Said notes in his own memoir, he himself retained this "unsettled sense of many identities—mostly in conflict with one another—all of my life, together with an acute memory of the despairing feeling that I wish we could have been all-Arab, or all-European and American . . . and so on."[9] The unflinching brutality of such seemingly benign questions of my "roots" and "origin" has often plagued the inmost fluids of my body/self, as if I were hanging over the bottomless depths of the Pacific Ocean, with one foot on the shores of North America and the other dangling over, if not firmly on, the shores of Korea.[10] Such questions are always an interrogation and challenge to one's sense of belongingness to a particular context by a particular group. Usually I am left speechless; my unspoken answers, too complex. I have not yet been able to make a witty, succinct, and sophisticated retort. Frequently I am silenced by my own bewildering and overwhelming sense of complexity.

Furthermore, not only has there been a psychological and spiritual silence but also a loss of voice. This sense of displacement due to various forms of constant departures, arrivals, and nonbelonging is not only connected with geographical disorientation but also with language/voice/reality. I have often been frustrated by my lack of thorough access to either the Korean or the English language. My limited grasp of either language continues to be indicative of my nonnative status at both sites. Those of us who are by necessity multilingual are often left in the end with an imposed silence and feelings of inadequacy and incompetence. Part of the trauma then is that most of us no longer speak our "mother tongue." "Living with resonances and reasoning . . . we are cut off from the body's nocturnal memory, from the bittersweet slumber of childhood"; we bear within ourselves like a "secret vault" that language of the past that "withers without ever leaving" one's psyche.[11] If the body is argued to be the terrain/site of most intimate memory, then the words of Mikhail Bakhtin serve as a great source of comfort and encouragement, for he argues that such "hybrid" people are not only double-voiced but also double-accented and more importantly double-languaged. Our memory embodies two sociolinguistic epochs pregnant with potential creativity to articulate new ways of perceiving the world as they come together to "fight it out on the territory of the utterance."[12] To use W. E. B. Du Bois's concept of "double-consciousness," people living in the interstitial space between two cultures have had to learn to think beyond language and to develop an epistemology that is emancipatory rather than complicit with the "ideology of monolanguaging."[13] For as Walter D. Mignolo reminds us, "bilanguaging" is a necessary emancipatory response to the use of monolanguage as a tool of imperialism.

Constant reminders that I am a stranger from a strange shore have driven me to what I have been told is the bosom of "where I came from." Kristeva writes of exactly this question that is often posed to "foreigners."[14] She derisively notes, "Blundering fools never fail to ask the question." This surface kindness hides the "sticky clumsiness" that exasperates the foreigner.[15] This issue of "my place" is challenged and forever questioned not only by the dominant society but also from those very places of origin to which I can supposedly always return. To whichever side I turn, I am constantly met with recognition and simultaneous disavowal. The recognition that both sides of the boundary challenge my identity has been both crushing and revelatory. The overwhelming weight of ignorance works powerfully as they put you "back in your place" of foreignness. This challenge of "go back to where you came from" always works effectively to render any theoretical response seemingly impossible. Thus, in terms of hybrid, split identity—a kaleidoscope of identities—one is compelled to ask, "Can we be a saga for ourselves without being considered mad or fake; without dying of the foreigner's hatred or of hatred for the foreigner?"[16]

COMPLEX ROUTE/DEEP ROOTS

Living on the boundary of multiple contexts, one is challenged to recognize that one's identity is fluid, shifting, and often engaged in one form of negotiation or another. These negotiations are often done from positions that might conflict with one another even as we find ourselves positioned simultaneously at both sites. Negotiation is not about resolving one position over and against another from an oppositional stand but often entails "two incompatible imperatives that appear to be incompatible but are equally imperative . . . one negotiates by engaging in the nonnegotiable in negotiation."[17] For those who live in the boundaries, our lives are often fraught with various negotiations on multiple terrains.

On my first return to Korea I raced there with open arms, with all the pain and anger I had gathered while living in North America. I have made many trips since then. Korea did not heal all my wounds or take away my anger, but it did bring a level of comfort that eased the inner wounds. There is a certain estranged yet comfortable sense of coming home, of belonging, whenever I return to Korea. When I am there, I miss North America, and when I am here, I long for Korea. People living in the interstitial space between differing worlds often experience feelings of unsettledness, for one is "neither completely at one with the new setting nor fully disencumbered of the old, beset with half-involvements and half-detachments, nostalgic and sentimental on the one level, and an adept mimic or a secret outcast on another."[18] One would have to admit to a certain presence of the "motherland" that is symptomatic of all split selves.

But with frequent returns to Korea, I realize that the initial sense of arrival is no longer enough to bring about that same sense of belonging. My identity is much more at home in North America, and, to use Said's phrase, that departed place of "origin" is "irrecoverable."[19] The complexity of this recognition brings the risk of aggravating even further my sense of displacement. Interestingly enough, this awareness has allowed me to reflect even more on the "placed-ness" of immigrants in this country and the political implications of our citizenship.[20] Our sense of belonging to this context forces us to reexamine what our role is when it comes to the participation in and construction of national identity in North America—recognizing that we have not only been colonized but that we inevitably are now part of the empire that continues to exercise oppressive imperialism on a global scale.[21]

A prevailing sense of displacement and being "out of place" has always been at the edge of my life and has often intruded unexpectedly into the center of my everyday living. Such unexpected intrusions, quite often from unsuspecting persons and situations, have led me to become much more acutely aware of how ambiguously and precariously our histories, origins, and identities are constantly recorded, constructed, claimed, and even disavowed.

For me as a Korean American feminist, the tensions between "home," "elsewhere," "roots," "routes," "Korean," "Korean-American," and "feminist" have in the past functioned as paradoxical, contentious pieces needing to be clearly categorized and somewhat pieced together in an orderly fashion. Edward Said reflects in his memoir, this task of valiantly trying to put all the pieces into a clear picture never comes to satisfactory fruition.[22] Postcolonial theory questions the often-dichotomizing tendency of identity politics[23] in favor of an understanding of identity as a complex and often shifting construct.[24] Postcolonial theory challenges the dominant dismissive views of hybrid identities. This project will draw heavily from postcolonial theory as a challenge to the oppressive links that have continuously marginalized hybrid identities for their lack of "purity" and "authenticity." This dilemma of multiple positionalities and kaleidoscopic identities is addressed by postcolonial theory. Above all, postcolonial theory "represent[s] an attempt at grappling with the meaning of location and belonging, of communities of interpretation and praxis, of home, in the increasingly diasporic panoramas of the contemporary world."[25]

ARGUMENT OF THE BOOK

This book examines theological reflections on Christology from a postcolonial feminist perspective. Postcolonial theology does not

> function as a supersession but instead as a supplement to the liberation tradition. In the deconstructive sense of supplementarity, it offers an internal challenge to the certainties and dichotomies that tempt every emancipatory discourse to render final judgement rather than justice.[26]

Minjung theology has already explored *han* extensively. The most favored definition is still one of the initial descriptions offered by the sociologist Han Wan Sang. He writes, "*Han* is a sense of unresolved resentment against injustices suffered, a sense of helplessness because of the overwhelming odds against one's feeling of total abandonment, a feeling of acute pain and sorrow in one's guts and bowels."[27] *Jeong*, on the other hand, has not been explored in depth.

Whereas *han* is now a familiar concept in North American theological conversation, I will propose *jeong* as a concept in need of new analysis and ongoing conceptualization. *Jeong* names a prevalent ethos in the history of the Korean people. Inasmuch as it expresses an integral part of relationality in Korea, it also resists definite categorical translations. The reader should be aware that the notions of both *han* and *jeong* resist easy translation into the Western vernacular. We are thus invited to stretch the boundaries of our familiar categories and experiences by the complexity of these two notions.

One cannot succinctly define *jeong* without losing the depth of its multiple and shifting dimensions. Moreover, *jeong*[28] embodies the invisible traces of compassion in relationships and is most often recognized when we perceive our very own self, conscious and unconscious, in the mirrored reflection of the other.[29] *Jeong* is a Korean way of conceiving an often complex constellation of relationality of the self with the other that is deeply associated with compassion, love, vulnerability, and acceptance of heterogeneity as essential to life. It not only smooths harsh feelings, such as dislike or even hate, but has a way of making relationships richly complex by moving away from a binary, oppositional perception of reality, such as oppressor and oppressed. I will argue that *jeong* is the power embodied in redemptive relationships.[30] It can even be argued that redemption emerges within relationality that recognizes the power and presence of *jeong* to move us toward life.

To my knowledge, *jeong* has not yet been defined for theological purposes. This book is an invitation to explore, imagine, and articulate a theopoetics of the nuanced yet inevitably obscure contours of the concept of *jeong*. In any act of translation, something is lost even as the trace of that something evolves into a new version.[31]

While avoiding essentialized and feminized concepts of *jeong*, I will argue for a politicized appropriation of *jeong*. This feminist appropriation of *jeong* is radically different from male/patriarchal perceptions of *jeong*. Even as *jeong* is acknowledged as a powerful way by which Koreans understand their relationship with one another, often it has been feminized, domesticated, spiritualized, trivialized, or psychologized and viewed as the "sticky" element of relationality not fit for the "rational" thinking *man*. When *jeong* is misunderstood in an essentialized way it effectively works to perpetuate the disempowerment of the suffering individual or the collective. It does so by stressing that *jeong* is something that only "women," ontologically speaking, practice due to their "inherent" female tendency to be relational. Thus, *jeong* is often understood as something that the "women" do; whereby *jeong* becomes domesticated. While I argue that *jeong* should not be essentialized, I recognize also that the politicization of *jeong* as a way of living and seeking justice is often recognizable in communities that emphasize the value of intersubjectivity and relationality.[32]

As previously mentioned, this book will focus on the juxtaposition of the Korean concepts *han* and *jeong* in relation to Kristeva's notions of abjection and love as a way toward articulating a Korean American feminist theology of *jeong*. Through an examination of the traditional doctrine of the atoning suffering/*han* of Christ in conversation with critical feminist christological discourse, I hope to give voice to a Korean American feminist Christology that, while understanding the *han* of Jesus the Christ on the cross, recognizes the power of *jeong*/love embodied in Jesus' life and death.[33] While mindful of feminist critiques of traditional atonement Christology, I will argue that the cross performs a double gesture as it simultaneously signifies abjection and love, *han* and *jeong*. I will draw from Kristeva's notion of the semiotic and love in terms of their relationship with the abject from a feminist perspective to argue that the semiotic/love/*jeong* and the abject are fully present on the cross. Moreover, I will suggest that the notion of *jeong* evokes this semiotic power. Simply put, Kristeva's understanding of the semiotic is distinctive from that of the symbolic. Her semiotic "precedes all unities, binary oppositional structures and hierarchical forms of organization. . . . It is the symbiotic space shared by the mother's and child's indistinguishable bodies."[34]

The semiotic is not a subject but the locus because it is the space and stage before the formation of subjectivity and identity. In Kristeva's work the semiotic is explicitly maternal and feminine while the symbolic is paternal, the Law of the Father. The abject then is all that is expelled, repelled, excluded in the process of identification and transition into the unified self and into the symbolic precisely because the abject threatens the stability of this transition from the semiotic into the symbolic. However, the subject is never stable in the symbolic because the abject, the repressed or the repelled abject, always haunts at the edges or in the depths of the self in the symbolic. We will discuss in more detail the relationship between the semiotic and the symbolic in later chapters.

Feminist Asian American scholarship on Christology will therefore be brought into conversation with postcolonial theory. My theological response will grapple with what Korean American feminist sociologist Jung Ha Kim calls the "double edged . . . symbol of the cross."[35] The cross, understood as mimicry, works both to pay homage to patriarchal notions of power and obedience and to "menace" those concepts at the same time.[36] Consequently, mimicry functions powerfully in the transformation of the cross from a tool of imperial execution and repression into a powerful subversive and revolutionary semiotic presence. I argue that the cross is double-edged; or to use Derrida's notion, the cross as a sign performs a "double gesture" from a Korean American feminist perspective.

A feminist reading of Jürgen Moltmann's Christology reveals a less than fully liberating picture of the cross. Although his emphasis on understanding the event of the crucifixion as a manifestation of God's resistance against oppression is appealing, it still echoes the classical expiatory Christology he himself attempts to disassociate from. I will pose challenges not to his liberating political theology but to what I perceive as remaining traces of patriarchal power dynamics in his theology of the cross. Traditional formulas on Christology not only distort concepts of power and love but also deprive the crucifixion of its political power for resistance against suffering and structures of oppression. Postcolonial theory on hybridity, mimicry, interstitial space, and rupture will come into play as I examine this edge of meaning of Christology from the "elliptical in-between" of a Korean American Christian feminist perspective.[37]

Kim states, "Sexism preached within the context of the sacred realm of Christianity produces a dangerous atmosphere wherein churched Korean American women may accept the self-less and pain-enduring image as an ideal Christian model for them. . . . Call for churched women's suffering is often reflective of the image of Christ as 'the suffering servant.'" She further writes, "But the inherent contradiction of the satisfied suffering servant, which resembles a sadomasochistic understanding of the meaning of Jesus' life and death, is justified."[38] Likewise, Dorothee Soelle, in her criticism of traditional Christology, insists that despite Moltmann's portrayal of God as the "God of the poor, the peasants and the slaves," his intention is weakened by his less-than-complete departure from the traditional patriarchal theological paradigm.

Soelle offers a crisp and fiercely honest feminist critique when she insists that such theology is ultimately "sadistic."[39] From a Korean American feminist standpoint, the patriarchal understanding of the cross reinforces the language of patriarchal power dynamics.

MAPPING THIS BOOK

Even though this interdisciplinary scope gives freedom to be creative, I will limit my reflections to key leading scholars from areas of constructive feminist theology, Asian/Asian American theology, poststructuralist feminist psychoanalytic theory, and postcolonial studies.

Chapter 1 begins by analyzing the current conversation around the issues of identity politics and antiessentialism via the politics of location. Postcolonial theory notes that identity is more fragmented and fractured than unified or singular. It is constructed across different and often intersecting and oppositional positions and practices. This chapter explores the complexity of feminist, postcolonial identity politics that many Asian Americans must negotiate as they construct their heterogeneous identities vis-à-vis the politics of location and how all this might relate and transform our theological reflections. The chapter will conclude with an introduction of *jeong* and *han*.

Chapter 2 begins with an analysis of *han* through the psychotheological analysis of *han* by Jae Hoon Lee. His work is important to our examination of *han* because he offers an in-depth psychological analysis of *han*'s effect not only on the collective but also on the individual consciousness. This chapter explores various ways *han* has been articulated and will further add dimensions of *han*-causing traumatic factors experienced by Korean American immigrants. It is in this context that the concept of *jeong* will be introduced. *Jeong* is understood to be at the heart of the Korean understanding of relationality. Unlike emphases on the construction of the self in opposition to the other, *jeong* bids us to see that we are always already in relation to the other as another self. Because *jeong* is even linguistically composed of vulnerability, heart, and life, we are asked to imagine *jeong* as that which fosters life-giving relationality through the transformation of the heart. To do so, the chapter will analyze a recent independent film from Korea, *Joint Security Area*, and a documentary, *Sa-I-Gu. Joint Security Area* takes place at the thirty-eighth parallel, the DMZ, and *Sa-I-Gu* records interviews with the victims of the April 29, 1992, Los Angeles riots. Both of these avant-garde films are postcolonial in their content and explore the multiple dimensions of *jeong* that are prevalent in the lives of Korean people.

Chapter 3 will examine my Korean American readings of postcolonial theory by highlighting postcolonial concepts such as hybridity, marginality, and mimicry as critical hermeneutic lenses for theological constructions. This chapter suggests how we might reconstruct the traditional understanding of the need to erase difference by arguing that "difference" is encouraged and appreciated by the relational concept of *jeong*.

Chapter 4 will bring the concepts of *han*, *jeong*, abjection, and love into conversation with Jürgen Moltmann's Christology from a feminist theological perspective. Feminist theologians' critiques have served as a corrective to the traditional expiatory atonement theology. Many feminists and liberation theologians have argued that this traditional Christology, especially the suffering on the cross with its emphasis on sacrifice, has worked to perpetuate powerlessness, self-abnegation, and even state-sanctioned violence. While I am critical of such atonement theories as well, I will insist here that there might be an alternative way of understanding the cross. While suffering is not redemptive, we must acknowledge suffering in the world and on the cross. Again, on the cross there is a simultaneous presence of both the horror of violence as well as a radical form of inclusive love, which I will link to *jeong*. In light of our examination of *han*, *jeong*, and abjectness, my critical conversation with Moltmann will be to engage his theology in order to challenge the still-remaining traces of patriarchal power dynamics within his otherwise liberating political Christology.

Chapter 5 continues to examine traditional Christology in light of feminist critiques. However, this chapter will add a psychological dimension by bringing Julia Kristeva into the conversation. Her articulation of the abject, the semiotic/symbolic, and love are fruitful for the previous discussion on *han* and *jeong*. This chapter will note that in order for difference to exist between the self and the other, there needs to be a radical form of love, which I link with *jeong*. The event of the cross then is not only about the horror of abjection and suffering but also about the return of the repressed. It is a disclosive event embodying not only suffering but also a radical form of inclusive love. Here we will shift towards a postcolonial Christology. By insisting on the power of *jeong* as apparent in the ongoing prophetic christological praxis, I seek to reimagine the concepts of suffering, atonement, and the cross through a subversive, open-ended, postcolonial "double consciousness" embodied on "the cross." By critically examining the theological implications of the ambiguous yet powerful concepts of *han* and *jeong* in dialogue with postcolonial theory and Kristeva's notions of abjection and love, this chapter will suggest a distinctively postcolonial Christology of *jeong*.

The conclusion of this book is an invitation to enter into a conversation around the different contours of the postcolonial theology of *jeong*. This chapter asks and explores different ways we might respond to the question of whether or not we might speak of the power of the cross while still being mindful of the oppressive ways it has been interpreted conventionally in the past. Is it possible to speak of the cross in *any* redemptive manner given the traditional interpretation that has worked to sanction violence and suffering? While noting the importance of emancipatory praxis from structures of oppression, a theology of *jeong* will argue that it must be done along with a praxis of *jeong*—a form of relational living that daily encounters the otherness of the self in relationships. As a form of postcolonial love, might the praxis of *jeong* invite an alternative postcolonial Christology that does not deny the historical *han* present on the cross but at the same time examines the subversive *jeong* that irrupts mimetically on the cross? *Jeong* allows us to reimagine love on the cross not as self-abnegation or sacrifice but as a radical inclusive love that is both transgressive and emancipatory. From a postcolonial perspective of *jeong*, the cross pays homage to the power of horror/abjection while at the same time using mimicry to make present the transgressive and transforming power of love.

Although a significant amount of research has been emerging on these issues, we have yet to encounter research done by Korean Americans that integrates postcolonial studies with feminist theological reflections. This book is not *the* Korean American postcolonial feminist theology but merely one among many voices emerging and still yet to be voiced. I hope the reflections in this book will contribute toward expanding the horizon of already ongoing and lively theological conversations, particularly within and around Asian Americans. This book is an invitation to think with and through the heart in order to rediscover a radical form of love that is startlingly both mysterious and emancipatory.

1

Identity Out of Place

There is a growing unease with the concept of identity politics, an idea that has become so highly contested people will often defer to another term, such as "the politics of difference." We might ask where and why this shift has taken place. I would argue that part of this shift took place with the recognition that identity and difference are intimately connected; identity, therefore, is no longer understood as singular or simple but rather as complex and multiple. The shift also has to do with the growing debate between what is referred to as essentialist or constructivist theoretical views. This chapter explores these dynamics and how notions of home, difference, and claims to identity enable the postcolonial subject to engage in the simultaneous task of deconstructing and constructing the diasporic subjectivity.

OUT OF PLACE

The supplement adds itself, it is a surplus, a plentitude enriching another plentitude, the *fullest measure* of presence. . . .
Jacques Derrida, Negotiations

Only by firmly putting down roots in fact and being nourished by them can one live truly and long. . . . An early awareness of oneness, that we are in reality limbs of one body, will end all suicidal convulsions.
Ham Sok Hon, The Queen of Suffering

Gayatri Spivak has mentioned that what she distrusts, above all else, and even has contempt for, are people looking for roots. As she derisively notes, "Anyone who can conceive of looking for roots, should . . . be growing rutabagas!"[1] According to Spivak, roots are not something stationary but something that we embody and carry around. Yet despite her contempt for roots, Spivak acknowledges and displays in her travels back and forth to India the yearning to search for if not grow rutabagas! As much as I am wary of calls for roots by purists, I am also deeply mindful of the roots that are life giving, as Korean activist, philosopher, and theologian Ham Sok Hon notes in the epigraph. The paradox for many marginalized people is unique: because one exists at the boundaries, one is able to bring a creative convergence to the dialectics of traditional thinking between object/subject, Western/Eastern, female/male, creature/ "non"-creature, earth/cosmos, spirit/body, roots/routes, margin/center.

At one's recognition of being an other who is never truly accepted into the dominant culture, one is often compelled to turn back and reclaim what one perceives to be a pure culture of origin. Often this drive is double-edged. While it affords a temporary sense of security and a sense of "return" to an "original place" of belonging, it also positions one to fall into the trap of essentializing and exoticizing that place of "origin." Such essentialism is dangerous because it runs counter to the very need for freedom from such dominant processes of "Othering."[2] Nonetheless, essentialism is often politically necessary; it can be embraced tentatively and strategically as a way of cultural affirmation and political empowerment. An example is Gayatri Spivak's take on "strategic essentialism." Essentialism is when certain traits are posited and understood to be an inherent part of that person or group's identity based, for example, on race or gender. This use of essentialism is problematized by deconstructionism. However, while one may argue for heterogeneity and deconstruction of false essence as racist or sexist, for an emancipatory political movement of resistance, oppressed groups have often used essentialism strategically. "Strategic essentialism" then is necessary at times while seeking justice. Straddling two dangerous edges leaves one precariously dislocated between the vacillating boundaries of "no place like home" and "no place is home." Such understanding of home as

> that place and time outside place and time appears to mingle promiscuously with its opposite—exile, the outside, elsewhere. Hence, its attraction for a critical practice that seeks to undo such binaries as belonging/unbelonging, loyalty/disloyalty, to unpack their ideological baggage. . . . And perhaps . . . get a glimpse of the double bind within which criticism is practiced today in a context where "home" is both a myth of belonging and the name of a state that criticism cannot avoid wanting to inhabit.[3]

The notion of home, traditionally understood in static terms, is being radically reenvisioned. "Home" is being reconstructed as a traveling, dynamic concept that simultaneously encompasses the political implications of locatedness. This diasporic identity is fraught with "double consciousness." Over time, the vicissitudes of such double consciousness result in a perennial crisis of self-doubt and self-abnegation. In this ineluctable process of constant renegotiation and reappropriation of one's history and identity, those who hold onto beliefs of purity see acceptance of hybridity as a form of co-optation by the hegemonic structures of oppression. On the other hand, we also hold ourselves up to constant self-scrutiny since we are suspicious of ourselves, too. Hence, a politics of identity will be most effective if it remains deconstructive and transformatively engaged with dominant discourses while also affirmative and proactive in the creation of its own history. Histories, origins, and identities most often lead to constructions of constraining boundaries that also afford a sense of shared belonging.[4]

Despite the uncertainties of being "out of place," ambiguities of refracted and layered identity cause such subjectivities to be necessarily complex. Diasporic subjectivity, then, is necessarily double as it acknowledges the imperatives of an earlier "elsewhere" in an active and critical relationship with the cultural politics of one's present home. The immigrant experience, then, comprises multiple traces, multiple origins, and diverse stories that resist the tendency to be easily commodified and homogenized. Put another way, as Kristeva writes, "Origin certainly haunts [the immigrant], for better and for worse, but it is indeed *elsewhere* that he has set his hopes, that his struggles take place, that his life holds together today. *Elsewhere* versus the origin, and even *nowhere* versus the roots."[5] Consequently, the paradoxical dynamic of identity is that one is always in the midst of unremitting shifts and tensions of disempowerment, indetermination, and displacement exacerbated by persistent awareness of being inappropriate.

The search to claim a static and coherent sense of identity, including that of being "in place," gradually leads to the recognition that identity is neither fixed nor simplifiable. The concept of living within the reality of double and multiple binds and thresholds not only reflects the complex layers within individual identities but also points toward a reality that is always and already changed. The progressive rhetoric of "purism" has often been more noticeably challenged in recent times with the growing emergence of people and children who have multiple roots and thus multifarious routes. Children of diverse racial unions truly challenge and complicate our notions of "pure" roots.[6]

The acknowledgement of such altering intricacy of our locational movements often brings our considerations into the realm of the effects of roots and/or routes on how our identities are determined, influenced, reappropriated, and repetitiously negotiated. Being positioned at the forever-shifting edges of reality, one is acutely attuned to the persistence of cultural roots while being aware of the inevitable process of hybridization of all roots as they become part of our routes.[7] R. Radhakrishnan argues, "All contemporary politics . . . exist dangerously suspended between a dominant universalism and a range of separatist and/or relativist terrains."[8] She further notes,

> Overdetermined, as it is by multiple histories, the postcolonial location feels like an intersection, fraught with multiple adjacencies. Identity often requires some form of displacement. . . . Belonging nowhere and everywhere at the same time, the diasporic subject may well attempt to proclaim a heterogeneous "elsewhere" as its actual epistemological home.[9]

Identity politics and politics of difference have been transformed by prevalent binary implications into recognition of sites of ambiguities internal and external to the self. Even the concept of one's nationality has become complicated. Postcolonial theory challenges the ambivalence of citizenship that has often been felt and experienced by immigrants. For example, many Korean Americans who were either born in North America or came to this country as youngsters with their immigrant parents often experience displacement. Furthermore, there are differences between political exiles and those who willingly leave Korea for various reasons. The former are often accepted as patriotic heroes who were forced to leave their country due to a repressive regime, while the latter are often portrayed as those who abandoned their country in times of economic crisis to improve their own personal lives.

This portrayal of selfish abandonment of Korea by immigrants often fails to acknowledge the hardships these immigrants faced first in Korea, then in the wilderness of North America.[10] This disavowal of Korean immigrants by Koreans in Korea is here mentioned because I believe that it is relevant to the emergence of political consciousness among Korean Americans.[11] My personal sense of ambiguity is rooted in part with my belonging to neither North America nor Korea. Stuart Hall observes that the concept of identity operates "under erasure" in the "interval between reversal and emergence."[12] Hence, identity is understood not in an essentialist way but in a strategic and positional one. Likewise, another concept conducive to the sort of postcolonial identity I seek here is the notion of "the trace," found especially in the works of Jacques Derrida, himself an important influence on much of postcolonial theory. The "trace" of our "origins" assumes *the supplement* necessary for living on the boundary, in the interstitial space, where senses of wandering and lostness prevail, but more importantly, where tantalizing memories of "the trace" work effectively to fuel the vision needed to *move into* flourishing and sustaining of life in between. Identity then is under continuous erasure even as it is reconstructed and reappropriated with close attunement to the "trace" that works as an enlivening supplement.[13]

ESSENTIALISM ON TRIAL

In recent years, feminist discourse on differences among women, emerging from critiques of the assumed universal notion of womanhood, has led to the conundrum that any feminist talk laced with possible essentialist thinking is suspect and under constant surveillance. Moreover, this discourse has unwittingly shifted the same dynamics onto notions of cultural differences.[14] Problematic in this shift is the reification of colonialist assumptions about seemingly inherent cultural differences. Universal essentialist notions of women have thus been replaced with culture-specific essentialist notions about what constitutes "Western" or "non-Western."[15] Put another way, it is an attempt to jam "the theoretical machinery . . . of suspending its pretension to the production of a truth and of a meaning that are excessively univocal."[16]

The debates on essentialism, whether on sexuality, race, or gender, have been emerging as many groups and communities struggle not only to construct theoretical responses to such structures of oppression but also to form counterresistance to these structures.[17] The clash of theory and praxis is evident in these debates. The convergence of the politics of difference/identity with the politics of overall struggles such as feminism might well produce a gridlock that is debilitating for women and feminists, or it might work to bring about a radically hybrid understanding that opens up a new space for feminism.[18] The challenge facing feminism is critically stated by Ellen T. Armour:

> Attempts to attack women's oppression without attending to systemic violence at work in the discourse that inscribes the institutions and individuals we hold responsible for oppression and ourselves is to risk following exits that either leave the system in place or reinstate it on new ground.[19]

The relationship between feminist theory, theology, and practice cannot assume division of labor and a split between language and reality.

Susan Bordo articulates several trends, but here I would like to point to one key observation. She notes the importance of feminist appropriations of deconstructionism. At the postmodern recognition of "interpretive multiplicity, of indeterminacy, and heterogeneity of cultural meaning and meaning production," there is a call for "new narrative approaches, aimed at the adequate representation of . . . 'difference.'" Specifically, theories on gender difference are under attack for their "fixed binary structuring of reality" and are "replaced with a narrative ideal of ceaseless textual play."[20] However, she argues that this idea,

> while arising out of a critique of modernist epistemological pretensions
> to adequately represent reality, remains animated by its own fantasies

of attaining an epistemological perspective free of the locatedness and limitations of embodied existence—a fantasy that I call a "dream of everywhere."[21]

Bordo's apprehension of this capacity to obliterate the power of movement in the name of difference seems to be a case of "cut our nose off to spite our face" of what she calls the "institution of knowledge/power that still dominates" and is active in the public arena. Such institutions applauding these divide-and-conquer tactics work to "harness and tame the visionary and critical energy of feminism as a movement of cultural resistance and transformation."[22] But, as Bernice Regan has observed, what feminism needs as a countermove is to engage in coalitional work that embodies and is attentive to the politics of difference in order to garner, mediate, and mobilize political power. As a result, the two issues of politics of location and a coalition politics should be the central issues for feminists.[23]

Bordo insists on the dangers of the "view from nowhere" since she notes that all perspectives are totalizing to a certain extent. No epistemological ground is innocent. She notes, "For no theory—not even one which measures its adequacy in terms of justice to heterogeneity, locality, and complexity—can place itself beyond danger."[24] In terms of essentialism, Bordo argues that feminism in recent years is less in "danger of totalizing tendencies" and more in danger of an increasingly "paralyzing anxiety" of being accused of essentialism, in addition to our danger of espousing what appears to be a "view from nowhere and the dream of everywhere."[25] Such accusations imply that one's theory is deeply conservative and/or racist. What we might want to hold in tension is our suspicion of the totalizing potential of essentialist moves and our awareness that essentialist moves are necessary even if it means treading on dangerous ground—a ground in which, for the sake of political exigency, we might fall into the trap of reifying sexist, racist, homophobic, and imperialist notions. One possible illustration of this slippery slope is feminist contestation and appropriation of feminist relationalism.

Theologian Catherine Keller maintains that there is a developing trend within feminist postmodernism to disassociate from, and even to attack discursively, feminist relationalism.[26] Feminist relationalism is the emphasis placed on the importance of understanding the self as always implicated in relation to another. Feminist relationalism itself is accused of harboring essentialism. As Keller notes, to many scholars who identify themselves as feminists, "relationalism seems to entail a spurious 'feminine' essence." Keller further argues that such antirelationalist moves, homogenizing moves "in the service of heterogeneity," should be questioned. The binary oppositions of individual versus sociopolitical, feminist versus feminine, and essentialism versus antiessentialism all run the risk of involvement in a slippery slope argument.[27] Keller goes on to charge, and rightly so, that antiessentialist feminists are guilty of an "epistemic essentialism" of their own.[28] What we need then is a constant deconstruction of the very space from which we theorize. This double gesture demands that we "historicize . . . examine each deployment of essence, each appeal to experience, each claim to identity in the complicated contextual framework."[29] It is not that we "possess contingent identities but that identity is contingent."[30] Often the contingency of an identity and possible dangers of reified essentialism could also be approached from a practical angle in which one uses "practical effect" rather than rigid principles, but also one makes calculated strategic decisions when deciding which universal might work or fail in a particular context.[31]

Here I would like to refer to Gayatri Spivak's much-cited notion of "strategic essentialism." This concept uses strategically positioned essential identity to combat the oppressive tactics of colonial structure. In line with Bordo, while adapting poststructuralist theories to subaltern studies (subaltern are those considered to be economically disposed radically), Spivak works through essentialism in her own terms and not those dictated by any institutions. For her, this need for strategic essentialism is explained as follows: "As a deconstructivist . . . I cannot in fact clean my hands and say I'm specific. In fact I must say I am an essentialist from time to time." To use universalism and essentialism strategically without making totalizing commitments to these concepts, Spivak notes that we are always already committed to such concepts whether we admit it or not. For she notes that

> even as we talk about feminist practice or privileging practice over theory, we are universalizing—not only generalizing but universalizing. Since the moment of essentialising, universalizing . . . is irreducible . . . [l]et us become vigilant about our own practice and use it as much as we can rather than make the totally counter-productive gesture of repudiating it. . . . Because you are an essentialist from time to time.[32]

While the debate about essentialism/antiessentialism is constructive, it is important to note that most of us at one point resort to strategic essentialism. Essentialism has become a tricky concept for the feminist political agenda. It is a case of "can't live with it, can't live without it." For feminist scholars, then, the debate should no longer concentrate on whether to have traces of essentialism in our theories. Rather, feminists must now concentrate on how best to converse among the provocative traces of essentialism, which we seem unable to elude. Toward this end, Tina Chanter notes that the word "essentialism" has

> come to embody rifts that established themselves along a variety of interconnecting faults and that structured diverse feminist terrains;

the rocky ground on which practice and theory jostle one another; the treacherous territory in which psychoanalysis falls prey to political critique; the slippery slopes on which sexual difference is liable to slide into biological reductionism; the marshy swampland in which any assertion of feminine specificity risks subsiding into a murky pool of universal claims that threaten to immerse feminism in a morass of its own making. Increasingly fancy foot-work is required of feminists who negotiate these difficult domains.[33]

Unfortunately, this controversy between essentialism and constructionism has become antagonistic in feminist discourse as it spills over even into areas of feminist theology.[34] Primarily, the controversy is focused on what, if anything, can women speak of as feminist without reifying an already sexist, racist, or imperialist construct? This debate on essentialism is also pertinent to postmodern and postcolonial theory. Under the rubric of identity politics, discussions on gender, sexuality, race, religion, and culture—to name a few sites of contention—are often under constant surveillance for traces of essentialism. Such critical zeal for a purity/orthodoxy of its own should be understood as emerging out of necessary, unflinching self-examination for any traces of totalizing and dominating rhetoric.

Julia Kristeva, whose work on psychoanalysis will be engaged in my discussion on Christology, has also been criticized for her essentialism. Kristeva remains unapologetic. In fact, for Kristeva, feminism itself is problematic and is inadvertently an extension of patriarchy. According to her, feminism is an extension of the "Symbolic," or "the Law of the Father." In *Strangers to Ourselves*, Kristeva recognizes the struggles in the name of group identities. She does acknowledge that the feminist movement has made much progress by using the group identity of "woman." At the same time, she notes the dangers inherent in such tactics. Problematic to her, then, is that often politics of liberation become merely politics of exclusion.[35] This process of abjection is what compels Kristeva *into* and *through* the self. As much as feminists are critical of her work, she herself is critical of feminism. She concludes that feminists should not fight for "woman" but against "woman." She argues that the mirage of the "we" is problematic as much as it is necessary because even while the individual participates in this "we," each individual becomes her own victim.[36]

According to Kristeva, what we must address is the difference within personal identity itself. This is the first step toward addressing difference without attempting to "totalize it, annihilate it or reconcile it."[37] By delving deeper into personal identity, Kristeva seeks to understand the subject as the other. This does not necessarily mean that the subject and the other share strangeness, but that the subject can relate to an other as other because she is an other to herself. Thus, crucial to Kristeva's thesis is that alterity lies within.[38]

POLITICS OF HOME

According to postcolonial theory, identity is more fragmented and fractured than unified or singular. It is constructed across different and often intersecting and oppositional positions and practices. A postcolonial theory of hybridity, then, seeks not to claim origin or roots but to claim our multiple routes.

For many people, home is always on many thresholds, such that these people are not quite fully allowed entrance but always live on the borderlands of many realities. Home then is not only contingent on many different dynamics but also always provisional so that we are strangers in our supposed "homeland" as well as in our new places of being. As a result one repeatedly feels out of place within what are familiar but also differing worlds. This unsettling feeling causes us to scrutinize questions of settlement so "as to make it easier for the diversely unsettled ones to bear the anxieties of unwonted seclusion."[39]

We might return to our origins, but the origins are forever changed and changing while we also change. However, hyphenated people are often seen, at worst, as cultural scavengers and abandoners of heritage and, at best, as watchdogs who keep progressive Euro-American liberals from being too complacent and too comfortable with their "totalizing" theories. It is from these experiences of fragmentation, indeed of a certain dismemberment, that I have come to realize that "home" and "elsewhere" are neither fixed, monolithic, nor unproblematic categories. As Sang Hyun Lee, a Korean American theologian, observes, this sense of homelessness might in turn be interpreted as a "sacred journey." This metaphor of "journey" embodies both the remembering of our past roots and the forging of new routes. According to him, the Asian American experience of marginality as liminality opens up new ways of reappropriating and reenvisioning biblical themes of pilgrimage and home.[40] Although he does not specifically use the postcolonial language of "interstitial space," by arguing for the necessity of "hyphenated" identities as an integral part of being open to God's household, Sang Hyun Lee is the pioneering Asian American to theologize about "in-betweenness" from both the immigrant context and a biblical standpoint.[41]

R. A. Saugiartha notes that the reality of homelessness is becoming a new hermeneutic framework that is provoking contradictory responses. On the one hand, we have theorists who advocate a global, borderless, geopolitical agenda while, on the other hand, we have those who are ethnonationalists struggling to reclaim/reconstruct indigenous histories. Saugiartha suggests a third alternative. He calls on people to position themselves "between and betwixt cultures and countries and engage in a processual hermeneutics."[42] He further cites Jan Mohamed's notion of "interstitial cultural space," similar to Homi Bhabha's "Third Space," as an alternative if not an "uncolonized space" from which contemporary hermeneutical praxis must above all reserve freedom to hybridize. The importance for Saugiartha regarding the postcolonial is not that it is about a new period but that it is a particular reading posture emerging from the colonized other.

The postcolonial task, then, is a discursive resistance against narratives of oppression.[43] As feminist cultural critic Trinh Minh-ha suggests, home is a place/space/time that locates the invisible traces of elsewhere in what is familiar, always locating already interlocking incongruities that are recognized as "home."[44] She further remarks,

> Home is a site that is constantly shifting. . . . Home can be said to be also a site of change, whose movement often reflects a different pace and a different sense of time. . . . Home has conveniently been considered to be the place of purity . . . yet the place of "impurity" can become extremely enabling since one can draw from it unthought of relationships . . . that [are] not defined by a dualist shuttling between native and non-native.[45]

The profundity of "no place like home" and "no place is home" pushes for the constant shuttling/doubling of the self and invariably reminds us of the otherness within. The question of "home" and locating this "home," whether by a sense of return or through imagined communities, has been drastically complicated by postcolonial theory.

Postcolonial theory has challenged the often-dichotomizing tendency of identity politics in favor of an understanding of identity as a complex and often-shifting construct. As Rita Nakashima Brock notes, "Interstitial life often feels like a process of being torn among several different worlds that refuse to get along."[46]

The hyphenation of identity into Asian American, for example, expresses the reality that Asia is not an unchanging ontological condition while pointing toward its specificity. This helps to avoid falling into the essentialist trap yet still recognize the trap's political necessity. Furthermore, hyphenation becomes a way of investing in the strategic, even as we open up utopian spaces beyond the regime of dominance-as-history.[47] Moreover, as much as we engage in identity politics as a way of opening up of multiple positions and more fluid identities, let us keep in mind certain vagaries of postcolonial theories that simultaneously resonate with and challenge poststructuralism.

Currently postcolonial disruptions of master narratives, which insist on the heterogeneity of all identities and cultures, are becoming much more persistent.[48] The insistence on such ongoing processes of hybridization of peoples and cultures allows for the seemingly incoherent pieces of identities to be loosely connected. This disruption allows the subaltern to reinscribe and revise metanarratives, including the mythology of white patriarchal supremacy. Along with the emergence of postcolonial theory, dissonant voices among a large network of postcolonial theorists are articulated. One of the serious critiques that we need to be mindful of is the critique that theories of hybridity tend to be academic and not rooted in the struggles of the subaltern. In short, postcolonial theory is accused of being preoccupied with existential/ontological navel gazing while lacking any political agency. While this might be true from a superficial discursive stand, we need to keep in mind the assertion that the personal is the political. Additionally, postcolonial theory cannot and should not be judged from a binary epistemological standpoint of what constitutes "political."

Critiques of postcolonial theory have asserted that its expression closely resembles that of poststructuralism, a postfoundationalist discourse deployed mainly by displaced Third World intellectuals in prestigious settings. These arguments go further to suggest that postcolonial theory underplays the importance of capitalism and its connection with the First World and the ensuing oppressions by avoiding analysis of material reality. Theorist Ella Shohat is adamant that postcolonial theory is theoretically and politically ambiguous in its "dizzying multiplicity of positionalities," in its "ahistorical and universalizing displacements," and in its "depoliticizing implications."[49] She notes that postcolonial theory is politically vague and ambiguous because of its tendency to blur the clear-cut distinctions between colonizers and colonized. While not completely wrong, this critique too easily dismisses postcolonial complexity. Postcolonial theory attempts to encompass the complexity of our postcolonial situation. If the starting point of postcolonial theory is a critique of various manifestations of capitalism, empires, and colonialism, how could one possibly level a critique to postcolonial theory that it is not political?

Critics also point out that postcolonial theory tends to collapse different histories and racial formations into the same universalizing categories. It dissolves the politics of resistance because it calls for no clear opposition.[50] Problematic to Shohat is "hybridity, cultural undecidability and the complexities of diasporic identification which interrupt any 'return' to ethnically closed and 'centered' original histories."[51] Rather than a complete disconnection, she does, however, suggest a gradual epistemological shift that is a movement of deconstruction-reconstruction. Theologian David Tracy offers a similar critique in a rather different fashion when he writes,

> Postmodernity releases the voices of the subjugated knowledge; the voices of all those marginalized by the official story of modern triumph. Often postmoderns are proud and ironic in their centerlessness. . . . Having killed the modern subject they too must now face their own temptation to drag all reality into the laughing abyss of that centerless, subjectless but very Western labyrinth.[52]

Many theologians from non-Western countries point to precisely this situation as the dangerous slippery slope in the praxis of liberation. Again, what constitutes "authentic" *subalternity*? What epistemological criteria do we use when we continue to refer to the bifurcation of colonized and colonizer; or to "original histories" as if we might truly return to some "pure," uncontaminated nativized place?

It is quite relevant here in the beginning to point out this particular and consistent critique of postcolonial theory even among the theorists themselves. It of course is the question of the relationship between dominant narratives, subjugated knowledge, and insurrection. This complex relationship questions, hints, and unfolds the subversive space, on the boundaries, from where we theorize. Radhakrishnan points to its very position as "rupturally from within the hegemonic body or from a position 'without' that is not complicitous with the mandates of the official body of knowledge."[53]

Most feminists, as an example of subjugated positions, have argued for the necessity to conceive of their positions as "lacks" or "absences" in need of retrievals and reconstructions within the dominant structures. Currently, there is a gradual shift that is moving less toward reconstruction than toward the recognition that feminist theory might be claimed as separate and disjointed from the official, master-theoretical discourse and capable of creating its own space without building on the structures of given dominant discursive practices. Feminist discourse no longer relies on master/patriarchal discourse in order to validate itself. Furthermore, such insurgent ways of doing theory move away from seeing these new theories always as "insurrections" and therefore always "transgressive," "progressive," and "reactive" in identity, which forces groups into a dubious if not dangerously paternalistic position of power.[54] I would suggest that the paradox of postcolonial identity lies within this matrix. Insistence on strategies of separation drives us right back to the position that vehemently believes in such misguided notions of purism.[55]

Perhaps the challenge resides in the embodiment of incommensurable multiple and complex identities. Being sharply attuned to the complexities, indeterminacies, and vagaries of theories and realities, I suggest that we work with a critical epistemology in its entire complexity, while being vigilant to the various attending politics. Because of the need to work with such interwoven and inexplicable complexities between poststructuralism and postcolonial theory, there is still an important difference that needs to be named. The difference is that notions of traveling and unfixed identity have less at stake within U.S. poststructuralism than in postcolonial theory. The daring and the risk taking seem to remain more epistemological in the former, whereas they take on a sense of constituency and politics in the latter.

FEMINIST, POSTCOLONIAL IDENTITY— TOWARD *JEONG*

Feminism has changed over the years, yet it also has not changed in certain aspects. Feminism, criticized for its own brand of universalizing tendencies, has undergone much change due to its unrelenting desire toward a utopian vision. Such self-critical reflections have not only facilitated shifts within feminist theory but also in their critical engagement with the emergence of postmodern deconstructionism. After the deconstruction of the subject, poststructuralist feminist articulations of ethical and political agency and practice are among the most debated within the academy. Poststructuralist critiques of the autonomous subject have been motivated by the totalitarian nature of subjectivity. However, as much as the subject has been deconstructed of its totalitarian shroud, poststructuralism has also inadvertently failed to provide any satisfactory alternative political agency. What seems to be an easy and natural alliance between feminism and postmodernism is actually a double-edged relationship. Feminism has argued that the fundamental categories of Western philosophy obliterate differences of gender in terms of how experience and subjectivity are shaped and structured.

The movement of "death of history" and "death of the subject" comes at a time when oppressed groups are claiming themselves as subjects of history. Hence, even while we critique and dismantle grand narratives, it is crucial for us to be mindful of what constitutes grand narrative and whose histories and narrative we are dispensing with in our grand, sweeping gestures. For as Kristeva points out, there is never a full and complete extrication, nor should we desire that. For how can we be free without "some sort of utopia, some sort of strangeness?" In short, then, we must accept that we are of nowhere without "forgetting that we are somewhere."[56]

Seyla Benhabib thus asks, "Can feminist theory be postmodernist and still retain an interest in emancipation?"[57] While she concedes the necessary emancipatory agenda of postmodern thought, she suggests that postmodernism has produced a "retreat from utopia" within feminism. Moreover, she is critical that feminist theory has become wary of any essentialist attempt to formulate a "feminist ethic, a feminist politics, a feminist concept of autonomy, and even feminist aesthetic."[58] According to Benhabib, while postmodernism may illuminate the traps posed by making narratives and claiming subjectivity, feminism still cannot retreat from envisioning utopias. Benhabib, in the vein of other feminist and cultural critiques that are critical of what seems to be an abandonment of praxis, goes on to note that "the postmodernist position(s) thought through to their conclusions may eliminate not only the specificity of feminist theory but place in question the very emancipatory ideals of the women's movement altogether."[59]

As much as feminism has worked toward emancipation from a patriarchal apparatus, it, similar to postcolonial theory, has generated much criticism from within and certainly from the outside as well. Feminist theory, including feminist theology, continues creatively and critically to be engaged with manifestations of patriarchal power in history. Much criticism has been generated especially from within feminism in terms of its identity. Thus, feminism has contributed to identity politics, politics of difference, and to poststructuralist thought. The emergence of critiques, especially from women of color, ensures that feminism widens its scope in terms of its identity. Problematic to postcolonial theory is the tendency to ghettoize, marginalize, tokenize, universalize, or essentialize particular complex identities into a seemingly simple unitary identity.[60]

Thus, identity is now understood in terms of "multiple oppressions" and of "triple or double jeopardy."[61] In this way, the difference among women and within feminism itself has begun to emerge. Hence,

> what is emerging in feminist writings is . . . the concept of multiple, shifting, and often self-contradictory identity, a subject that is not divided in, but rather at odds with, language; an identity made up of heterogeneous and heteronomous representations of gender, race, and class, and often indeed across languages and cultures; an identity that one decides to reclaim from a history of multiple assimilations, and that one insists on as a strategy.[62]

Out of this, another trend has emerged to broaden our understanding of identity politics for feminism. One of the dangers of constructing an identity solely based on one subject, such as race, is that we tend to overlook the "epistemic violence" that takes place within the complex web that constructs identity.[63] Within this context, the self is analyzed in depth with the recognition that the self is not singular but rather multiple. This view is also connected with feminist theories on multiple and contradictory subject positions within the self. The emergence of all these different contours to feminism has also led to engagement with other emerging theories, such as relational and situational epistemology of the subject.[64] From both within and without, Western feminism has challenged the ethnocentric myth of sisterhood but, more importantly, the problematic universalizing of gender.[65] Such awareness has led to a deconstructive analysis of the complex relationships between women and politics of identity.[66] Thus, gender can no longer be posited as an essential and universal category that takes exigency over and/or against other relations. Perhaps one important observation is that we practice not "feminism" but "feminisms."[67]

Chandra Mohanty has also argued that feminism should rethink the inadequacies of how we evaluate experiences and conditions, especially of women in the postcolonial context. Mohanty calls for a theory of relational agency that understands the "complex relationality that shapes our social and political lives" in order to rewrite oppression by particularizing the struggles of fragmented subjects in interstitial sites. These sites are often fraught with indeterminacies but also with knowledge that interrupts the "grand narratives."[68]

A politics of difference encourages a dialectic that neither represses difference nor privileges identity. A politics of difference struggles for the rights of oppressed groups to seize the power of naming the difference, and it explodes the implicit definition of difference as deviance in relation to a norm.[69] Thus, difference now comes to mean not otherness or exclusive opposition, but specificity, variation, heterogeneity. Difference names relations of similarity and dissimilarity that can be "reduced to neither coextensive identity nor non-over-lapping otherness."[70]

While being mindful of the double-edged relationship between feminism and postmodernism, Judith Butler strongly writes, "Identity categories are never merely descriptive, but always normative, and as such exclusionary."[71] This translates into responsibility for feminists to be on guard whenever identities are being constituted in nationalist, gender, or class terms. Butler notes that deconstruction of identity is not the "deconstruction of politics; rather, it establishes as political the very terms through which identity is articulated."[72] She does not, however, suggest the death of categories but rather that categories/terms ought to be opened up from totalizing tendencies. She further voices that

> the rifts between and among women over the content of the term ought to be safeguarded and prized, indeed, . . . this constant rifting ought to be affirmed as the ungrounded ground of feminist theory. To deconstruct the subject of feminism is not, then, to censure its usage, but, on the contrary, to release the term into a future of multiple significations, to emancipate it from the maternal or racialist ontologies to which it has been restricted, to give it play as a site where unanticipated meanings might come to bear.[73]

Feminist work on relational positionalities seems to be more aligned with the postcolonial perspective on hybridity and ambivalency. Such relationality should be read differently from pluralism, which runs the risk of erasing or repressing the analysis of structural power relations and systems of domination. This is a reminder that most often our hasty celebration of difference either erases difference or domesticates difference into ineffective politics. As Audre Lorde's much-cited insights indicate, difference must be not merely tolerated, but seen as a fund of necessary polarities between which our creativity can spark like dialectic. Only then does the necessity for interdependency become unthreatening. . . .[74]

Relational positionalities understand that the flow of power in multiple systems of domination is not always unidirectional. Rather, they embrace the possibility of double-edged identities coexisting within the self. Thus *han* and *jeong*, oppressor and oppressed, coexist within the individual. Therefore, current theorizing about concepts such as hybridity allow feminism to move beyond the exclusive focus on difference. In her call to go "beyond" the politics of difference, Friedman explicitly advocates a "post-difference feminism." In her use of the word "beyond," she does not abandon the existence of racism or sexism. Rather, by "beyond" she confronts the "grid-lock" or "the difference impasse" faced within feminism and other emancipatory movements.[75] She is adamant that we have much to learn in order to work together despite our differences. Hence, for Friedman, "beyond" is used in terms of

hither and thither, back and forth, between our competing needs to understand difference and to chart the spaces in between difference . . . a dialogic movement between sameness and difference, between mimesis and alterity . . . and between "universalizing" and "minoritizing." . . . Feminism . . . should refuse polarized choices between difference-talk or hybridity-talk.[76]

Problematic to Friedman is the loss of people's visions for emancipation. By seriously taking into account the utopic visions that have powerful material effects and that have often fueled the resistance to unequal distribution of power based on group identification, she insists that utopic vision is not a luxury but a necessity that we cannot afford to abandon. Friedman pushes us to think that perhaps in resisting the ethnic or gender absolutism that underlies the dominance of difference talk amongst feminists, we might be able to think of a possible move "beyond" difference. According to Friedman, one of the dangers of difference-talk is that it tends to "suppress attention to sameness produced in the liminal spaces in between racial, ethnic, sexual, religious, or geopolitical difference."[77]

For Trinh, our search for identity is often our search for a "pure," "true," "original," authentic self that is often situated within a "process of elimination of all that is considered other, superfluous, fake, corrupted, or Westernized."[78] Simultaneously, whatever is said, claimed, and accessed is already suspected of totalizing maneuvers. Hegemony works to level out differences. Difference should not be defined by the dominant sex nor by the dominant culture. The self-marking or the speaking as so-and-so, as an Asian American or Korean

American feminist, turns out "to be a form of validating one's own voice within permitted boundaries."[79] Not surprisingly then,

> understanding a strategy as strategy changes the way you speak. Each one of us has more than one subject positioning, and the demarcation of "speaking as" is always shifting according to circumstances, contexts, or historical moments. . . . Therefore, what you offer is not a solidified boundary but a positioning whose ability to shift and to remain multiple defies all reductive attempts at fixing and classifying.[80]

Therefore, Trinh maintains it is necessary for people who are always specifying to question such boundaries as we reclaim our identities. These identities that have been denied or undermined historically cannot be used to confine us now.[81] Theory of difference, as it is being constructed within feminist discourse, is brought to a practical level. Many marginalized people note that it is always up to us to specify ourselves whereas those who are in the dominant position retain their sense of power through the absence of their specificity. This idea resonates with bell hooks's observation that the relationship of women of color to feminists has in the past been solely limited to discussions on race.[82] We often recognize the need to be specific while at the same time we feel the closures that are placed by such need for specificity. For Trinh, difference can be inclusive of similarities in addition to being beyond and alongside conflicts. Difference furthermore is not something that is only between the outsider and the insider; it is also at work within the outsider or the insider herself. She observes that "difference" is "essentially division in the understanding of many."[83] Identity politics for Trinh takes on the complex contours of deconstructionism in that the moment something is named is also the moment that can only be positional and transitional; so for her, the process of naming is to "dive headlong into the abyss of un-naming."

There is then a need for an interplay of cultural signs of identity that oscillate with sameness and difference that is "historically embodied within the context of complex power relations." Difference has been the bone of contention not only among feminist discourses but also in areas such as racism. Theories on difference have opened up new ways of analyzing relations of power and oppression.[84] On the other hand, eruption of difference has created deep chasms that stand in the way of coalitional politics. Perhaps what is necessary for postcolonial and even for feminist politics is a "critical tactic that will call into question both the economy of identity and the axiology of binarity that underwrites the nomology of identity."[85] This is the interstitial space for feminist and postcolonial contentions along the axis of theory and praxis. For in the postcolonial situation, "identity is shot through and through with difference, and yet identity is direly needed."[86] Postcolonial theory, however, recognizes such contrary positions and opens up new sites to explore and embody the complexities within us. Friedman thus notes that

> the exclusivity of difference-talk fosters politically dangerous balkan-ization and suppresses both the utopic longing for connection and the visibility of the everyday realities of intercultural mixing. . . . The exclusivity of hybridity-talk can in turn slip into a romantization that elides the existence of collective identities on the one hand and the structures of power that construct them on the other.[87]

Friedman therefore argues for a promotion of both/and ways of thinking rather than either/or responses. She further insists that such suppressive binary thinking jeopardizes heterogeneity in the name of difference-talk. As a Korean woman, the tension continues to be placed between my need for polit-ically potent ground to stand on and the totalizing narratives of racism, sex-ism, and classism, to name a few. On the other hand, I am pulled by the call of radical freedom that is critical of boundaries and totalizing narratives.[88]

My discussion of postcolonial identity, location, essentialism, and difference was done with a feminist appropriation of *jeong* in mind. The "backbone" of *jeong* is relationality of the self with the other. Feminists' appropriation of "relationality" has often come under fire from different feminist sectors as reifi-cation of yet another "false" and "contaminated" patriarchal concept. The concept of relationality has been critiqued as unwittingly embracing a patriar-chalized "feminine" concept for the liberative works of feminism. Certainly, this debate on feminist appropriation of relationality centers on the issue of essentialism. My appropriation of *jeong* might also be construed as reifying a concept conducive to patriarchal notions of femininity. By engaging in the debate over essentialism, I have attempted to highlight some of the key issues pertinent to this debate. This chapter has focused on the politics of identity and difference and then on the contested meanings of essentialism as a way into our introduction of a feminist appropriation of *jeong*. Having highlighted my awareness of this persistent conflict over relationality, I will now introduce the concepts of *jeong* and *han*. The next chapter will plunge deeply into the concept of *jeong* via *han*, particularly through feminist psychoanalytic and postcolonial theories. These two concepts have been briefly introduced because they will provide the basis for articulating what I propose as a Christology of *jeong*.

2

Han and *Jeong*

This chapter will examine the Korean concept of suffering through the idea of *han*. The individual and collective suffering of Korean people are deeply interwoven within history, and Korean theologians have articulated a liberation theology through an analysis of *han*. This chapter delineates the concept of *han* through Minjung theologians' use of the term and also shows how it might be understood through Julia Kristeva's notion of "abjection" and Jae Hoon Lee's psychoanalytical perspective. I will also analyze an avant-garde Korean film, *Joint Security Area*, and a Korean American documentary, *Sa-I-Gu* (4-29). The former illustrates a profound sense of *han* in a particular time and space of the Demilitarized Zone while the latter portrays the violence, injustice, and complexity of U.S. systemic racism as encapsulated in the Los Angeles riots of April 29, 1992. In unfolding *han* in these ways we also here introduce *jeong* as a related but distinctive notion.

PSYCHOANALYSIS OF *HAN* AND *JEONG*

> The pain of suffering is inscribed deep in the backbone, the face, the voice and the heart.
>
> Ham Sok Hon, *The Queen of Suffering*

Ham Sok Hon was a passionate activist, critical philosopher, prophetic theologian, and lover of Korea and Korean people. In his life, he challenged Russian, Chinese, Japanese, and American imperialism. He was not only passionately critical of these "outsiders" but also critically vigilant of his own country's move toward becoming a democratic nation. Even before postcolonial theory emerged in academia, he was already engaged with his own form

19

of postcolonial consciousness as a person who came to critical consciousness in the March First Movement in Korea as a student. Moreover, he struggled with Marxism, capitalism, and Christianity. In the end, he became known as a Christian heretic, critical of the orthodoxies of Marxism and capitalism as well. He argued that Korean people could not uncritically import these philosophies but that the liberation of Korea and Koreans must emerge from Koreans themselves, from the Minjung. His metaphor of the mustard seed for everyday people, the Minjung, was the catalyst for Minjung theology, and I consider him a forerunner of Minjung theology itself. His awareness of Korea is in a paradoxical position between roots and routes.

Minjung theologians have argued that *han* (a form of suffering) is caused predominantly by social, political, and economic oppression. Their analysis of *han* was mainly from a Marxist theoretical perspective.[1] Korean feminist theologians have argued, furthermore, that for Korean women, all these oppressive factors are compounded by sexism; thus Korean women are the "Minjung of Minjung." Both Andrew Sung Park and Jae Hoon Lee insist that even though as the concept of *han* is uniquely Korean, the experience of *han* is universal to those who suffer and are oppressed. As Lee observes, "*han* is a . . . broad and deep image that speaks to all human beings about the mysterious source of both suffering and creativity."[2] Lee's methodology of understanding *han* is through depth psychology since he is insistent that *han* is not only social/structural but also a psychological reality existing in the deeper layers of the psyche.[3] In his consideration of those who experience *han* in history, Park not only refers to the Minjung of Korea but also to those who suffered at the hands of white Christianity—for example, Africans who were forcefully enslaved and removed to North America. He refers as well to the *han* of racism and sexism, and to the *han* of nature.[4] Park offers further illustration of *han* by noting that

> *han* can be defined as the critical wound of the heart generated by unjust psychosomatic repression, as well as by social, political, economic, and cultural oppression. It is entrenched in the hearts of the victims of sin and violence, and is expressed through such diverse reactions as sadness, helplessness, hopelessness, resentment, hatred, and the will to revenge. *Han* reverberates in the souls of survivors of the Holocaust, Palestinians in the occupied territories, victims of racial discrimination, battered wives, victims of child-molestation, the unemployed and exploited workers.[5]

Park also contends that *han* is brokenheartedness—the woundedness of the heart. When the "ruptured heart" is wounded "again by external violence, the victim suffers a deeper pain. . . . The wound . . . is *han* in the heart."[6] By linking *han* and the traditional doctrine of sin, Park argues for a wholistic approach to sin whereby we not only understand sin from the perspective of those sinners who cause sin but also of those who are victims of sin and injustice. According to Park, *han* is not only the "abysmal" experience of pain; it is also dominated by feelings of abandonment and helplessness.[7] Individual and collective *han* result, therefore, through individual and collective sin. Park makes a general assessment that there are arguably three dominant modes through which *han* is generated: the capitalist global economy, patriarchy, and racial/cultural discrimination. Moreover, Park observes that in order to unravel *han* "we must understand that patriarchy is one of the major matrices in which the *han* of the world is produced."[8] Park, Chung, and Lee have all made notations regarding the link between the experience of *han* and patriarchy. Park explains that *han* has the possibility of being active or inactive. Active *han* manifests in aggressive emotion while inactive *han* is closer to acquiescent spirit.[9]

Lee closely aligns his research with that of Melanie Klein. Similar to Park, Lee notes the double-edged manifestation of *han* as *won-han* and *hu-han*.[10] I would argue further that *han* itself is also double-edged because it is present not only in the oppressed but in the deeper psyches of the oppressors. Recognizing the prevalence of *han* in both the oppressors and the oppressed allows us to admit that a dichotomy can no longer function as the only critical hermeneutics of resistance. According to Lee, depending on the depth of this "original *han*," a person's reception to present external *han* will vary. Citing Korean analysts Kyu-Tae Lee and Bou-yong Rhie, Jae Hoon Lee attests that *han* results from both the serious, negative mother complex and the split-ego complex.[11] Lee concludes that, depending on their prior loss and ego fragmentation, individuals also experience the external experiences of *han* differently. Lee maintains that the present experiences of *han* often activate "the original fragmentation of the ego, existing in a deep layer of one's personal unconscious."[12] Interestingly, he calls this deep fragmentation within the unconscious the "original wound" and "original *han*."[13]

After having examined diverse manifestations and expressions of *han* through folklore, shamanism, literature, and psychology, Lee concludes that there exists a "layer of an original type of *han*."[14] He makes a clear distinction between this "original *han*" and the present external experience of *han* as "secondary *han*." Lee goes on to make a case that the "original *han* is beyond the reach of conscious memory, since it is formed during the early days of childhood. Since the original *han* remains in the personal unconscious and is unavailable to conscious memory, it thus exerts great influence."[15] Due to an overriding sense of self-preservation, the ego suppresses and represses this painful memory of original *han*. However, as much as this original *han* might harbor a tremendous sense of pain and loss, it nevertheless also embodies what Lee calls "life energy" that must be released.[16] Here one must ask whether this "life energy" could be connected to the dynamic experience of *han*. I would say that this "life energy," this "chi," manifests itself through relational *han*, which often disarmingly tunes one into a sense of mutual vulnerability.

Such repression inevitably works against the ego because it cannot then respond to an external present experience of *han* in a healthy manner. Repression of original *han* as the ego's way of protection instead functions to paralyze one from responding to an external, present experience of *han*. Lee goes on to insist that only when the original *han*, the original wound, is healed can the secondary *han* be "sustained, overcome and creatively sublimated."[17] He maintains that analysis of secondary *han*, as has been done by Minjung theologians, is not enough. Rather, in order for us to really heal and unravel *han*, we must also delve into the deepest layers of our unconscious where our original *han* lies dormant. Lee also adheres to the dominant psychoanalytic theory on *han* that the seedbed of original *han* lies within the negative mother complex. He goes on to declare that because original *han* is formed during early childhood, the role of the mother is extremely important to study. Lee's work on *han* relies on Melanie Klein's analysis of childhood, which resulted in the concept of the "bad mother's breast." Lee goes on to correlate these two states as *hu-han* and *won-han*.

Han is inevitably interwoven with the presence of *jeong*, so much so that we can write *jeong-han*; yet Koreans have often highlighted this *jeong* as depressive rather than liberative. Previous understanding of *han* has been limited to what was known as *hu-han* in the past. However, I am insisting that the androcentric perspective of both the social context and the scholars has been a limitation in the past. Through depth psychology, especially that of Melanie Klein, Lee notes that the inner dynamics of *hu-han* are similar to those of psychic depression. The most important feature of *jeong-han* is that love and aggression coexist. We might allude that *jeong-han* could be likened to a release of a long sigh by the person who has experienced *han* while a person experiencing *won-han* might articulate and demand justice. Moreover, a person who experiences *won-han* without any change in the status quo and who continues to experience even more pain and suffering might become hopeless, and in that hopelessness, a person's *won-han* will express itself through *hu-han*. *Hu-han* expresses its outlet through aggressive attack against the object of his/her oppression. It no longer sees justice as a possibility but rather its aggressive impulse is instead revenge. The main concept of *hu-han*, as is proved in the long history of Korean culture, is that love is entangled with hate such that "in *hu-han* the focus is not on the survival of self under the threat of annihilation but on the well-being of the object that the ego relates to."[18] According to Lee, *hu-han* could be divided into two phases: the early phase, dominated by masochism, and the second phase, wherein melancholy comes on strong. *Han* in its complexity often works to blur distinctions and to clear divisions and separations.[19] *Han* could also be then understood in terms of melancholy.

Intriguingly, Julia Kristeva's portrayal of melancholy resonates deeply with definitions of *han*. For Kristeva, the best symbol of melancholy is the "black sun":

> It is an abyss of sorrow. . . . A devitalized existence . . . the inner threshold of my despondency, the impossible meaning of life whose burden constantly seems unbearable. . . . I live a living death, my flesh is wounded, bleeding, cadaverized, my rhythm slowed down or interrupted, time has been erased or bloated, absorbed into sorrow.[20]

As Lee observes, in the first stage of *jeong-han* one experiences an overdose of sorrow and self-reproach. One regresses back to *won-han* as a defensive measure when the pain becomes too overwhelming. Lee argues that if one becomes stuck in this early phase of *won-han*, one will suffer from pain without articulating the reasons for such suffering.

According to Lee, *won-han* contains feelings of sorrow, love, reproach, and emptiness, and *won* means resentment and/or hate. The confrontation between *won-han* and *hu-han* is, in short, a confrontation between love and hate, or between "life and death instincts."[21] Lee's work indicates that *han* is double-edged in its embodiment of love and hate. Love and hate thus coexist in the experience of *han*. When hate gets stronger, it becomes *won-han*, whereas when love becomes the stronger force, *han* turns into *jeong-han*. Lee argues that the fluctuation between love and hate, between *won-han* and *hu-han*, are not done arbitrarily, but that experiences of *han* tend to drive one toward either *won-han* or *hu-han*.

Most often, women experience, and are allowed by patriarchy to experience, *han* as *jeong-han* whereas men are dictated by the norms of patriarchy to experience *han* as *won-han*. In the practice of *dan* (the practice of severing/cutting off forms of oppression), the male experience of *won-han* is often encouraged to lead to the practice of *dan*. The transition of *won-han* to *hu-han*, as Lee observes, is a rather slow and painful process, during which "regression to *won-han* takes place repeatedly."[22] Thus, when the suffering of *jeong-han* is felt too painfully and accumulated for too long without signs of healing or justice, *won-han* is brought to the foreground as a defensive measure against the crushing weight of *jeong-han*. Clearly, this view is more acute given the nature of the patriarchal perception of *jeong-han* as a passive, ineffective, compromised, and domesticated way of exorcising *han*. The theological articulation of *han* and the ensuing discussion of *jeong* are crucial to understanding the possible power of *jeong* in overcoming *han*.

Lee further notes that the predominant feeling of *jeong-han* is depression, through which anxiety leads to hate, which is often expressed in self-reproach.

For example, this experience of *jeong-han*, embodied by Korean people, and especially by Korean women, has caused much grief in those who have experienced catastrophes in the United States. Instead of this *han* being projected onto others, such incidents among Koreans often lead inward. The harshness of the self-reproach in *jeong-han* often becomes "reduced along the course of its maturation into guilt proper, which is capable of taking responsibility based on a more realistic assessment of reality."[23]

Lee suggests that *han* turned to anger appears as *won-han*, which calls for vengeance and revolution. *Han* turned pessimistic and regressive is known as *jeong-han*, which tends to encourage resignation and adaptation to reality. I would like to suggest here a feminist critique of this explanation. Most often Minjung scholars have associated *won-han* as the energy that fuels social and historical change by crying out for revolution. As tremendous as Minjung theologians' contributions to liberation theology have been, their articulation of *han* and *won-han* has also been vicariously associated with what I see as a binary response to the experience of *han*.

A categorical distinction or separation between *hu-han* and *won-han* is not only difficult but also hazardous to make, for in reality they are two sides of the same coin: *han*. In reality, they coexist saliently and fluidly in the personal and the collective unconscious. The contents of *won-han*, as noted by Lee, include feelings of grudge, hate and vengefulness, and emptiness.[24] Citing Korean scholar Yul-kyu Kim on aspects of *han*, Lee notes, "*Won-han* is born from death, grows from death and yields to death."[25] Lee observes that when the depressive pain of *jeong-han* is felt as too painful, *won-han* emerges as a defense against the *jeong-han*. When *won-han* goes deeper and becomes extreme, people often experience complete withdrawal, feelings of persecution, and a paranoiac sense of threat. Lee defines this stage as *won-han* turned into *hu-han*.[26]

Those who experience *hu-han* feel they have to choose the most extreme line of activity as a way of overcoming what they perceive to be their own fear and contempt for their weak existence. They are often "gripped by the logic of extremity."[27] Throughout his writing, Lee is most notably concerned with the dangers of *hu-han*. Lee observes that

> *hu-han* people try to justify destruction and violence in the name of future creation, so they become revolutionaries . . . but in the destruction itself, they have no hope for the future. Hopelessness and despair are their plight. . . . Extreme idealization of someone of a certain cause is a feature of *hu-han* phenomenon. They tend to idealize and praise suicide in the name of great cause, and avoid looking at the tragic aspect of death.[28]

The terrorist acts that occurred on September 11, 2001, come to mind as a manifestation of explosive *hu-han*. The site of the destruction at New York's

World Trade Center has been called Ground Zero by the media. The site of *han* is most often the place of Ground Zero in our lives. At Ground Zero, we witness the convergence of death and life, hatred and love, extreme *jeong* and *han*. At the same time, the majority of American citizens' reactions to Sept. 11 emerged from the *han* of their individual lives that found a target in this incident as a way of coalescing individual *han* into collective *han*. The initial reactions of outrage, anger, bitterness, and dumbfoundedness seem to be rooted in *won-han*. *Won-han* is distinctive for its deep awareness of injustice and justice seeking. *Hu-han* has given up on justice as a possible goal and seeks instead retaliation and violent revenge.

The instinctive *won-han* reaction to seek retribution and retaliation—to "hunt" down the perpetrators—seems to come from a militarized sense of *dan* in reaction to the government's call for the "eradication of evildoers from the world." For some Americans, the response was double-edged: we struggled with *won-han* in the face of such tragedy while, through introspection, we also recognized our sense of *han* with others, even with the plight of those in the world "who hate us so much." The Ground Zero of *han* embodies the complexity and the ambivalency of love and hate, recognition and disavowal, and the need for "cutting off" and "coming together." Lee's observations on the inner dynamics of *han* and its many phases are crucial in understanding the power of *jeong*. Though he includes the works of Minjung theologians in their exploration of *han*, Lee is at the same time critical of what he perceives to be a lack of distinction between "healthy symbols that deserve to be lifted up to the level of social or religious symbols and the unhealthy symbols originated from individual or collective pathologies."[29] He further insists that creativity is often mixed with pathological phenomena.[30] While most Minjung theologians assume the innocence of *han*-ridden people as the victims of oppression, Lee insists that such is not the case. This binary thinking would further deepen the problem of unresolved *han*. *Han* and *han*-ridden people's experience are much more complex and fluid than one would like to believe. Against such beliefs of binary divisions between clear victims and victimizers, Lee hints at the possibility of complex relationships and fluid identities that all coexist in a web of power structures. Lee observes that *han* is more than the social oppressions that are experienced by the people. Lee insists,

> *Han* is not innocent. Innocent suffering is one cause of *han*, but once it becomes *han* it loses its innocence by becoming the source of evil forces that seek revenge on other innocent victims. *Han*, however, can be transformed, just as one personality can be transformed, into a more mature form.[31]

Lee argues that the nature of the human psyche is much more complex and that *han* is never created by external sources alone. For Lee, the simple dichotomy of oppressed and oppressor is contrary to what seems to be a complex and dynamic psychic reality. As he notes, we not only experience *han*; we also cause *han*. This is clearly illustrated in Korean folktales that illustrate *han* as not only the victim of evil but also "the creator of evil."[32]

In the phase of *jeong-han*, melancholy is replaced with sympathy for others. This empathy is generated through one's recognition of *han* in other people. This genesis becomes a way in which one is empowered to go beyond individual interest or suffering to understanding the plight of others. Hence, an aggressive need for justice is tempered with love and understanding. Thus, Lee notes, "love overcomes hate not by splitting it off and projecting it outward or turning it inward,"[33] but by the recognition of *han*'s complexity, *jeong-han* is transformed into a deeper quality of love that could also contain and temper aggressive feelings.

Jeong-han then has enough recognition of the sufferings of others to turn into what can be called *jeong*/love that is inclusive of aggressive energy to fight against injustice in society. On the other hand, the aggression of *won-han* could easily turn into a destructive force whose "target" is indiscriminate. Not surprisingly, the destructive, aggressive forces of *won-han*, without the power of *jeong*, shift into *hu-han* that seeks violence, which in turn calls for more violence. Consequently, *won-han* produces a cycle of violence in history and in relationships. This compels one to ask, "Where is the love?" For some, perhaps, *jeong* is what transforms destructively aggressive *han* into constructive resistance against the very forces that gave rise to structures that cause *han*.

This form of aggression based on love can be used toward the transformation of individuals and communities. Whereas *won-han* calls for the cutting off of individuals and societies that caused their *han*, *jeong-han* searches for healing the wounds of individuals and collective society. Furthermore, Lee maintains,

> *jeong-han* in its premature form can be a source of pathology individually and collectively. . . . [I]n its mature form it can also be the source of individual creativity as well as of social development . . . in contrast to *won-han* or *hu-han* which are rooted in a psychic structure that is marked by . . . ego mechanisms of splitting, excessive projection and suicidal wish.[34]

A noted Korean Minjung philosopher, activist, and poet, Kim Chi Ha, argued for the practice of *dan*, in which churches must accept an eruption of "limited violence" in the process of liberation. While Kim Chi Ha's call for revolutionary changes for the liberation of the Minjung is believed to be a necessary component toward emancipation, I maintain that the practice of *dan*, as "cutting-off," is not enough, even though sometimes it is a necessary part. It is not enough because it does not seriously take into account relationships of systems of oppression to complex human experiences of *jeong*. Kim Chi Ha's critique of the "feminized love" of the Korean church is correct, yet his call for "the violence of love" also carries certain patriarchal malignancies. Kim's earlier works emphasized the negative depiction of what he perceived to be debilitating for the process of "cutting off." For Kim, symbols such as "home" are feminized and critiqued as a "tomb" or a "nest of amnesia," which obstructs true revolutionary work. This dichotomization of femininity and masculinity must be challenged from a feminist standpoint in order for us to arrive at a wholistic move toward understanding and overcoming *han*. But it is interesting to observe Kim Chi Ha's works as they have progressed. His later works actually move away from such a dichotomizing tendency and toward a wholistic understanding of what it might take to overcome *han*. These works dwell on the notions of "relationality" and "diversity of life" while he notes that spiritual and conversational encounters between people might arguably be just as effective. Thus, his image of the revolutionary is changed from the fighter to the caring mother.[35]

Jae Hoon Lee's work has extensively analyzed the inner complexities of *han* and its different stages. However, it is only toward the end of his work that he hints at the power of traditionally feminized *jeong* to achieve what *dan* has not been able to do. I will suggest in a later chapter that perhaps it is in relationships that we best overcome *han*. Since *jeong* has not been systematically analyzed using conceptual methods either in the West or in Korea, I would like to explore *jeong* via avant-garde Korean films that portray the gradual infiltration and arising of *jeong* in what appears to be a *han*-ridden relationship.[36] The lack of analysis of *jeong* does not point to insufficient work by Koreans. I insist here that such an undertaking would in many ways be presumptuous since *jeong* defies attempts to be categorized even by the natives of Korea. Asian women's diverse understandings of suffering and *han* will be further discussed in the chapter on Christology. Korean feminist theologian Chung Hyun Kyung has argued for an integration of Korean shamanism as crucial to the unraveling of *han* in the process of "*han-pu-ri*."[37] Suffice it to note here that Korean women's affinity with shamanism and their dominant participation as clients and priestesses opens up and taps into the semiotic power inherent in shamanism. The embodiment of the semiotic power within shamanism creates ways for Korean women to become disentangled from *han* and thereby subversively eschew the need for male authoritative power in the unraveling process.[38]

TALES OF *JEONG*

One nation's misfortune is the ache of the whole universe—God's grief.

Ham Sok Hon, *Queen of Suffering*

> Love is the necessary corrective to the violence of systems of con-
> trol and oppression; bilanguaging love is the final utopic horizon
> for the liberation of human beings involved in structures of dom-
> ination and subordination beyond their control.
>
> Walter D. Mignolo, *Local Histories/Global Designs*

During my trip to Korea in the summer of 2001, I was able to visit what is
known as the Demilitarized Zone (DMZ). The Korean DMZ is now the most
heavily armed place in the world today, given its small size. It is a 2.5-mile strip
of land that has sliced the Korean Peninsula in two since the end of the Korean
War, and the 800-yard-wide Panmunjom Joint Security Area is the sole crossing point between the Koreas. Each side is allowed to station only thirty-five
men carrying sidearms, and Northern and Southern adversaries have stood eye
to eye in a grotesque and painful stalemate for over forty years. Such tight
security and heavy military presence makes this seem like a wasteland, yet,
ironically, this place fosters a nature sanctuary, giving space and freedom to
some of the most endangered species in the world. The nearly dehumanized
area is one of the world's greatest wildlife sanctuaries, protecting species such
as the magnificent Manchurian crane from extinction.

Korea remains one of few divided countries in the world today. Ironically,
this division within "one family" is maintained by the "Peace-Keepers" from
the outside. As David Suh notes, tremendous amounts of money, food, and
weapons, as well as approximately two million soldiers, are dispersed in order
to maintain this so-called "peace and security," supposedly for the good of the
Korean people. The political reasons for such division are also ambiguous. As
Suh observes, unlike the division of Germany due to its aggressive politics, the
aggressive nation of Japan was not divided. Rather, Korea was divided by the
superpowers based on their political interests.[39] According to Suh, there are
many diverse explanations for such division. Some predominant explanations
are that the demarcation was drawn to disarm the Japanese soldiers, that it was
a form of American imperialist expansion, or that it was Soviet aggression.
However, according to Suh, Koreans did not participate as active decision
makers in the process of Korean division: "Korean people were innocent of
the cross; that is, Koreans received the cross despite the fact that they were
innocent of any crimes committed against the world or the superpowers."[40]

It did not surprise me that foreign citizens were allowed to tour the DMZ
whereas Korean citizens were not, but I struggled with my reactive feelings of
anger, pain, and sorrow. The tourism company indicated that about one hundred thousand foreigners flock annually to gawk at the immutable terrain.
They have recently made concessions to allow older Korean citizens to visit,
but the application procedure takes more than two years of waiting.

The DMZ reminds one of a visible scar, a wound running along the body of Korea, unable to be healed even by its own body, and only gawked at by bystanders. This wound is constantly poked and torn open fresh with barely enough time to form a scab. It was not only discomforting to be on the bus with so many European and Japanese tourists; it was also disquieting to realize that the ease with which I gained permission to take the trip to the DMZ made me a foreigner to Koreans. With my U.S. passport, I am no longer part of their national identity. When going through customs at the point of entry into Korea, I often find it disarming to have to go through the line marked for non-Koreans. In the final analysis, Koreans do not know how to claim me as part of their national identity, yet I know that they also hesitate to include me fully into the mantra of "Yankee go home!"

The visit to the DMZ was a life-changing experience for me. To actually see the division of Korea, the heavy Korean and non-Korean military presence, the barbed wires, the modern buildings that seemed vacant and hollow, and the green fields of North Korea, pressed against my heart. One wonders if the sensation of longing and yearning might have been similar to those gazing into the Promised Land and knowing there's no point of entry. To witness Korean brothers ever ready and watching each other in opposition as enemies from a few feet apart was painfully disturbing. At the truce camp, the only official point of contact between North Korea and the "free world" is within a blue-painted hut with an iron roof. A microphone wire drew the border down the middle of a green negotiation table. Such a flimsy and tenacious border was both ironic and humiliating. Here, the tourists are allowed to have the privilege of "crossing over" to the other side without military consequences. I could not let myself cross to the other side as I watched other tourists who delighted in doing so. Such crossing over the boundary was done with playfulness while the guards looked on with what appeared to be inscrutable gazes. The display was vulgar, barbaric, and insensitive.

Inside the "hut," the Korean soldiers on guard are commanded by American military officers to pose for tourists taking pictures of them. The soldier obeys with precision-like movements that bring him into a robotlike position ready for battle. I felt a swell of resentment as I witnessed this ironic interchange. What was most outrageous was the sense of commodification of what was and is a deep collective wound of a people. My visit to the DMZ was like a visit to an open grave. It was the first time I was able to participate in the collective *han* of my ancestors, of people who gave birth to me. I experienced grief for people I did not know intimately but who I realized then were part of my body and my memory. At the DMZ I also recognized that though my relationship to the nation is ambivalent, there were ways for me to respond to this injustice. To do so, I needed to recognize and own up to my citizenship and all the ramifications that went with living in the United States.

I remember thinking that despite feelings of ambiguity about my returns to Korea and life in North America, it was at the scar of the DMZ that I had a sense of "my people." Here the collective experience of *han* and my sense of *han* for Koreans and Korea became most tangible. Our collective roots go deep into our psyches. Their traces are clearly present, yet they follow many routes. Our roots are part of who we are, and their imprints are visible in unexpected places at unexpected times. Ham Sok Hon, whose passionate love of Korea and Korean people and whose life commitment to peace, justice, and reunification I have come to deeply admire, wrote that

> commitment to peace is done not because it is possible, nor is it not done because it is impossible. Such labor for peace must be done no matter whether it is possible or impossible. It is a Way we must travel. . . . Although the division of Korea is caused by outsiders, reunification must occur through the works of the Minjung even if it takes 100 years.[41]

Ham's prophetic voice has influenced many Minjung theologians. It is poignant that after his death his voice has become heard even by this Korean American living so far removed from Korea and his generation.

Clearly, the historic meetings between the leaders of the Koreas—South Korea's Kim Dae-jung and North Korea's Kim Jong il—have made reunification an obsession for at least the South Koreans. *Joint Security Area*, a domestic film, became an all-time box office hit, even surpassing *Titanic*. *Joint Security Area* continues to receive critical acclaim, yet the reviews have been mixed. Some have heralded it as a groundbreaking work, while others accuse the film of unrealistic predilections. *Joint Security Area* has received much attention by the independent film sector and was even favorably received at the Berlin Film Festival. It was also shown all over the United States starting in the fall of 2001.

TRANSLATED TRANSLATOR

Films are translations, and filmmakers are translators. As the viewer and writer of this particular reinscription of the film, I also find myself in the role of translating—a role that is ambivalent and fraught with anxiety, for I anticipate mistranslations and misreadings. While translation is one of the most intimate acts of reading, in the process the translator earns the "permission to transgress" from the closest places of the self. Gayatri Spivak concedes that every act of reading/translation risks fraying at the edges, yet our agency as translator somehow keeps the "fraying down to a minimum when it is done in love." The task of the translator is to "facilitate this love between the original and its shadow, a love that permits fraying."[42] Bearing this in mind, as well as the notion that every translation is also composed of some betrayals, I am mindful of Trinh Minh-ha's observation that

> the best translation of a text is precisely a translation that can take off and depart from literal meaning. In taking off it creates for itself another space. This occurs so that it can remain loyal not simply to the letter, but also to the spirit . . . of the text . . . or the lived quality of that experience. The process involved in the work of translation is in itself a creation (or a re-creation) rather than a mere illustration, imitation, or transfer of meaning.[43]

My decision to use a film in this book was a strategic decision. *Jeong* resists easy translation into the Western vernacular categories precisely because of its many complex layers of meaning. Because of its multifarious complexity, I have chosen to analyze a film that I believe unfolds the layers of ways that *jeong* expresses itself relationally. Keep in mind, however, that this analysis is a translation, and something does get lost. I would hope that the reader would find the analysis intriguing enough to want to view the film him/herself. Again, though the film gives glimpses of *jeong*, it is in no way a definitive take on *jeong*.

Directed by Park Chan-Wook and based on the novel *DMZ* by Park Sang-Yeon, *Joint Security Area*[44] is a murder mystery set at the only meeting point between North and South Korea. The film's tragic solution reveals the war zone's tension and ambivalent embodiment of both *han* and *jeong* and opens up a wide-ranging exploration of *han* and *jeong* in the Korean Peninsula. The content of the film relies deeply on the symbol of the DMZ/Joint Security Area and the Bridge of No Return. Threading through these symbols are the concepts of *han* and *jeong*.[45] Ideology is a dominant presence at the border.

However, what makes this film interesting is that presences of *jeong* seem not only to counter such *han*-filled ideology but also overcome a powerful militaristic ideology. Thus, in the interstices of *Joint Security Area* we find neither clear heroes nor clear villains. The only clear and powerfully redemptive aspect of the film is the experience of *jeong*, which changes the lives of those who come into it relationally through their recognition of mutual vulnerability and humanity. The power of *jeong* allows for a particular kind of audacity, as characters risk the consequences of disobedience by crossing militarized and ideological boundaries and as they risk their hearts by becoming vulnerable relationally.

JOINT SECURITY AREA: LIFE AND STRUGGLE AT THE DMZ

Before a scab forms it hemorrhages again, the life blood of two worlds merging to form a third country—a border culture. Borders are set up to define the places that are safe and unsafe, to distinguish *us* from *them*. A border is a dividing line, a narrow strip along a steep edge. A borderland is a vague and undetermined place created by the emotional residue of an unnatural boundary. . . . The prohibited and forbidden are its inhabitants. Ambivalence and unrest reside there and death is no stranger.

Gloria Anzaldua, *Borderlands/La Frontera*

The DMZ is a scab in the minds of Koreans that refuses to heal completely. Healing can only come through reunification. The DMZ is the borderland where, at such close range, one might even forget why it is there in the first place. It is at the borderland that one feels a presumably unbridgeable distance of separation but also a particular kind of deep intimacy. In *Joint Security Area*, two North Korean soldiers manning a post along the demilitarized zone have been shot dead, and another is wounded. Most of the scenes are filmed in the post overlooking the Bridge of No Return and in the cabin looking at the Bridge of No Return on the Northern side. The Bridge of No Return is significant to the story as the Korean guards, first Soo-Hyuk and then Sung-Shik, cross this bridge multiple times with very little hesitation. As the film unfolds, it becomes clear that such military symbols of boundary and division bear hardly any significance in relationships filled with *jeong*.

The Bridge of No Return is legendary as the place in 1953 where thousands of prisoners of war from both sides were repatriated. The POWs were allowed to choose which side they wanted to return to but could never return to the other side. We discover later that Sophie's father was one of these POWs from North Korea who took the option of not returning to either the South or the North but instead took flight to Argentina. One South Korean soldier, Soo-Hyuk, has confessed, and Sophie is handed his written account of what took place. According to his account, he was kidnapped by North Korean guards, taken across the Bridge of No Return, and held hostage in the little cabin by three North Korean guards. He then freed himself from his captivity and shot the North Korean guards, killing two and wounding one while himself being shot once.

He flees by crossing the Bridge of No Return, by which time the alerted South Korean guards come to his rescue. It is the job of Sophie Lang, an officer from the Neutral Nations Supervisory Committee that has jurisdiction in this matter, to interrogate the confessor and the wounded man and to determine what happened. She is informed by her colleague that she is the first female to set foot into the area since 1953. When she is briefed by her superior to stay neutral, she is highly skeptical and derisive as she ironically asks, "So I'm supposed to stand at the borderline and ask, 'Could you tell me why you pulled the trigger?'"

Tensions are escalating between the two governments, so the observer's ability to reconstruct the events is crucial. It is interesting to note that military representatives who spout hysterical ideology represent both sides of the government. Through their words, we hear the elements of *won-han* that has turned into undiluted *hu-han*. We witness a brief scene between the South Korean commander and his soldier. The commander reprimands and slaps the soldier, as he stridently demands, "We had a perfect opportunity to kill them! Why were you not able to at least kill one!" Whereas the soldier responds, "I did not want this to escalate into a serious incident . . . this could lead to war." The commander then tells the soldier, "A soldier should never be afraid of war." At the same time, he commends a numb, shocked, and very silent Soo-Hyuk that he "did well to have rid the world of at least two of them!"

In her first encounter with this South Korean commander, Sophie bears the brunt of his derisiveness and ridicule as he mocks her neutral stance and resentfully points out to her that there are only two kinds of people on earth, the "red communists" and their adversaries. The plot of *Joint Security Area* is convoluted, and its reconstruction is managed via conversations and flashbacks. Through these techniques, we find that the supposed killer of the North Koreans is a South Korean soldier, Soo-Hyuk, and the name of the wounded North Korean is Gyung-Pil. Both are not being completely honest with Sophie, who is the investigator in charge. As she attempts to reconstruct what took place, Gyung-Pil's account reveals that Soo-Hyuk crossed the Bridge of No Return and barged into the cabin, killing two of Gyung-Pil's Northern colleagues and wounding him.

There are also two other soldiers involved: Soo-Hyuk's nightly partner, Sung-Shik, and Gyung-Pil's nightly partner, Woo-Jin. Woo-Jin has been shot to death, and the other officer, the Northern superior, has also been killed by a few shots. Only one man, however, had incurred a head shot distinctively done in military-assassination style. According to his sister, Sung-Shik grew up as an orphan yet still has much *jeong*. During the investigation, he attempts suicide and is of no help to Sophie.

Sophie comes to realize that Soo-Hyuk and Gyung-Pil are the major players in this unfolding story; one is reluctant to disclose the truth of what took place, and one is trying to protect the other. When Sophie begins to suspect the extent of their relationship, she brings them and their superiors together in order to reconstruct what she believes took place. Recognizing how accurate her reconstruction is becoming, Soo-Hyuk, sitting by Gyung-Pil and surrounded by military presence, begins to have a major breakdown. When Gyung-Pil senses Soo-Hyuk will disclose and confess what took place, he physically attacks Soo-Hyuk with incoherent nationalistic and North Korean ideology, which results in momentary chaos but accomplishes his goal: he stops Soo-Hyuk from revealing full disclosure to the military powers and thus protects Soo-Hyuk from punishment. Through this quick and spontaneous intervention, Gyung-Pil's action indicates his choice to maintain the integrity of their newfound yet subversively *jeong*-filled relationship. It signifies not only his willingness to protect Soo-Hyuk, who is supposed to be his South Korean enemy, but his inner move from *won-han* to *jeong-han*. Just as Sophie is about to be discharged from the investigation, Soo-Hyuk approaches her in order to disclose what really took place. Through his narrative the sequence of events is disclosed.

Through the recollections of Soo-Hyuk, we are told that the soldiers practice many scouting military exercises. Frequently, mistakes take place. On one such exercise, Soo-Hyuk's group crossed the border into North Korea unknowingly and had to retreat hurriedly. While the group is retreating, Soo-Hyuk becomes separated while taking care of bodily business in the midst of some tall reeds. Once he realizes his group has disappeared, he makes great haste to find them and inadvertently steps on a land-mine wire. He knows he cannot move, yet none of his group members are around to hear his plea for help. While he is in this desperate situation, two North Korean guards come upon him. All three men draw guns and make hateful comments to each other. Soo-Hyuk informs them that he is on a land mine, and they should stay away from him. At this point, Gyung-Pil and Woo-Jin (the North Koreans) start to walk away from Soo-Hyuk.

Seeing this, Soo-Hyuk's frustration and desperation comes through as he shouts to them, "Why the hell are you walking away? I told you to move back not leave me! Please, help me!" Gyung-Pil and Woo-Jin mock Soo-Hyuk's tears, as big brothers would tease younger brothers. Gyung-Pil works to free him, thereby putting himself in danger. Once the wire is neutralized, Gyung-Pil hands Soo-Hyuk the key piece of the land mine as a token of what he went through. In their parting shot to Soo-Hyuk, the other two men offer a familiar Korean farewell: "Take care and be careful of your health." This is a common *jeong*-filled farewell in Korean culture. Rather than say, "I will miss you," or "Good-bye," one focuses the farewell on the care for the other's health. *Jeong* forms attachments that are difficult to sever.

The second encounter takes place during the winter in which another patrol along the border is being exercised, this time in broad daylight. In this incident we glimpse disregard of borders and boundaries by the patrolling soldiers. Both North and South guards meet in a desolate and isolated place along the border with guns positioned and everyone facing each other across a few feet. Here the leaders from each group casually walk to the center, light each other's cigarettes, and walk back to their respective lines to continue with the patrol. The scene captures the soldiers' ambivalence about and mockery of the military exercise designed to keep them apart. As they completely disregard military sanctions against such meetings, these soldiers cross borders and thus mock the dominant military powers. It is here that Gyung-Pil, Woo-Jin, and Soo-Hyuk make eye contact one more time. As Soo-Hyuk gazes at the two men who saved his life, it becomes a little secret amongst the three.

The next scene is right at the Panmunjom. Gyung-Pil and Soo-Hyuk are directly facing each other across the line, as Gyung-Pil jokingly says to Soo-Hyuk, "Hey, be careful, your shadow's coming over." After these incidents, Soo-Hyuk decides he wants to communicate with Gyung-Pil. During one of his nightly watches he wraps a pack of cigarettes with a letter and flings it across toward the cabin on the other side. As the letter goes flying across the starry moonlit night, we hear Soo-Hyuk's voice: "I'm sorry last time, and I didn't think to offer my gratitude properly. Do you mind if I call you older brother?" It is after this that we witness the tossing back and forth of letters and small gifts. As Gyung-Pil writes in one of his letters, "I have been called comrade for so long, and hearing 'Older brother' really feels nice." Their relationship begins to form through such letters, regardless of their place along the DMZ. Soon though, for Soo-Hyuk, this tossing of letters and gifts is not enough. He takes one of Woo-Jin's joking invitations for a visit to heart and dares to cross the Bridge of No Return to the utter astonishment of Gyung-Pil and Woo-Jin. Thus begin the nightly border crossings. During these nightly visits, Soo-Hyuk boasts of his speed with his pistol. Gyung-Pil counters him by saying that in a real confrontation, accuracy rather than speed is the most important aspect.

Soo-Hyuk soon introduces Sung-Shik to these nightly visits. Sung-Shik, who grew up as an orphan but is full of *jeong*, eagerly soaks up the friendship that is apparent during the visits. What is inherent in these nightly visits and their conversations is the growing sense of *jeong* they have for each other. Through the sharing of stories, laughter, jokes, and idiosyncrasies regarding each other, as well as through the sharing of their personal *han* and mutual collective *han*, they experience *jeong*. The depth of *jeong* that they experience becomes the most important disclosure at the end of the film.

What is interesting is that the experience of *jeong* among the four men produces a safe space that allows each to feel free enough to criticize each other's government. They also uninhibitedly share their poignantly negative regard of "the Yankees," whom they perceive to be an unnecessary third party, and they share their aspirations and yearnings. Woo-Jin confesses, for example, his sense of guilt as an only child who has not seen his widowed mother for the thirteen years he's been stationed at the DMZ. All of these men know what that *han* is like and can feel compassion, in this case, even for their "enemy." *Jeong* is what allows them to see one another's vulnerability.

During a false emergency-alarm response, Soo-Hyuk and Sung-shik face the reality that they must discontinue their nightly visits. Sung-shik worries to Soo-Hyuk that he feels he is betraying his country through such visits, whereas Soo-Hyuk argues back, "It's not like we are anybody so important. We have no secrets to be spies since we do not know anything. We're just nobodies here anyway." Even as they make this decision, they plan one more farewell visit to their friends across the border. In Korean thinking, this last visit is not just to say good-bye but also to pay respect to their friends. Ending their visitations without warning or closure would not only disrespect Gyung-Pil and Woo-Jin but also discredit the relationship.

Sophie's investigation centers on this farewell visit, during which one of the most poignant scenes in the film takes place. The men bring gifts to each other, and we watch as they play the innocent traditional Korean children's game of "chicken leg." They drink and share a last meal together. Interestingly, all these subversive, furtive activities take place at the "womb" of the lookout shack. The semiotic expressions of and the men's articulations of *jeong* spill over in a hidden, womblike secret space "below," which is accessible through a door on the floor. In one scene, Sung-Shik bends down on his knees to polish Woo-Jin's boots. Reading through theological lenses, I cannot help but see symbolic gestures of the last meal and foot washing. Yet here we do not have one lone figure as the focus of these rites, but rather a mutual giving, sharing, loving, and servicing. In fact, the film's portrayal of this particular visit is reminiscent of childhood memories of boys playing innocent games of tag laced with uninhibited laughter and bodies freely touching and bumping. They speak of how they are tired of the "war games" and just want to return home. They have such hope of reunification that they exchange addresses. As the camera circles the room, we see hanging on the walls pictures of North Korean leaders and words of "reunification" framed. Sung-Shik even asks Gyung-Pil, Woo-Jin, and Soo-Hyuk to pose together for a picture. Sung-shik cannot frame the shot to his satisfaction until they are close enough together to completely obscure the framed photo of the North Korean leader hung in the background.

As the time draws near for Soo-Hyuk and Sung-shik to return to their post, we feel the palpable tension of reluctance mingled with heavy sadness that *jeong*, as vulnerable intimacy forged in the borderlands, must end. In Korea, a familiar ritual occurs when one does not want to send someone away and when the other does not want to depart. They engage in dialogues of "Shouldn't you be going?" "I must be going," yet nobody leaves or is pushed to leave. Such reluctance is *jeong*'s attempt to savor and make the relationship continue. It is often in the experience of such sticky *jeong* that past, present, and future seem to converge, for *jeong* is impervious to the demands of the boundedness of time.

As they are about to leave, Gyung-Pil's ideologically fanatic superior suddenly walks into the cabin. Soo-Hyuk, who had boasted of his speed, has drawn his pistol and so has the superior. The intrusiveness of the superior brings the film to its denouement. As the superior and Soo-Hyuk face each other with pistols drawn, Gyung-Pil is caught in the middle, and Woo-Jin and Sung-Shik hover in the background, stunned and speechless. The superior brutally smashes Gyung-Pil's face with his gun as Gyung-Pil attempts to explain the situation. During this tense moment, Soo-Hyuk's inheritance of collective *han* emerges to shadow his recent experience of *jeong* with these Northern guards. With fear and adrenaline shooting through his eyes, Soo-Hyuk responds to Gyung-Pil's plea to put the gun down by saying scathingly and desperately, "In the end, no matter what, we must play enemies." To this Gyung-Pil responds, "Let's begin over again." This plea to begin again was directed not only to that situation but also to the plight of the Koreans caught in this life-threatening web of ideological differences.

Gyung-Pil is able to pull both guns down simultaneously. However, chaos breaks loose when the tape recorder goes on automatically, playing loud music unexpectedly in a crucial moment fraught with indecision, fear, *han*, yet threaded with a sliver of hope and possible *jeong*. At this moment guns go off, killing both Woo-Jin and the superior. Sung-Shik has shot many bullets into Woo-Jin, his younger Northern brother, and into the superior. In a moment of stunned silence, Gyung-Pil acts quickly to put one more accurate assassination shot into his superior, then hands the gun to Soo-Hyuk and tells him to start running and to confess that he had been kidnapped by Northern soldiers. Soo-Hyuk's *han* and *jeong* emerge in a torment as he turns toward the door with Sung-shik. Gyung-Pil calls quietly to Soo-Hyuk. As Soo-Hyuk turns around, he reads in Gyung-Pil's eyes forgiveness, understanding, friendship, and regret that they must never meet again. This recognition brings a cry from Soo-Hyuk as he shoots Gyung-Pil in the shoulder, wounding him to create in the eyes of North Korean military superiors the illusion that somehow Gyung-Pil was a victim.

By using the technique of recollection and memory, *Joint Security Area* shifts reality and memory constantly, thus making history and time seem indeterminant. With such constant shifting and repositioning of the telling and making of the accounts, we come to realize that often history is changed as it is retold.

As this recollection is being confessed to Sophie, Sophie's roots are revealed: her father was a North Korean POW, and she was born in Geneva to a Swedish mother. This information leads the South Korean commander to demand her release from the investigation. Sophie is an ethnically Korean, Swiss military lawyer flown in to conduct the investigation, at the end of which she is to certify one of the country's official lines and go home. However, it becomes apparent to Sophie that the evidence does not match the official statements, and the major begins to look for another explanation. By the end of the film, in fact, she has discovered a far different and more tragic truth from the one that everybody wants her to certify.

Through the investigation, we thus witness Sophie's own history, her roots, and her routes. Such subjectivity and history become suspect and unacceptable in someone who is supposed to be a neutral representative. From the South Korean commander's perspective, Sophie must be replaced. As her investigation turns to a reconstruction that neither side would dare acknowledge, Sophie is admonished by her superior: "You haven't learned much about the Panmunjom; here the peace is preserved by hiding the truth. What they both really want is that this investigation proves nothing at all." Read disruptively, the "peace" at the Panmunjom is maintained through active suppression of *jeong* and thereby through active maintenance of *won-han*.

We do not yet understand the extent of Soo-Hyuk's *han* turned *jeong* turned once more into a different *han* until the last scene. In his last departure from Sophie, Soo-Hyuk discloses the depth of his *han*. Here we discover his self-reproach and regret at his own lack of trust in the power of *jeong*. It was he, the one with the fastest speed, who pulled the first trigger, killing Woo-Jin and wounding the superior. Despite this, he has experienced the depth of Gyung-Pil's *jeong* as he continues to protect Soo-Hyuk in spite of his own suffering. Soo-Hyuk experienced the depth and expanse of Gyung-Pil's *jeong* for him in his simultaneous acceptance and forgiveness of Soo-Hyuk for the death of their mutual friend, Woo-Jin. Recognizing this, Soo-Hyuk can no longer live with his own betrayal of their relationship and thus commits suicide in front of Sophie. As Sophie witnesses this scene, the full tragic nature of the Korean division seems utterly incomprehensible, while at the same time the complexity of *han* and *jeong* at Ground Zero of the DMZ is clarified. Here, the viewer must ask why it is that Soo-Hyuk chose to confess the full extent of what really took place and then take his own life. Why did he confess all to Sophie?

The ubiquitousness of the Korean division becomes tragically apparent in Soo-Hyuk's death. As the blood from Soo-Hyuk flows on the ground, we see a piece of metal from a land-mine wire hung around Soo-Hyuk's neck. This memento, which marked the beginning of their relationship embodied by *jeong*, becomes washed in a pool of his blood, in the pool of Korean people's blood. The keepsake worn close to his body invokes a symbol of both attachment and separation, of stagnant boundaries and fluid borders: a symbol of *han* and the power of *jeong*. The constant shuttling across the Bridge of No Return unfolds to displace the boundary of the DMZ and the hardened *won-han* from its physical and spiritual settled location toward the fluid, unsettled, and complex areas of liminality and *jeong*. At the heart of the film is the tragic dilemma of the Korean soldier and perhaps of the peoples of both Koreas. The dilemma is double-edged in that bitter enemies are also brothers and sisters yearning for reunification in the deepest part of their hearts. This film exposes the ambivalence of what seems to be a binary border separating the country. The ambivalence of division is forced upon relational realities that still embody remnants of abiding *jeong*.

According to Korean Minjung theologian David Kwang-Sun Suh, the division of Korea is a visible wound in the Korean peoples' psyche. Such division is the "cross of division" imposed upon innocent people.[46] Thus the "cross of the division is a cross of *han*."[47] Moreover, it is my contention that this directly affirms and reflects the ultimate theological thesis of this project, which will be developed further below: that the cross works symbolically to embody both *han*/abjection and *jeong*/love. As this film clearly illustrates, the suffering caused by the DMZ in Korea is a visible scar of abjection and *han* that ironically becomes a site of powerful *jeong*. This "cross of *han*" was imposed on all Korean people, both in the North and in the South. Suh goes on to observe,

> As long as we are nailed to the cross of division there can be no resurrection. . . . We are left to die, forever nailed on the cross of division. . . . We hear the agonizing cry on the cross of division. . . . This cry of *han* is a cry to God from a forsaken people. Has God forsaken the Korean people on the cross of division?[48]

Perhaps the best response to Suh's question is to ask not whether God has forsaken the Korean people but to ask how the Korean people understand the cross of Jesus. Postcolonial theory offers ways by which we might assess not only the cross but also the suffering of the Korean people as illustrated in this film.

The irony and mimicry embodied in the reality of the DMZ for Korean people, for example, could be further analyzed through key concepts offered by Homi Bhabha. Bhabha argues that his notion of "mimicry" is double-edged. Mimicry is a process by which the colonized subject is reproduced as "almost the same but not quite . . . so that mimicry is at once a resemblance and menace." Bhabha clarifies here that mimicry is "stricken by indeterminacy." It is also a sign of "double articulation," a complex "strategy of reform, regulation, discipline, which appropriates the Other as it visualizes power." Mimicry is also the sign of what seemingly is "inappropriate."[49] This film portrayed the mimicry of the soldiers stationed at the DMZ. By their surreptitious nightly meetings, they engaged in subversive relationality countering the military apparatus. *Han* and *jeong* are juxtaposed distinctively in this film. The border demonstrates in a symbolic way the divergence and the convergence of both *han* and *jeong* in the collective experience of Korean people.

Here I would like to suggest that the military boundary at the DMZ works as a zone of mimicry for the characters in *Joint Security Area*. The power of the boundary to separate and keep apart loses its power when those who maintain the border experience *jeong*. The emergence of *jeong* then functions to open up a space through which the *han* of the Korean people's division can be healed. I suggest that the film's portrayal of the DMZ, which mocks military power, works to pay homage to patriarchal notions of power and obedience while at the same time "menacing" those concepts.[50] The power of *jeong* and its subversive potential is also seemingly yet unconsciously recognized by the military powers that want to maintain such divisions and thus further maintain the illusion of *won-han*. The intrusion of *jeong* poses as the power to shift *won-han* to *jeong-han*, as is the case in *Joint Security Area*. However, as much as this film delves into the potential of *jeong* even in the midst of such collective and individual *han*, the film's conclusion is pessimistic. Soo-Hyuk's newly experienced *jeong*, mingled with not only awareness of collective *han* but also the *han* created by the shootings, is too fragile and too new to withstand the demands of patriarchalized *won-han* forces. From the postcolonial perspective, *jeong* works, in Bhabha's term, to create a "Third Space."

Rather than a symbol of separation, the boundary in *Joint Security Area* is the site that allows cultures to come together. In this film, *jeong* eases differences, whether they are the tangle of *han* or political ideologies associated with *han*. *Jeong* in such space does not erase differences between cultures but rather recognizes difference while creatively undermining biases. In this particular film, respect of differences is quite clearly apparent in one particular scene. During one of their nightly gatherings, Soo-Hyuk has brought a very popular Korean snack to share. While Gyung-Pil is feasting on this snack, Soo-Hyuk utters a thought that in other circumstances should not have been and could not have been uttered without causing a serious breach of trust. Soo-Hyuk offers a possible invitation for Gyung-Pil to defect to South Korea by saying, "You could eat Choco pie until your stomach splits."

The ensuing silence leaves the viewer in suspense. We are forced to hold our breath to see how Gyung-Pil will respond to such a daring presumption. Gyung-Pil's serious yet humorous response both creatively undermines biases while respecting differences. "Do you know what my dream is?" he responds. "My dream is that one day soon, we will create a delicious snack we can be proud of. In the mean time, I have no recourse but to thoroughly enjoy this Choco pie!"

The site of the DMZ brings to mind Homi Bhabha's observation in *The Location of Culture*, where he invokes the trope of the stairwell as the liminal space:

> The designation of identity . . . becomes the process of symbolic inter-
> action, the connective tissue that constructs the difference between
> upper and lower. . . . The hither and thither . . . prevents identities at
> either end of it from settling into primordial polarities.[51]

This interaction creates a unique space where hierarchy and relationships of power are challenged. As the men become impervious to military borders and political allegiances, we witness the emergence of *jeong* that is capable of see-ing beyond the aggressive *won-han* of the other. This dangerous act of cross-ing the Bridge of No Return signifies the repetition and iteration of *jeong* in the hearts of Korean people. *Jeong* experienced at the edges often provokes and evokes power of radical change. However, *jeong* rooted within the center of power, advocated within the dominant power structure, works as an accom-plice in the oppression of people in the name of *jeong*. I suggest that the expe-rience of *jeong* needs to be distinguished into aspects of *who* is the experiencing agent and *where* it is being experienced.

We have explored *han* and *jeong* as they are portrayed in *Joint Security Area*, which encapsulates a vital collective experience for the Korean people. This wound in the collective experience of the Korean people helps us better to understand the notions of *han* and *jeong*. Those Koreans who immigrated to North America encountered and continue to encounter different forms of expe-rience, such as economic hardship in a foreign land compounded by racism that creates deeper scars in their experience of *han*. Korean immigrants already bore the scars of *han* in their lives when they emigrated from Korea. Moreover, their experience of *han* and the experience of *jeong* in their communities to overcome *han* seem best portrayed in the event and responses to the Los Angeles riots. The year 2003 marks one hundred years of Korean immigration to North America. Koreans have long believed that if they lived the life of the "American dream," they would be accepted in this foreign land. They truly believed in the myth of the American dream. However, this belief was tested and reassessed after the events of the Los Angeles riots of April 29, 1992, when the Korean Americans experienced their own sense of the apocalypse in North America.

SA-I-GU: LIFE AND STRUGGLE IN THE L.A. RIOTS

> The tide of racism is not only rising in the U.S. against people of
> color . . . as the dominant race feels increasingly threatened by the
> growing number of the racial others and the influx of new immi-
> grants and refugees into previously white enclaves, more brutal
> expressions of racism are to be expected.
>
> Eleazar Fernandez, *Reimagining the Human*

> White misunderstanding, misrepresentation, evasion, and self-
> deception on matters related to race are among the most pervasive
> mental phenomena. . . . [The] cognitive and moral economy psy-
> chically required for conquest, colonization, and enslavement . . .
> requires a certain schedule of structured blindness and opacities in
> order to establish and maintain white polity.
>
>   Charles Mills, *The Racial Contract*

On April 29, 1992, a jury acquitted those officers accused of using brutally
excessive force to beat Rodney King. The ensuing rage resulted in what is
now commonly called the Los Angeles riots. In Korean memory this event has
become known as *Sa-I-Gu*, 4-2-9: April 29. Black/white tensions in the United
States are still present, and race relations continue to be charged. Before we
examine *Sa-I-Gu*, the documentary film, it seems pertinent to remember some
of the history of Korean immigrants. We are always located somewhere, but
we know we come from "elsewhere." Scholars argue that Korean American
communities in Los Angeles were created by the changes in international cap-
ital flow. Korean immigration to the United States is directly connected with
the role of both the U.S. government and U.S.-based multinational corporations. With the onslaught of economic changes in America during the 1970s,
and with the Immigration Reform Law of 1975, South Korea received much
of the dislocated industry from the United States. Relatively low wages in
Korea helped U.S. investments to flourish. The decision for many Koreans to
leave Korea had much to do with the dislocation and demographic change
brought about by the rapid industrialization of an export-led economy. Of
course, other factors also contributed to many Koreans' decisions to emigrate,
particularly to the United States. Some of these factors were housing short-
ages, an intentionally racist zoning law policy, depressed wages, underem-
ployment, decreasing educational opportunities, and Koreans' exposure to
American culture via the ever-present U.S. military. These changes, combined
with a new immigration policy toward Asians, resulted in an increase of the
Korean American presence from about 70,000 in 1970 to more than 350,000
in 1980.[52]

Los Angeles in the 1970s lost many jobs, and economic depression was
prevalent. Koreans' arrival in South Central Los Angeles signified to many
African Americans the replacement of white storeowners by Asians. The cyclical distrust fostered by racist images between the two groups and exploited by
white power served to narrow the scope of their conflict. Moreover, the
boundaries were so concretized it made it rather difficult to see beyond
the African American and Asian American relationship that had replaced the
black-white racial dyad. By reacting and responding solely to each other, both

Korean Americans and African Americans unknowingly identified themselves as the source of their conflicts and frustrations, such that their relationship became more or less a "metaphorical fight over the slice of pie."[53] Feminists commonly refer to such examples as falling victim to the tactic of "divide and conquer" by the dominant group.

Other parties, such as Los Angeles economic elites, city officials and, metaphorically speaking, the "bakers of the pie," are not addressed and are thus relieved of their responsibility and compliance in the continuation of the conflict on a micro level. Prior incidents of disrespect for Korean American shop owners and for African American clients, many of which resulted in deaths, tragically set the stage for what was to happen on April 29. The simmering frustration and anger between the diverse ethnicities, particularly between Korean American store owners and African American and Hispanic residents, erupted out of their accumulated sense of *han*. As David Li notes,

> strangled between the authentic white subject and the oppositional black subject, the Asian American is at once defined and "derealized"; [his] claim to a distinctive self and national embodiment will have to be fought out not only between the East and the West, Asia and America, but also between black and white, labor and capital.[54]

Interestingly enough, most Korean Americans converged in their conviction that the "black/Korean" conflict was not at the root of the riots, which to them seemed inevitable given the historical situation of racism in North America. Many Korean Americans observe that they are most often invisible when it comes to race relations in North America, which are mostly about the black-white conflict. Asian Americans continue to be the "invisible minority" in the United States.

The bifurcation of racial tensions as solely between Asian Americans and African Americans perpetuates the absence of structural and systemic analysis. A Korean American who was interviewed after the riots argued that such tactics were aimed to "divide and conquer" minority groups and that "it anesthetizes Americans to accept this racialized version."[55] The "black/Korean conflict" reifies racialization of both African Americans and Korean Americans and the conflict itself. African Americans are portrayed as homogeneously poor, and Korean Americans, as homogeneously all shopkeepers.[56]

The cultural dissemination of such stereotypes in the media work to put concrete boundaries to interethnic conflict. The media's focus on the Los Angeles riots as the manifestation of deep conflict between African Americans and Korean Americans assumes there are no conflicts between Latinos (who were the most arrested looters) and Korean Americans, and it dismisses the possibility of conflict between "whites" and Korean Americans. Additionally, the media's continued coverage and emphasis on the "black/Korean" dyad argued and reified the myth that such conflict, while it may be economic, was mostly due to cultural roots. Unsurprisingly, the media never delved into white supremacy as an issue and as the possible core cause of the Los Angeles riots.

The promotion of such overgeneralizations alongside restrictive Manichaean constructs, such as *us* versus *them*, diverts people's attention from structures that are in place and systematically undermines coalition politics among diverse ethnic communities and across racial divides. The interpretation of *Sa-I-Gu* by Korean women who directly experienced this event indicates the depth of *han* caused by economic disenfranchisement, cultural misunderstandings, and racism from within and from outside their own intimate communities. The documentary also points toward ways to work through *han*-causing factors by the empowering and sustaining presence of *jeong*, which, in the film and through the voices of these women, signifies the power of *jeong* to bridge and resist the racial divide.

The documentary film *Sa-I-Gu* is told from the perspective of Korean women shopkeepers. It was directed and produced by three Korean American women scholars who felt the urgent need to hear the coherency and the particular reflections of Korean women who were directly touched by this riot. These producers, Elaine Kim, Dai Sil Kim-Gibson, and Christine Choy, were particularly driven to produce this documentary to counter the detrimental portrayal of Korean women during the riots by the media. In the introduction, Elaine Kim notes that the purpose of the film is to give voice and visibility to those portrayed as voiceless, incoherent, weeping, and selfish Korean women.

This live-action documentary was broadcast on PBS's "P.O.V." series. The interviews are of the little-heard thoughts, feelings, and reflections of Korean American women shopkeepers who owned many of the businesses destroyed in the violent aftermath of the Rodney King verdict. The film uses news footage and family and newspaper photographs along with current footage of the Korean American community in Los Angeles, who are demanding reparation from the U.S. government despite their lack of trust in that same government. The riots occurred in the afternoon and went on all through the night to the next day. Buildings were set on fire and businesses looted while the police looked on; owners were physically brutalized; people even drove trucks to carry out looted merchandize. Police officers came to South Central L.A. and rather than intervene stood by and gawked while the riot took on a life of its own. One must ask what was the purpose of the police force? Furthermore, what was the purpose of thousands of National Guardsmen called into the area? These guards were deployed not to put an end to the riots but to contain the riot within the perimeter of the South Central area and to prevent its possible spread west into Beverly Hills. This outrage is what motivates a very elderly woman to attend every possible demonstration to seek justice for the Korean community. As she says in the film, "I want to end my last days demonstrating against the injustice of what happened." The film is also interlaced with news footage of the riots, which evoke a sense of the apocalyptic. My reaction to the film was a sense of South Central Los Angeles as Ground Zero.

What we see in this film is the overlapping of *han* from community to community. More specifically, these Korean American women experience *han*, yet it does not go over to the *hu-han* stage. Interestingly enough, these women engage in their own hermeneutics of suspicion by critically reflecting on what brought about the riots. Furthermore, what is evident from the media footage that covered the Korean community's response after the riots is that women are the key spokespersons and leaders working with many of the demonstrators, who were also mostly women. Korean Americans' response to the Los Angeles riots was mobilized amazingly by Korean American women.

The film is dedicated to Edward Jae Song Lee, the nineteen-year-old who was the only Korean death, and to fifty-three other sons and daughters who died during the riots. The film begins with the reflections of his mother, Jung Hui Lee. Even after she witnessed his dead body, she is a mother who is still waiting for her son to walk through her kitchen door. In the telling of her story, she goes all the way back to Korea and the reasons why they immigrated to America. She also speaks about the hardship of immigrant life, the hours they worked, the struggle of raising children as conscientious parents in spite of their economic difficulties. She speaks of being a foreigner in a foreign land and having to trudge onward for the sake of their children. Another Korean who mistook him to be a looter shot Edward, the only Korean casualty. Jung Hui Lee confesses that she had blamed this individual person initially. However, as time passed and she was able to think coherently, she observed, "It is not just an individual. There is something so very wrong here in the U.S." The voice of the narrator notes that 200,000 Koreans live in Los Angeles and they suffered the most during the riots. The estimated financial loss by the Korean community was at least 800 million dollars.

Only one woman in the interview is not translated with English subtitles. Young Soon Han, after three months, still has a difficult time understanding why her business was burned to the ground. Hearing her speak, we hear echoes of the myth of the American dream. She had worked hard and, as she says, she had "not been a bad citizen, staying out of trouble and minding [her] own business." Her confusion is made explicit as she asks, "Why? I didn't do anything wrong." Her experience of limited *jeong* with her African American coworkers, and her experience of *han* because of the riots, leads her *han* to be directed to her inner self, for she states that above all she is angry with and blames herself. The myth of the American dream is so instilled in her that she fails to direct critical reflections to somewhere else. So even while Han states she has done nothing wrong, she can only direct the anger inward.

Choon Ah Song is another women interviewed. She seems to have had the most intimate relationships with her coworkers, who were Latinos and African Americans. Her relationship was such that her employees not only warned her to leave her business because the rioters were heading toward it, but also went in her stead to protect her business for her. She is one interviewee who had developed a strong relational sensibility with her employees. Although she experienced the total loss of her business, she maintains that she does not regret immigrating to the United States. She is also the only interviewee who seems, despite the pain of the loss, still to have more *jeong* than *han*. She is optimistic and clearly supported by other ethnic people in her neighborhood as they urge her to open her business again. Choon Ah Song is also the only interviewee who speaks about religion and faith. She shares the complaints voiced by African Americans and tells of the extent to which she went to create a caring relationship with their customers. She was actively engaged with the African American community, and they created a shared sense of respect and *jeong* for each other. She argues that Koreans must learn to respect African Americans because "they are also God's children just like us."

These women and others who are interviewed briefly all share a common perception. Contrary to the media's negative portrayal of them, these women have critically examined what took place on April 29, 1992. To them, there is clearly a racial problem in the United States. They have often felt that America was on their side, and before April 29, racial conflict was to them a white/black issue. They had known of racism against blacks but unconsciously felt they were exempt from racism. They had, up to this time, bought into the notion of the model minority. But April 29 clearly showed that Koreans are a minority and thus also victims of white racism. They know well from experience what Howard Winant argues, that

> Democracy . . . can be pragmatically measured by the degree and scope
> of racial inclusion and racial injustice. . . . Our modern political sys-
> tem lies in racial dictatorship; it should not be surprising that where
> racial difference is concerned, democracy continues to be in short sup-
> ply. . . . So racial politics have their origin in the ravaging of the globe,
> in the consolidation of European rule . . . the interpellation of all
> humanity along racial lines.[57]

These women reflect that the rage and violence of April 29 were not sudden or singular reactions to the Rodney King verdict, but rather indicative of a systemic failure to address larger structural evils: for example, the justice system for acquitting the four white police officers who had been recorded making racist comments and alluding to other incidents of the use of excessive force before and after beatings. These women now also question economic structures in the United States; one woman notes in a despairing and commensurably compassionate voice, for example, that most of the looters were poor. As one woman observes, "I now see a huge hole in America."

Andrew S. Park observes that there are several sources of *han* within Korean American communities. He names several of these: racial conflict, transnational corporations, classism, and a crisis in identity.[58] Among these several *han*-causing factors, he argues that racial conflict and identity crisis are predominant. Clearly, Park's analysis of the Korean American context indicates the unique experience of *han* for many immigrants. Their response to these new forms of *han*-causing external factors further aggravates their external experience of *han* in Korea, which in turn aggravates the dormant "original *han*" in the deepest part of the psyche. *Sa-I-Gu* as an event in Korean American immigrant history is crucial for understanding Korean American identity politics. *Sa-I-Gu* is an experience of *han*/suffering in the Korean immigrant history. It is a brutal experience of abjection such that "they are neither objects nor subjects of their environment; rather, they exist as abjects, along fluid lines of demarcation, undecidedly both inside and outside, precariously inerasable yet vulnerable."[59] The Los Angeles riots, for Korean American immigrants, were the in-breaking of a crisis in identity politics. This tragic history allowed Korean American communities to reflect on what it means to be a political citizen of this country. Perhaps one might even argue that this was the decisive event for Korean Americans to actively participate in civil rights and to engage in critical reflections on racism.

In light of April 29, 1992, Korean Americans can no longer accept the myth of the American dream without critically reflecting on race relations, which often push Korean Americans to the edge of any discussions on racism. April 29 marked the end of innocence for Korean Americans as they recognized what Rey Chow has termed the "liberalist alibi." This is the myth that in America everyone has certain rights. In the case of April 29 the "right" to protection was seen to be a myth. In the documentary, the myth is clearly recognized by a young Korean American man who had served in the U.S. military reserve and had believed in this right to protection, which failed to exist for the Koreans during the riots.

The feminist perspective of this documentary not only highlights this key event for Korean American history, but it offers the reflections of Korean women who were victims of the riots. The women recognize the economics of the looters who were poor; they recognize that the riot was symptomatic of something deeper; they recognize that all are God's children; and most important, they realize, as the mother who still waits for her son notes, that "there is something really wrong here." What I find most interesting is that these women have experienced a tremendous sense of *han*, yet they do not let such *han* be carried into *hu-han*. They clearly, though reluctantly, have some remnants of *jeong* because they understand the collective pain and the anger of *Sa-I-Gu*/4–29: all have been victimized.

Theological reflections on *han* have most often centered on the much-needed critical analysis of systemic structures of oppressions. This chapter focused on the deeper dimensions of *jeong* not in opposition to prior reflections on *han* but in order to add other possible dimensions. The next chapter will proceed into conversation with postcolonial theory through notions of hybridity, mimicry, negotiation, and the interstitial space/Third Space.

3

Postcolonial Theory and Korean American Theology

Racism is one of the key experiences through which Korean Americans experience and accumulate *han* in their lives. For many Korean Americans, the experience of *han* frequently comes from a sense of deep "dislocatedness" from both inside and outside of their intimate community. In time, their sense of racial ethnic identity is no longer easily identifiable but becomes ambiguous and much more complex. Identities become multiple, as people pass through the myriad differing realities that hybridize their identities and their perception of the world.[1] This chapter will delve into the experience of *han*, particularly that of Korean Americans, through the analytic lens of postcolonial theory. The Korean American experience of *han* cannot be reduced to merely that of racism. However, I will proceed in this chapter by exploring our racial politics before delving into my reading of postcolonial theories on hybridity, mimicry, and interstitial space. My aim is to emphasize that the hybridization of Korean American identity allows for the emergence of a distinctively postcolonial identity of difference that does not rely on dichotomy to validate itself.

ALIEN/NATION

Racial minorities, specifically Asian American, have in the past repeatedly sought inclusion within the American community, within the promise of American democracy, within the ideals of equality and human dignity, and have, just as regularly, been rebuffed and excluded from that company and ideal.

Gary Okihiro, *Margins and Mainstreams*

49

> There is no white world, there is no white ethic, any more than
> there is a white intelligence. . . . I am not a prisoner of history. I
> should not seek there for the meaning of my destiny. . . . In the
> world through which I travel, I am endlessly creating myself.
>
> Franz Fanon, *Black Skin/White Masks*

Recent racial theory could be illustrated by three common approaches to race
and race relations based on the categories of ethnicity, class, and nation. Ethnicity theory has been changed due to the rejection of two central aspects of
an ethnicity approach. The first approach is the European immigration analogy, which suggests that racial minorities can be incorporated into American
life in the same way that white ethnic groups have been and assumes an American commitment to equality and social justice for racial minorities. This
assumption of equality for all in the American dream becomes quite clear in
the *Sa-I-Gu* interviews. The second approach is to use racial ethnic categories
that homogenize ethnicity by oblique racial identification.[2]

Frequently, for both white and nonwhite groups, the temptation is to think
of race as an "essence," as something fixed, concrete, and objective. An
opposite temptation is to imagine race as a mere illusion, a purely ideological
construct that some ideal nonracist order would eliminate. Clearly, such
dichotomous views run the risk of essentializing the category of race. Racial
formation is a process that is historically situated and in which human structures and bodies are represented and organized.[3] A third approach is to think
of the process of racial formation as occurring through diverse linkages
between structure and representation. Race continues to signify difference and
structure in equality. Society is suffused with small and large racial projects
that allow race to become a common-sense way of comprehending, explaining, and acting in the world.

Thus, the centuries of what Omi and Winant term "racial dictatorship" have
had three significant consequences. First, they defined "American" identity as
white. Second, they established a "color line." Third, racial dictatorship and its
diverse racial projects consolidated the "oppositional racial consciousness and
organization originally framed by marronage . . . just as the conquest created
the 'native' it also created 'black' where before there were distinct tribes."[4] Both
coercion and consent was and is entailed in the racial project of America.

Whites tend to locate racism in color consciousness and find its absence in
color-blindness. In so doing, they see the affirmation of difference and racial
identity among racially defined minority groups as racist. Nonwhite persons,
by contrast, see racism as a system of power, and argue that blacks cannot be
racist because they lack power.[5] I suggest, however, that such binary thinking

needs to be critically explored despite the need to dismantle racism. The issue of having total power and the notion of absolute lack of power seem to fall into the trap of either/or thinking. I suggest that even this issue must be reframed since power cannot be so easily taken and so easily had. Rather I would agree with Charles Mills's critical race theory, which says the issue is not about the dichotomization of race "as non-existent or race as biological essence." Rather, "race is sociopolitical rather than biological, but it is nonetheless real."[6] We can best understand racial formation through the mechanism of its operation in not only institutional structures but in everyday experiences. There are many racial/political projects. However, a racial project can be defined as racist if and only if it creates or reproduces structures of domination based on essentialist categories of race.

IDENTITY AS A "SWEEPING FORCE"

Cultural spaces are unfixed, unsettled, porous, and hybrid. It becomes difficult to either defend the notion of singular essentialized identity or deny that different groups and people are bound to each other in a myriad of complex relationships. The spaces, borderlands, identities, and crossings have created a growing panic among those who control "dominant regimes of representation."[7] Ethnicity becomes a constantly traversed borderland of differences in which identities are formed in relationship to the shifting terrains of history, experience, and power. Ethnicity as a "representational politics pushes against the boundaries of cultural containment and becomes a site of pedagogical struggle in which the legacies of dominant histories, codes and relations become unsettled and thus open to being challenged and rewritten."[8] Hence, in the rest of this chapter I will trace how postcolonial theory revisions identity—i.e., cultural identity—as a kind of sweeping force.

Similarly, Gayatri Spivak rejects all definitions of identity, which are fixed in essentialist conceptions of origins or belonging. She insists that within and around this complex issue of origin, return, identity, and history is the serious issue of "epistemic violence." Keeping the complexity of the postcolonial situation in mind, Spivak does not easily do away with such ambivalence but rather suggests that the idea of "pure" subaltern consciousness is a necessary "theoretical fiction" that enables an emergence of counterresistance and critique. To this end, her "strategic essentialism" emerges because she "reads it then as a strategic use of positivist essentialism in a scrupulously visible political interest."[9] Just as one embraces and utilizes strategic essentialism, Spivak seeks simultaneously to put it under erasure so that postcolonial subjectivity is made to choose between its contemporary hybridity as sedimented by the violent history of colonialism and an indigenous genealogy as it existed prior to the colonial chapter. . . . The dilemma then is not between two pure identities . . . but between two different narratives and their intended teleologies.[10]

I would suggest here that the journey into *jeong*, by way of recognition of the commonality of *han* in others, is a similar process of unsettling, shifting, and rewriting histories of the oppressed. Race and racism are important to this writing, just as gender and debate on essentialism work as a thread within this argument. As I position myself within the postcolonial sites of ambiguity and ambivalence, I am also constantly reminded of the politics of race and gender. The violence of sexism and racism, to name just two forms of oppression, are still rampant and active.

Along with postcolonial theory, we also witness a proliferation of discussions on identity emerging out of Pacific Asian American communities. Lisa Lowe writes that cultural identity is a "matter of becoming" as well as of "being."[11] Thus, identity belongs to the future as much as it does to its various pasts. Cultural identities come from somewhere (perhaps convoluted and hybrid origins), but also like anything that is historical, identities have undergone transformations (routes). Hence, identity is not fixed in some essentialized past but always and already transformed and unsettled.

The boundaries and definitions of Asian American culture are being continually challenged and shifted.[12] Lowe stresses "heterogeneity, hybridity and multiplicity in the characterization of Asian American cultures."[13] Heterogeneity, hybridity, and multiplicity are not used as rhetorical terms but as attempts at naming the "material contradictions" that characterize Asian American groups. One should then be suspicious of the "uncritical nativism or racialism" that would be appealing to the essentialized notions of precolonial identity. Lowe resonates with Spivak's call for a "persistent recognition of heterogeneity."[14] Here, I would agree with Lowe and go even further by noting that any claims of "authentic" Koreanness, for example, would be suspect—at best, an innocent appeal to essentialist identity and, at worst, a complicitous posturing and denial of hybridization of identity.[15]

For Lowe, the key notion of hybridity plays an important role in understanding Asian American identity. Hybridity for Lowe is always in the process of being appropriated and commodified by the commercial culture and, on the other hand, of being rearticulated for the creation of oppositional resistance.[16] Similar to Gayatri Spivak's notion of "strategic essentialism," Lowe also argues the possibility of utilizing specific signifiers of ethnic identity for "the purpose of contesting and disrupting the theoretical groundwork excluding Asian Americans while simultaneously revealing the internal contradictions and slippages of Asian Americans."[17] Because we can no longer claim any "original" or "authentic" precolonial identity, what is helpful and constructive is to examine the complexity of postcolonial identity through concepts of hybridity, mimicry, and interstitial space in order to discover the creative power of our hybrid identities.

HYBRIDITY

> The social articulation of difference, from the minority perspective, is a complex, ongoing negotiation that seeks to authorize cultural hybridities that emerge in moments of historical transformation. The "right" to signify from the periphery of authorized power and privilege does not depend on the persistence of tradition; it is resourced by the power of tradition to be reinscribed through the conditions of contingency and contradictoriness that attend upon the lives of those who are "in the minority."
>
> Homi Bhabha, *The Location of Culture*

Theorists note that views on the politics of hybridity take three basic trajectories. The first trajectory views hybridity as the product of oppression. This perspective maintains that hybridity is something that emerges out of coerced assimilation or deculturation or is an identity misappropriated by the dominant group. This framework suggests that hybridity is largely negative and is used as a strategy of containment and policing by the hegemonic powers. In this analytic mode, binary divisions are predominant. The second trajectory on hybridity actually deconstructs the first trajectory by suggesting that hybridity functions to undermine authority and to displace the binary thinking on which its power is based. Hence, in this framework, hybridity "disturbs, intervenes, unsettles, interrogates, ironizes, denaturalizes, and transgresses by refusing to 'fit' into established categories."[18]

   The third trajectory, which I would like to accentuate, suggests that hybridity is not an effect of inevitable political mixing but is instead a "thick description" of historical and geographical situations. Thus, this framework suggests mutual agencies on all sides. Here power flows in multidimensional directions.[19] Certainly one of the salient characteristics of hybridity is ambiguity. The indecision inherent in ambiguity is the source of its very power for being open-ended. While the third trajectory seems much more viable than the other two, I am still keenly aware of the tension between the power of my roots and the pull of my routes. We need to maintain the urgent need for political resistance against structures of domination, but in order to mobilize and strategize resistance or emancipatory movement one almost always does so with a certain level of antagonism against those very structures. Simply put, the work of resistance against oppression often entails that we name these very structures. And in the process of naming structures as oppressive, we must be careful not to fall into the dynamics of demonizing and othering that invariably seem to occur.

I must confess here that my own struggle with postcolonial theory lies in the danger toward depoliticized and eroticized notions of hybridity. Perhaps the fear is the possibility of hybridity itself becoming a commodified term that becomes so easily accessed and claimed that it loses its insurgent potency. My hesitation and ambivalence, as I have indicated earlier, also have to do with the relationship of postcolonial theory to resistance against structural power discrepancies, such as its ability to critique oppressive material reality.

The theory of hybridity needs to emphasize mutuality and negotiations across the colonial divide. To many postcolonial theorists, the relationship between the colonized and the colonizer is complex and nuanced because of contradictory patterns of psychic affect in colonial relations, such as desire and fear of the other. The colonial experience is not just an uninterrupted experience of oppression. These relations undermine assumptions that the identities and positionings of the colonizer and the colonized exist in unitary terms distinct from each other. The colonial discourse is always "less than one and double." In a later chapter, I will further develop this from Julia Kristeva's perspective on the notion of the strange/other/abject.

Hybridity creates a sense of the new as "an insurgent act of cultural translation."[20] Hybridity works to disturb the questions of the images and presences of authority. Contrary to popular commodified notions, hybridity is not a term that resolves and dissolves the tension between two cultures. Rather it is always the splitting and the doubling that disallows for the easy self-apprehension of the colonial power. Colonial hybridity is not a "problem of genealogy or identity between two different cultures which can then be resolved as an issue of cultural relativism."[21]

The power of hybridity is in the emergence of subjugated knowledge to enter into dominant discourse and thereby shift the basis of its authority. Consequently, hybridity and mimicry are inseparable. Moreover, the most estranging above all is the presence of the hybrid itself, for it confounds the given. The hybrid strategy opens up a space of negotiation where "power is unequal but its articulation may be equivocal." This negotiation should not be understood as assimilation or collaboration. Hybridity is "a problematic of colonial representation and individuation that reverses the effects of the colonialist disavowal."[22] Hybridity and mimicry then are less likely to involve accommodation and complicitous moves than they are strategic negotiations. Hybridity is the difference "within" a subject that inhabits the "rim of an in-between reality." This hybridity is similar to the practice of "herethics," as discussed in Kristeva's writings, which seeks to integrate the notion of the abject as part of the subject. Kristeva moves toward the practice of alterity that emerges out of love rather than sacrifice. This will be further discussed in chapter 5.

MIMICRY

If hybridity is understood as more than the sum of all its various parts, we might ask, what might be the subversive side of hybridity if it is not just merely a "mixing" of different entities? Here I would suggest that the subversive, transformative, and emancipatory power of hybridity lies in how it functions when faced with dominating/colonizing powers and structures. The subversive and resistant move comes from the dynamics of mimicry—a move that is simultaneously a recognition and a disavowal of potentially dominating power. Mimicry functions as both a resemblance and a menace. For example, within the Asian American context, a term used to refer to particular kinds of identity in a self-deprecating manner is "twinkie." This derogatory term alludes in racialized terms to the idea that though a person "looks" Asian, s/he is white-identified. A similar derogatory and self-deprecating term used by African Americans when referring to their and others' colonized identity is "Oreo." What is interesting about these terms is that they embody identities that are not stagnant or static but rather shifting and unstable. The unexpected ruptures from such colonized identity is what is potentially seen as a threat of instability to the colonizer.

At the heart of mimicry then is a destabilizing "ironic compromise . . . the desire for a reformed, recognizable Other, as a subject of a difference that is almost the same, but not quite."[23] The consequence is very different from the intention of the colonizer in that mimicry produces subjects whose "not-quite sameness" acts like a distorting mirror that fractures the identity of the colonizing subject. In view of this we can say that mimicry is constructed around ambivalence. In order for mimicry to be effective, it must continually produce its "slippages," its "excess," and its "difference." This is its creative quality. It is a mode of creative production that is subversive. Mimicry thus is always and already stricken with indeterminancy. Bhabha notes,

> Mimicry emerges as the representation of a difference that is itself a process of disavowal. Mimicry is, thus, the sign of a double articulation; a complex strategy of reform, regulation and discipline, which "appropriates" the Other as it visualizes power. Mimicry is also the sign of the inappropriate, however, a difference or recalcitrance, which coheres the dominant strategic function of colonial power, intensifies

surveillance, and poses an immanent threat to both "normalized" knowledges and disciplinary powers.[24]

Such ambivalence of mimicry not only ruptures dominant discourses but introduces a level of uncertainty, or rather a partial presence of the subject. Mimicry then problematizes the dominant signs under discussion much like irruptive, uncanny moments that one encounters with the Strange. Moreover, mimicry not only problematizes by its intrusive uncertainty but also mocks its power to be a model. In particular, Bhabha's understanding of mimicry is double-edged since it constitutes both homage as well as menace to the colonizer's identity and authority. As a result, mimicry becomes simultaneously a resemblance and menace. The failure of the never-totalizing, colonizing process of mimicry is that it has its own slippages that throw into question the normalizing authority of the colonial power. Simultaneously we must ask whether we are able to locate agency in the "internal fissures" within the process of mimicry.

While Bhabha dwells much on the effect of mimicry *on the colonizer*, I argue that perhaps the performance of mimicry and the agency of mimicry affect the mimic much more profoundly.[25] For as Anne McClintock critiques, particularly Bhabha's notion of mimicry is "flawed identity imposed on colonized people who are obligated to mirror back an image of the colonials but in imperfect form."[26] As a result, the perennial tug for the "mimic" is that she or he is "obliged to inhabit an uninhabitable zone of ambivalence" that "bequests neither identity nor difference."[27] Though there is a subversive agency within mimetic movement, it is nevertheless infused with its own compromises and thus "ensures its own strategic failures." The ambivalence of mimicry is infused not only with the power of subversion but also with the *sublimated power of complicity* with colonial powers. The question that one must raise is to ask whether or not ambivalence is inherently subversive. This challenge must be closely linked with McClintock's crucial question: If mimicry always betrays a slippage between identity and difference by illuminating the indeterminancy of each,

> doesn't one need to elaborate how colonial mimicry differs from anti-colonial mimicry? If colonial and anti-colonial mimicry are formally identical in their founding ambivalence, why did colonial mimicry succeed for so long? If all discourses are ambivalent, what distinguishes the discourse of the empowered from the discourse of the disempowered?[28]

As much as I recognize the potential of postcolonial concepts of mimicry, hybridity, and interstitial space, questions like McClintock's emphasize the need of keeping a critical posture to postcolonial theory's other potential: that is, its vulnerability to becoming commodified, which would diffuse its subversive power. Notions like ambivalency, while embodying a subversive power, might

surreptitiously corrode the agency of the colonized. Poststructuralism that saturates postcolonial theory must therefore be aware that writings must be kept in constant tension with the historical emergence of the oppressed as subjects of history.

The performance of mimicry, whether it is done consciously or unconsciously, primarily affects the psyche of the performer before it ripples out to the recipient. The primary effect of mimicry—the gaze—should perhaps be viewed inwardly if one is to emancipate from the gaze of the colonizer. I suggest that the effect of mimicry on the performer is also double-edged. Mimicry causes the colonizer both to pay homage and to pose as a menace, while at the same time this performance of mimicry is satirically directed inwards to the very agent who is the performer. How one embodies this double-edged power of mimicry, traveling both externally and internally, will determine one's liberation into *jeong* or one's burial under the nihilism of *han*. For "mimicry rearticulates presence in terms of its 'otherness,' that which it disavows."[29]

The menace of mimicry is its element of doubling and its disruptiveness of authoritative discourse.[30] By illuminating the partial presence of authority, mimicry disturbs and challenges the "narcissistic demand of colonial authority" by displacing such authority.[31] Pushing this more inwardly into the self, as Kristeva does in her analysis, such mimicry disturbs the "narcissistic demand" of the self and the abject that has not been completely expelled.

Mimicry "marks those moments of civil disobedience within the discipline of civility" and is a sign "of spectacular resistance."[32] Such is the case in *Joint Security Area* as Soo-Hyuk and Gyung-Pil allow for the emergence of *jeong* in the midst of deep *won-han*. Crossing the Demilitarized Zone and forming a profoundly life-altering relationship is an act of "spectacular resistance." The interviews in *Sa-I-Gu* also disclose the transgressive power of *jeong* when the women recognize that it is not "black people" who should be blamed but that there is "something really wrong here" in the structures of domination in the United States. Their hermeneutics of suspicion and solidarity with others through *jeong* is yet another appearance of "spectacular resistance" or "resistant spectacle." This resistance takes further recognition when they voice the thought of how sad it was that the "looters were mostly people of color and almost all poor folks." It was recognition of their selves reflected in these others. We can further note that the cinematic renderings (i.e., the films) are themselves examples of subversive mimicry as well as tales about others' resistant mimicry—an important solidarious aspect of *jeong*. A later chapter on Christology will examine the role of mimicry in the crucifixion, especially as it pertains to the emancipatory reappropriation of its "signs to be taken for wonders."[33]

This double-edged mimicry is similar to W. E. B. Dubois's "double consciousness" and is something with which most marginalized/colonized people are familiar. Such double consciousness becomes apparent in uncomfortable, unexpected, and unconscious slippages by those who mimic.

From a postcolonial perspective, the colonial doubling is a "strategic displacement of value through a process of the metonymy of presence."[34] A process that involves mimicry in such an inappropriate way that it becomes a menace to the colonial process. It is through such partial processes, often-inappropriate signifiers, that we begin to recognize the specific significance of cultural colonial discourse. In terms of mimicry and hybridity this eluding nonresemblance "produces a subversive strategy of subaltern agency that negotiates its own authority through a process of iterative 'unpicking' and incommensurable, insurgent relinking."[35] Postcolonial use of hybridity is often accused of reification of imperialist/racist biological justifications of superiority based on essentialist notions of gender, race, or ethnicity.

From just what place, what location, does mimicry emerge? It is "in the interstices—the overlap and displacement of domains of difference—that the intersubjective and collective experiences of nationness, community interest or cultural value are negotiated."[36] As an illustration, *Joint Security Area* embodies the opening, the emergence of interstitial space that allowed for the subjects formed "in between" to come together despite differences. On further note, the *Sa-I-Gu* interviews are also indicative of how even violent ruptures become interstitial time/space by and through which "signs" are "negotiated." The interstitial experience opens up between colonizer and colonized a space of cultural and "interpretive undecidability produced in the 'present' of the colonial moment." As is apparent in the interviews of *Sa-I-Gu*, the margin of hybridity where "cultural differences 'contingently' and conflictually touch, becomes the moment of panic, which reveals the borderline experience."[37] The "slippages" in colonial discourse are primarily a consequence of the process of "translation" of particular ideas and narratives. This process was evident in *Joint Security Area* as the men from both sides discuss so nonchalantly the third party, the "Yankees." As was evident in the film, particular characters are intensifiers of mimicry through their performances in/at the interstices. I will later return to this notion of "slippages" as it appears in the translation of the cross.

Interstitial passage between fixed identifications opens up the "possibility of a cultural hybridity that entertains differences without an assumed or imposed hierarchy."[38] To highlight the liveliness and the fullness of this site, let us note Martin Heidegger's suggestion that the boundary "becomes the place from which something begins its presencing."[39] All cultural systems and stances are constructed in the ambivalent and contradictory space that Bhabha has named as the "Third Space of enunciation."[40] Accordingly, cultural purity is untenable because cultural identity emerges from this Third Space, which is both ambivalent and contradictory and teeming with hybridity. Once again, we see cultural identity as "sweeping" from/across boundaries or as overflowing. Bhabha views hybridity primarily as an empowering force because it displays the necessary "deformation and displacement" of all sites of discrimination and domination.[41] Mimicry as a "liminal moment of identification—eluding resemblance—produces a subversive strategy of subaltern agency that negotiates its own authority through a process of iterative 'unpicking' and incommensurable, insurgent relinking."[42] It is exactly this dynamic that takes place in *Joint Security Area.*

Hybridity "intervenes in the exercise of authority not merely to indicate the impossibility of its identity but to represent the unpredictability of its presence."[43] Bhabha argues that both the dominant colonial power and those who seek a return to "original," "native," "separate" space have denied what he terms the "metonymic" hybrid strategy. Such strategy, by employing mimicry, often has an effect of turning the gaze of the colonial power back upon itself. It functions as a mode of appropriation, in an often-inappropriate way of resistance to colonial power. A postcolonial concept of hybridity is relevant to the Korean American immigrant experience not only because it recognizes the ambiguities of our diasporic existence but at the same time recognizes the vagaries of our politics of identity. Immigrants live in the interstices, caught between nativism/nationalism and assimilation into the dominant culture. One of the key important concepts for Korean Americans is the notion of hybridity because it acknowledges that identity is constructed inevitably by way of negotiation of differences. Such "negotiation" allows that the presence of fissures, gaps, fragmentations, and contradictions is not, contrary to what has often been said, necessarily a sign of failure or shortcoming in terms of assimilation. Rather, in its radical form, hybridity, understood from a postcolonial perspective, stresses that <u>identity is</u> not the combination of right parts, an accumulation or a fusion of various parts, but an energy field of different forces. Thus, hybridity's "unity" is not measured by the sum of all its parts. New possibilities, in fact "newness," enter the space between fixed identities by way of interstitial openings.

At its best, hybridity and mimicry function not arbitrarily or capriciously but rather intentionally to unsettle any notions or pretensions to totalizing identity, orthodoxy, and purity, and it does so within the matrix of the interstitial Third Space.

As an Asian American woman, Trinh Minh-ha reflects that the challenge of the hyphenated reality is within the hyphen itself, in becoming Asian American, which is where "predetermined rules cannot fully apply."[44] In identifying intentionally with the in-between world, one understands the predicament but also the potency of the hyphen. The hyphenated person is constantly reborn in his or her refusal to settle down to one world or another. Thus, hyphenated reality does not limit itself to a duality between two cultural heritages. The desire to be both "here" and "there" implies a radical ability to shuttle across borders[45] and often leads to an active "search for our mother's garden" and consciousness of our "roots" while we are simultaneously acutely aware of our hybridity. The question of "roots" and the postmodern celebration of "difference" in the name of multiculturalism are often fraught with not only ambiguity but also another subtle form of exclusion. As Trinh notes,

> we no longer wish to erase your difference, we demand, on the contrary, that you remember and assert it. At least, to a certain extent. Every path I/I take is edged with thorns. . . . I play into the Savior's hands by concentrating on authenticity, for my attention is numbed by it and diverted from other important issues; on the other hand, I do feel the necessity to return to my so-called roots, since they are the fount of my strength, the guiding arrow to which I constantly refer before heading for a new direction.[46]

The question of "roots" and "routes" continues to plague/empower my reflections on identity; however, the pressing question emerging these days seems to be that of citizenship and the question of nation. One yearns for a return to "roots" while one is physically "rooted" to a particular nation even in the midst of travel and globalization. I have often struggled with this question, this tension, this ambivalency of wanting and not wanting somehow to be located and settled. For those who have had the privilege of being "rooted" and "settled," this yearning might seem naïve, especially for one whose theoretical works are aligned with deconstructionism.

The notion of shuttling almost always brings into question one's loyalties and betrayals to one's "roots." This shuttling, however, really is about loyalty to one's own self. Hence, it is a "working out of and an appeal to another sensibility, another consciousness" and condition of marginality.[47] The margins become "our sites of survival . . . our fighting grounds and their sites for pilgrimage. . . . Without a certain work of displacement, the margin can easily recomfort the center in its goodwill and liberalism."[48] Ambivalency with dichotomy is articulated as "essential insider in there, an absolute reality out there, or an incrupted representative who cannot be questioned by another incrupted representative." For the tension of sameness/differentness leads her to

> stand in that undetermined threshold place where she constantly drifts in and out. Undercutting the inside/outside opposition, her intervention is necessarily that of both a deceptive insider and a deceptive outsider. She is this Inappropriate Other/Same who moves about with always at least two/four gestures . . . [A]ffirming . . . persisting in her difference . . . unsettling every definition of otherness arrived at.[49]

To elude the dangers and pitfalls of commodification and reappropriation, one would have to reaffirm difference in terms of hybridity, constantly "reopening it and displacing it in order to keep its space alive . . . it is a question of survival . . . in every process liberating notions will be reappropriated and congealed."[50] Thus, the traveling and the repetitious circling never returns to the same point of connection. This traveling and rhythm of inevitable repetition keeps even the concept of hybridity from "congealing" and from "reappropriation." Each repetition becomes a moment of liminality, a form of constant regeneration that yet does not reproduce the same result.

Dominated and marginalized people have been "socialized to see always more than their own point of view. . . . It is therefore vital to assume one's radical 'impurity' and to recognize the necessity of speaking from hybrid place . . . saying at least two, three things at a time."[51] This is especially so for those colonized to always "please" and "understand" the shortcomings of the colonizer.

As an Asian American woman, Trinh deconstructs, for example, the Western perception of silence. For her silence is not just submissiveness or absence. Silence is tactical, powerful, and, most important, readable.[52] Although Trinh brings diverse and often-contradictory perspectives to the idea of visibility, she nevertheless continues coherently to historicize and situate the radical politics of indeterminacy. Trinh sheds light on this constant struggle by asking,

> How do you inscribe difference without bursting into a series of euphoric narcissistic accounts of yourself and your own kind? Without indulging in a marketable romanticism or in a naïve whining about your condition? How do you forget without annihilating? Between two chasms of navel-gazing and navel-erasing, the ground is narrow and slippery. . . . We have all let ourselves be infected with the leprosy of egotism.[53]

This dilemma continues to plague those with hyphenated identities. As Kristeva notes, one of the best ways to deal with the conflict between the subject and the other is to look within ourselves to find the other: There are contradictions from the outside and also those from "within such that for every I there is always an inappropriate 'I.'"[54] These dynamics continue to plague feminists as we explore limits of identity politics in conjunction with radical emancipatory praxis. For those whose voices have been "subjugated" in the past, the negotiation and navigation through the terrain of "metanarratives" often end with a prevalent sense of desperation and urgency as we become weary of the continuous demand for a sense of "unsettledness." The question/challenge that perhaps we are "rebels without a cause" in a postmodern/postcolonial context is echoed not only from critics outside but also from the critics within ourselves.[55]

Postcolonial identity, rather than the commodified metropolitan, capitalistic notion of hybridity, is in search of political identity. Hybridity then becomes an "excruciating act of self-production by and through multiple traces."[56] Thus, postcolonial identity is primarily beset with ambiguities of location. As a Korean American immigrant, I have often felt a deep sense of the "unhomely." This sense is the paradigmatic postcolonial experience. It is the "shock of recognition of the world-in-the-home and the home-in-the-world" that thus "relates the traumatic ambivalence of a personal, psychic history to the wider disjunctions of political existence."[57] Remembering such disjunctive experiences, however, has led me to recognize that the connective tissues have been the fragile yet tenacious thread/web of *jeong*.

INTERSTITIAL THIRD SPACE

The "interstitial space" is an open site that refuses the logic of binarism. The power of hybridity and the interstitial space is that the partial culture from which they emerge is unleashed to "construct visions of community, and visions of historic memory, that give narrative form to the minority positions they occupy; the outside of the inside: the part in the whole."[58] Postcolonial concepts of hybridity, interstitial openings, and mimicry are all relevant in analyzing Korean American immigrant experiences. They not only help in the naming of the often-ambivalent experiences of hyphenated identities, but more important, postcolonial theory recognizes the potency of these interstitial spaces. The dubious state of constant inner and outer challenges leads to the deepening sense of displacement and fracturedness in the collective experience of *han* for Korean immigrants. Yet, amazingly, it is the power of *jeong* that sustains the creativity, mimicry, and hybridity within the interstitial, in-between space. And so the notion of cultural identity as a "sweeping/overflowing" force grows ever stronger.

Although this Third Space is unrepresentable because of its complexity and constantly shifting terrain, this is precisely why it ensures the conditions for enunciations to emerge. Such enunciations of symbols of culture have no primordial unity or fixity. Moreover, even the same signs can be appropriated, translated, rehistoricised, and read anew. This split-space, this Third Space of enunciation, the in-between space, is the space that carries the "burden of culture" by exploring hybridity. It is here that identity performs the process of doubling and/or splitting within the subject. Identity emerges between "disavowal" and "designation." This process unsettles and erases any simplistic polarities and binarism so that one "may elude the politics of polarity and emerge as the others of our selves."[59] *Jeong* is what allows for the life in between to flourish. Because interstitial space is the contact zone of all relationality, even seemingly oppositional ones, *jeong* is the way of being in this space. And because *jeong* is relational, this relationalism can also not be anything but creative and political.

Contrary to some scholars' assumptions, Asian American identity is not homogeneous; rather, we need to be constantly reminded of its heterogeneity in a nation under the guise of universal "American" identity. Moreover, in terms of politics of difference, heterogeneity is crucial in coming to terms with the indeterminant number of positions that Asian Americans continually and repeatedly negotiate. The push and pull of being, for example, Korean American is not only fraught with ambiguities of nationalism, gender, social, cultural, and other divergent and adjacent boundaries, but it is also compounded by the question of what it means to be a Christian.

The experience of living in between that is experienced by some Asian Americans has much to do with the "unresolvable conflict between the impossibility of letting go of one's own ethnic . . . belonging and at the same time realizing that the assertion of one's own particularity is perceived as deviance by the society at large."[60] Asian American theologian Fumitaka Matsuoka writes of an interviewee who noted that the Cantonese have a name/word for Asians born in North America. The word they use is *jook sing*, which means empty bamboo. More important, I think, is the idea that *jook sing* has no roots at either end. Matsuoka continues by noting, "The search for Asian American identity is also a quest for freedom to live in a world of ambiguity, in the midst of the 'holy insecurity' of our liminal existence."[61] For this reason, most Asian Americans are estranged from Americans who think they are not "American" enough, not fully assimilated into a comfortable zone for them; they are also estranged from Asians who think they have become too "Americanized" and have thus betrayed their loyalty to their "roots." Of course using the term "America" instead of "United States of America" is an exclusionist power play in the context of the American hemisphere.

Asian Americans are fully aware of postmodernist epistemology that has unveiled the claims to universalism as a form of domination. On the other hand, Asian Americans are also critical of postmodernist epistemology that goes too far in its insistence on particularity of social location, which becomes prey to the dangers of what is "contradictory relativism." Hence, a growing number of Asian North Americans actively reject postcolonial notions of the "incommensurability" of different points of view.

Korean American theologian Jung Young Lee has noted that marginality and centrality are mutually inclusive and relative to one another. Owing much to the Taoist principle of yin/yang, the notion of change and interrelatedness is also apparent in his discussions of margin and center. There are multiple centers and margins. Furthermore, there are centers within margins and margins within centers.[62] A relevant implication emerges from this complex space of thought: borders and boundaries are salient. One might pursue this even further to say that not only cultural and religious borders and boundaries but also boundaries of the self are permeable. By stressing marginality over centrality we are able to restore balance between the polarized areas.

Binarism exists yet often fluctuates. Unlike most postcolonial theories emphasizing hybridity over and against Manichaean divisions, Taoist thinking seems to suggest that dichotomies exist in separate realms but that they are traversed and shifted. Marginality is more than a boundary itself; "it is many boundaries encompassing two or multiple worlds."[63] In marginality then, two or more worlds are not only congruous and juxtaposed but also brought together and separated from each other. Neither world is dependent on the other for its existence, but each is relative to the other's understanding. Here we are able to make connection with the notion of the interstitial space.

Marginality then is best understood as a nexus, the matrix where two or more worlds are interconnected yet none is central. Thus to be in between two worlds, Asian and American for example, means to be fully in neither.[64] Most often, when one is placed between these two-world boundaries, one feels like a nonbeing, a "schizophrenic." It is the radicalization of this negative and often dehumanizing feeling of being "in between" that reenvisions it as the interstitial space of creativity and life affirmation. Employing Taoist notions of both/and marginality is thus a condition, an opportunity for creativity. Furthermore, the idea of interrelatedness, of being "in between," leads to understanding marginality as being "in-both." The implication of this is that the space that touches the self and the other, that boundary, is the interstitial space of *jeong*. It is in this space that one is able to see the self reflected in the other and able conversely to understand the mandate to "love your neighbor as yourself." Living by *jeong* we know that often the life of the self is inextricably connected with the well-being of the other and vice versa. We are, in effect, locked into life with the other. We are permeable selves, and this boundary of the permeable self breaches the impossible possible.

Such affirmations sometimes have the danger of moving the marginal person toward an ethnocentricity that becomes an act of exclusivity. As marginal people, we must not fall into the very trap that forges "margins" and "centers." Similar to poststructuralists' assertions, we are not only "in-both" but also "in-all."[65] Marginality itself is redefined from a deconstructive standpoint when Lee insists, "Marginality imposes a new reality that transcends marginalization, for it means to be truly in both or in all worlds."[66]

By way of being "in-both," Lee suggests what he terms as "in-beyond" to signify a new hermeneutics of marginality. The shifting boundaries of margin/center have become familiar to many feminists, perhaps best exemplified in the writings of bell hooks, Susan Friedman, and Trinh Minh-ha. Lee, through his methodological connection with the Taoist concept of the Way, strongly emphasizes the notions of change/shifts as the only constant factor to marginality. It is not a question of marginality replacing what he terms as the realms of "centrality"; rather, by the laws of change itself, change comes about inevitably. Marginality then is about being at the margin that connects both worlds. To be "in-beyond" means to be in between and in-both. In postcolonial theory, the convergence of multiple identities and positionalities gives emergence to hybridity. Likewise, Lee notes that the margin and the "creative core are inseparable in new marginality . . . the margin is the locus—a focal point, a new and creative core—where two (or multiple) worlds emerge."[67] This interstitial space, the creative core, does not work to replace the status quo or the centers.

Ultimately to be "in-beyond" two worlds, one must be in both worlds but also in between them at the same time. The paradox of coexistence of in-between and in-both has much to do with the concept of "in-beyond." Perhaps in the language of postcolonial theory we might offer that the ambivalency of being in-beyond has much to do with the indeterminancy and constantly shifting borders/boundaries of multiple margins. Accordingly, "essence of being in-beyond is not a by product of being in-between and being in-both; rather, it embodies a state of being in both of them without either being blended."[68] Differences are distinctively recognized and embodied rather than the pluralism of differences that often results in indifference to differences. As further evidence of his Taoist hermeneutics, Lee pushes his thoughts to the very limit, which I suggest is illustrated in his notion of in-both and neither/nor. He explains that

> the neither/nor and both/and are opposite but complementary. . . .
> The total negation and total affirmation . . . coexist in the way of thinking of new marginal person. Such paradoxical reasoning is close to a mystic mind-set. . . . Negation is not a rejection of affirmation but an indispensable part of it.[69]

The concept of in-between and in-both worlds coexists in marginality. Hence, they are not only the most inclusive "but also the most relational form of thinking." It is "relational because yes exists always in relation. . . . Neither/nor and both/and ways of thinking de-absolutize the 'either/or' way of thinking."[70] One of the key determinants in terms of Asian American experiences in this country emerges from our experiences of racism. Race is a determining factor in Asian American experience. However, I suggest that as much as race is a determinant, it is one of many, such as gender and class. Anselm Min notes,

marginality is not a natural but a historical category, which is a "result of marginality in a social struggle for power not an ontological characteristic of
human being as human."[71] Min, another Korean American theologian, emphasizes the material conditions of Korean Americans as a contributing factor to
our experience of marginality. Min notes the dangers to Lee's embodiment of
marginality by explaining that

> the racial explanation of marginality tends to cover up the reality of
> marginalization, which is most concretely expressed in the political
> economic forms of abject poverty, economic exploitation, political
> powerlessness and cultural deprivation.[72]

Particularly in light of the riots of *Sa-I-Gu*, this critique is especially important as postcolonial Korean American politics/theologies emerge. From a
postcolonial perspective, it is all and not strictly one of them. As I mentioned
before, there are multiple adjacent determinants, such as gender and class. As
Min rightly observes, marginality could possibly reduce what is clearly a political and power issue to merely an epistemological problem of a "paradox and
apparent contradiction to be resolved in a mystical intuition rather than deal-
ing with it as a political problem of contradiction and conflict of power to be
resolved in a political praxis of liberation."[73]

DEBATING "POSTCOLONIALISM"

Postcolonial theory is shaped to a large extent by its methodological affiliation with French "high" theory, especially that closely associated with
poststructuralism/deconstructionism: Jacques Derrida, Jacques Lacan, and
Michel Foucault. In fact, most criticisms directed at postcolonial theory have
much to do with what is considered the intrusion of such "high" theory. As
previously mentioned, there is a rising controversy about postcolonial theory
for its conceptual framework, its institutional locale, and its middle-class emi-
grations from the Third World.[74] Some critics have argued that such statements seem to invoke the traditional romantic trope of the "self-made"
individual who invents him/herself in the American frontiers. Such celebration of hybridity, syncretism, and multiculturalism needs to be critically examined because such "reinvention" of self-writing from the cultural interstices is
inherently the conceit of modern bourgeois culture. According to critics, postcolonial theory's notion of hybridity has little revolutionary potential since it
is part of capitalism and modernity, which it claims to displace.[75]

One of the most direct critiques of postcolonial theory comes from Aijaz
Ahmad.[76] For Ahmad, postcolonial theory is one more medium by which the

authority of the West over the formerly imperialized parts of the globe is currently being reinscribed within the process of neocolonialism. He also focuses on what he regards as the privileged institutional affiliation of postcolonial theory. Connection to privilege indicates that it is cut off from the material realities of the Third World struggle. Theory is appropriated and domesticated into an unchallenging intellectual commodity only accessible and largely circulated within Western academic settings. The other contention is that postcolonialism's focus most often has to do with the era of clear, formal imperialism, a thing of the past, while not examining the dynamics of current neocolonialism, the new face of globalization disguising old imperialism.

Above all its methodological procedure, Ahmad argues, which derives largely from contemporary Euro-American critical theories, which are politically "regressive" in many ways, is suspect. Western cultural criticism is often severely detached from cultural political movements. Moreover, poststructuralism is represented as the most clear and debilitating example of which material forms of activism are replaced by textual engagement.[77] These criticisms are important, but I would suggest that they do not critically examine postcolonial theory in its full complexity.

Pnina Werbner and Chandra Talpade Mohanty take postcolonial theory seriously enough to have examined its methodological affiliations more extensively and critically. Both point to one of the key dangers to postcolonial theory by highlighting hybridity as an example. Werbner and Mohanty note that we need to guard "against essentializing all essentialisms as the same, a confusion that ends up criminalizing ethnicity and exonerating racism."[78] Critics argue that the postcolonial approach might interpolate essentialism in spite of denying it. The postmodernist deconstructionist approaches then are seen as not necessarily immune to essentialist constructions of their own.

Spivak, like other postcolonial theorists, consistently counters such criticism by acknowledging the ambiguities of her own position as a privileged Western-based critic and continues to draw attention to her "complicitous" position in a setting that produces neocolonialism. I would argue that there is no uncontaminated space outside of analysis to which the postcolonial critic has access by virtue of "lived experience" or cultural origin of some purity.

Postcolonial theory has worked to accept ambiguities, contradictions, and hybridity as being potentially powerful, and furthermore has recognized the presence of interstitial space. However, there is no sense of satisfaction, no sense of finally having "arrived" at a destination, no sense of belongingness. The only resting places of momentary comfort are found within the temporary interstices of the pendulum that swings from home to unhomed, from arrivals to departures, from recognition to disavowal.[79] Postcolonial theory is betwixt and between construction and deconstruction, between recognition and enunciation, in the hither and thither of subjectivity and in between unsettling residences and in unsettling "returns." Postcolonial theory should keep in mind that there is no "view from nowhere" position. Our ways of knowing and being are always located and specific. The key is to put our locatedness under constant deconstruction. And for me, "locatedness" would mean acknowledging the decolonizing resistance of communities in struggle (living hybridity/mimicry/Third Space) to make possible postcolonial theory.

Criticism suggesting postcolonial ties with poststructuralism as reinscribing colonialism seems unfair in light of other theories and their connections with what is seemingly the master narrative. For example, feminist criticisms' affiliation with deconstruction is not overtly criticized for reinscribing patriarchy. Moreover, questions of postcolonial theory's detachment from political endeavors seem to lack support. Though they are methodologically similar and owe a certain amount of debt to poststructuralism, they also depart radically from such "high" theory by critically pushing it to its limit. To say that postcolonial theory has no political activism and that it is at best a domesticated and appropriated form of activism that is compliant with colonialism seems unfounded. Perhaps the tension between "Continental" theory and U.S. theory, emerging out of our history of pragmatism, creates the "fault line," an interstitial space of its own, for production of new theory. Though postcolonial theory continues to be charged with depoliticizing relativism, it has always emerged out of anti-imperialism and a critique of colonialism.[80]

The drive of postcolonial theory is political emancipation while actively examining and acknowledging that the relationship between the colonizer and the colonized, the oppressed and the oppressors, is fraught with complexity from within and without. Likewise, postcolonial theory attempts to undermine the authority of Western epistemologies and regimes of representation. Its base is both ontological and political. Granted, at times agency, resistance, and politics seem to be pushed aside in favor of emphasis on the metaphysical and ontological, especially in light of the absence of a critical analysis of repressive systems based on gender, race, ethnicity, nationality, sexuality, and class. Moreover, I acknowledge as well that notions such as "sly civility" when connected with mimicry becomes problematic. Why might this be? This notion of "sly civility," while workable for colonized men, should not, from a Korean feminist perspective, be encouraged for women. This roundabout way of achieving a goal in a male-dominated society has encouraged women to always negotiate and strategize from a hidden space. It is not that "hidden scripts" lack power and agency, but they must be in conjunction with other forms of political insurgency that have often been the legitimate means allowed only to men and/or imperialists/colonizers.

While postcolonial theory should be aggressively critiqued and honestly challenged, politically "purist" critiques like those of Ahmad are dangerous because they construct a division of labor in which the Third World acts while the First thinks.[81] In other words, Ahmad assumes this division further reinforces an already-prevailing sense that the Third World is not much of a place for theory making. Here we must be mindful once again that theory, as a discourse, can be seen as a form of political praxis.[82]

As a Korean American feminist, I also have a double-edged relationship with postcolonial theory. One area that is problematic in my predominant acceptance of postcolonial hybridity is the absence of theorizing, specifically about material expressions of racism. In postcolonial critiques, it appears as if race and ethnicity become so conflated that the work of critically analyzing racial oppression becomes difficult.

It would seem that effective antiracist moves depend on the evolution of common, unitary narratives and the suppression of cultural differences between victims of racism. Thus, despite my antiessentialist leanings, I find myself in search of powerful hybridizing and strategically essentializing categories that can mobilize a wide group of people across differences to struggle against institutional and systemic forms of oppression. It seems that to "lump all forms of objectification together as essentialist is . . . to essentialize essentialism."[83] Moreover, in attempts to claim fragmentations and contradictions, and in its critique of totalizing "origins," I find myself asking yet again, "Who am I? Where am I from?" Such questions of "home" have not been answered even by postcolonial theory.

Postcolonial theorists do not ignore the critiques leveled at them. However, they do ask back, "Are we trapped in a politics of struggle where the representation of social antagonisms and historical contradictions can take no other form than a binarism of theory vs. politics? Is our only way out of such dualism the espousal of an implacable oppositionality or the invention of an originary counter-myth of radical purity?"[84] For Bhabha, the answer exists somewhere in between political polarities and in between theory and political praxis. Accordingly, we might concede that not only is culture hybrid but the method of theory has also become hybrid. Theory, as a hybrid form of approach, must now simultaneously seek to subvert and replace the theoretical apparatus of power/knowledge.[85]

This hybrid understanding of theory itself emerges so that "theory becomes the negotiation of contradictory and antagonistic instances that open up hybrid sites and objectives of struggle, and destroys those polarities between knowledge and its objects, and between theory and practical-political reason."[86] The function of theory within the political process becomes double-edged. Whether theory or culture, hybridity signifies its transformational value in its translation of "neither the One nor the Other but something else besides which contests the terms and territories of both."[87] A postcolonial version of hybridity comes, I suggest, foremost from an extreme sense of pain, of loss, of agonizing dislocations and fragmentations.

Postcolonial theory is necessary for doing Korean American theology. It not only delves into the politics of identity and location but also allows for the acknowledgment of the dynamic hybridic contours to identity and epistemology within the Korean American feminist experience. In the previous chapters, we have examined *han* and *jeong* from various perspectives. We have also examined postcolonial theory as a way of entry into the analysis of Korean American immigrant experience. The next chapter will engage in christological reflections. Jürgen Moltmann's articulation of Christology will be examined in light of our discussions on *han* and *jeong* and in conjunction with postcolonial concepts of mimicry, hybridity, and interstitial space.

The Crucified God:
The Way of *Jeong*

Korean American Christians have experienced the cross as both empowering and disempowering. The cross continues to empower people as it signifies radical solidarity with their experience of *han* and *jeong* as embodied in their lived immigrant experiences. However, it continues to be disempowering to many for precisely the same reasons. The cross signifies disempowerment to many who experience powerlessness and subjection because of its traditional interpretation of self-abnegation and its acceptance of sacrifice even unto death, as Jesus is understood to have demonstrated on the cross. Here, I would like to examine the complex ways in which a traditional understanding of the cross (1) has perpetuated subjection and submission to self-abnegation as a "true" sign of Christian discipleship and (2) continues to be embraced as a sign of challenge to those very dynamics of subjection, submission, and powerlessness.

VIOLENT UNDERTONES AND RADICAL SOLIDARITY

How cruel and wicked it seems that anyone should demand the blood of an innocent person as the price for anything, or that it should in any way please him that an innocent man should be slain—still less that God should consider the death of his Son so agreeable that by it he should be reconciled to the whole world.

Peter of Abelard

Theologian Anthony Bartlett claims that Christ disclosed a "radically new continuity of love . . . as opposed to that of sacred violence."[1] Thus the believer is called to the fullness of love revealed by Christ. The cross is the disclosure of the abyss "both as absence of the God of the sacred and the revelation of the biblical God fully in and through the abyss."[2] I suggest that this notion of the cross as both "absence" and "presence" can be fruitfully interpreted as both abjection and *jeong* in its fullness. In a similar vein, "through mimetic anthropology the face of the victim of human violence is declared to us. . . . [T]he scene of the abyssal Christ is the locus of human transformation."[3] In this chapter I will explore Christology, especially the symbol of the cross, as it has been conventionally interpreted, and the ways it has effectively functioned to sanction violence. The logic of this sanctioning of violence has more to do with the patriarchal relational contours of christological reflections and less with their subversive potential to be radically liberative. The cross can be read as much more than a "sacred violence" or abjection; it also is simultaneously inclusive of a radical form of love that I have linked with the concept of *jeong*. After engaging Mark Taylor's political Christology, which asserts that the crucifixion was in fact an imperial execution, I will bring works of Jürgen Moltmann into the chapter's christological conversation.

Mark Lewis Taylor claims that "Jesus' death on the cross is best viewed as what that event concretely was, an imperial execution."[4] Suffering has been traditionally made "holy" by the glorification of the crucified God. Taylor rejects the often-criticized notion of Jesus' death on the cross as advanced by styles of Anselmian atonement theory that sacralize "destructive sadomasochistic impulses."[5] To sublimate Jesus' death on the cross as a plan of God is to reduce the importance of what it means that Rome executed Jesus. The perception of Christology as part of a divine plan perpetuates the notion that God does not suffer from political realities like imperial domination and execution. As we later bring in Moltmann to bear on the discussion, we will notice that this particular christological boundary is stretched, though not transgressed, by the question of patripassionism, i.e., that it is God who is executed on the cross. I am not in complete disagreement with Moltmann's understanding of the cross; however, because I read Christology from the postcolonial Third Space, my perspective is closer to that of political liberation theologians like Taylor. Similarly, while I agree with various feminist christological critiques that view the conventional accent on the suffering and love on the cross as detrimental to women, I also argue that the suffering on the cross is not solely about self-abnegation. It is also comprised of powerful elements of *jeong*, which subversively fosters power rather than powerlessness.

Taylor argues that "Jesus was not possessed by some 'will to die' in order to make a 'redemptive death.'" Taylor's claim is that Jesus was executed on the cross.[6] What difference does "execution" make over and beyond "crucifixion"? In most Christian spiritualities, the latter often signifies a benign form of suffering and death and in fact often involves the sacralization and glorification of suffering; in other words, it perpetuates what one might construe as a worship of suffering that tends to sacralize "destructive sadomasochistic impulses."[7] The former, "execution," moves away from thinking of Jesus' death as a "sublime divine plan," and instead pushes for maintaining the horror of the material conditions that were bound up with his and thousands of others' victimization by the imperial regime of his time. Taylor goes on to insist that the executed God cannot be limited to the specific historical event of Jesus' death but rather that the phrase "executed God" signifies "greater, deeper, and wider forces" that he calls "the way of the cross." This particular event then is not solely about and contained in the figure of the historical Jesus but is a disclosure of a way of the cross in which Jesus himself participated. My own Christology finds resonance here, in that the execution, the cross event, discloses both the horror of abjection/*han* and the power of *jeong*/love. The execution, then, is the way of the cross; *it is a particular way of living out of the praxis of* jeong.

Traditional Anselmian theory understands Jesus' death on the cross as a form of payment that was willed and demanded by God from humanity. To say that Jesus was executed not by the will of God the Father but by a repressive empire sheds a radically different light on Christology. Traditional atonement theory depicts Jesus as passively suffering for the sake of the world. This is a form of depressive *jeong* that was mentioned in earlier chapters. This depressive *jeong* is not liberative but rather fatalistic and passive, and, as such, it plays into victimization. Taylor's Christology, on the other hand, suggests a Jesus who was marked for execution by a powerful empire. According to the empire, Jesus had enough power to be a threat to the powers that be. His death then might be construed as the result of the liberative *jeong* that is at the heart of liberative action, a living by the way of the cross.

The horror and the power of the abject on the cross also resonate through Taylor's observation that the call to remember Jesus' death as "execution is to renew our awareness of the official terror that crucifixion was."[8] This distinction is important in claiming the subversive power of the cross in the continuous struggle towards freedom, which he refers to as "the way of the cross."[9] It is a way that was powerfully highlighted by Jesus' life and ministry. Consequently, the cross embodies the complex and extensive power of God by directly pointing towards the "way of the cross" in which Jesus was and is one among many participants.

A Christology of the executed God calls for a deep understanding and practice of love that resonate with *jeong*. The cross reminds us of commonalities that traverse boundaries as there are certainly victims and executioners. Revolutionary change, as practiced for example by Jesus, must inherently embody a love ethic that includes the enemy. However, this concept of a love ethic is not a form of capitulation to the oppressors. Rather, it is a "strategy of revolutionary change

. . . to rival that of the enemy's power."[10] The issue of the cross is not a matter of "bearing one's cross" but rather of learning to "wield the cross for a liberating change."[11] The cross, with its powerful love ethic, is not a tool for perpetuating victimization and powerlessness but rather, according to Taylor, a powerful symbol that is inclusive of the love of the enemy while pushing towards emancipatory action. Similarly, while the concept of *jeong* can be problematized because of the way it has been traditionally domesticated, I suggest that the cross, when understood in light of *jeong*, works effectively to encompass incommensurable aspects of life: mainly the coexistence of both life and death, hate and love. The cross, with its powerful love ethic, is the symbol of the inclusive relationalism embodied by *jeong*. *The way of the cross must be sustained by living with, in, and through the power of* jeong.

Taylor's call for an "adversarial politics of resistance" is unearthed from what he maintains is a long tradition of resistance that includes the Galilean identity of Jesus.[12] His observations of the apostle Paul's use of "adversarial politics" resonate with the postcolonial strategy of revolutionary change through the dynamics of hybridity and mimicry. While Taylor does not draw from postcolonial theory, his claim is more than amply supported by distinctive traces of Paul's use of such strategic mimicry. As postcolonial theory has indicated, mimicry is a double-edged concept in that as much as it pays homage to the adversary, it also functions as a subversive threat and challenge.

A form of mimicry through adversarial politics, the cross effectively "steals the show from imperial power."[13] In this way, Jesus' execution "was not a salvific event . . . it was his creative and dramatic contestation with imperial-religious powers."[14] This claim is similar to my argument that the cross, as a semiotic rupture within the symbolic, functions to make present the abject in its fullness as the ultimate return of the repressed. Herbert Marcuse asked the question that I now pose here: How can the historical return of the repressed be understood? For Marcuse, taking his cue from Freud, Christians are "badly christened" insofar as "they accept and obey the liberating gospel only in a highly sublimated form—which leaves the reality unfree as it was before."[15] After naming the most heinous crimes committed by and in the name of Christianity, Marcuse explains the return of the repressed as follows:

> The executioners and their bands fought the specter of a liberation which they desired but which they were compelled to reject. The crime against the Son must be forgotten in the killing of those whose practice recalls the crime. It took centuries of progress and domestication before the return of the repressed was mastered by the power . . . [that] *releases a hatred and fury which indicate the total mobilization against the return of the repressed.*[16]

To Marcuse, we now again face the irrepressible return of the repressed in the global movements of liberation. Resistance to the imperial powers calls for a form of resistance that is nonviolent. More specifically, this nonviolence would have to be "creative, strategic practice" that must be done best with what oppressors do not usually expect: "the surprising force of imaginative nonviolence," which seems to echo our descriptions of *jeong*.[17] Moreover, Taylor, who is adamant that resistance is found most noticeably in the people's liberation movements, observes that our living by the way of the cross, in "the fullness of rebellion" must "*blossom new ways of love*."[18] These "new ways of love" might blossom through recognition and embodiment of *jeong*. "Rising out of" the connectedness of heart, *jeong* emerges in a transformative becoming within the interstitial space between the self and the other, a becoming that transcends *han*. Here, transcendence does not connote flight but rather a movement into and in spite of the structures of suffering.

JÜRGEN MOLTMANN'S *THE CRUCIFIED GOD* AND TRINITARIAN CHRISTOLOGY

> The crucified god is in fact a stateless and classless God. Nevertheless, that does not mean that he is an unpolitical God. He is the God of the poor, the oppressed and the humiliated.
>
> Jürgen Moltmann, *The Crucified God*

I wish to test the above claim by reading Jürgen Moltmann's Christology, which offers a powerful alternative to traditional Christology when he argues that God is crucified on the cross. While his emphasis on understanding the event of the crucifixion as a manifestation of God's resistance against oppression and God's presence on the cross is appealing and comforting, I am compelled to wonder if it does not continue to echo the classical expiatory Christology that has been often criticized by feminist theologians. His Christology gets its toes wet in the oceanic depths of the divine semiotic presence but still retreats, in the perspective of the present reading, from what could be construed as a possibly turbulent engulfment. In what follows, I will present my reading of Moltmann in relation to critiques directed at him by feminist theologians. By bringing feminist interventions into these conversations, I hope to draw attention to some problematic aspects of his christological framework. Through this conversation with Moltmann, I will indicate what I find to be problematic and what I suggest might, in conjunction, work fruitfully toward an alternative Christology.

Jesus as the Christ allowed for the full embodiment of *jeong* not only in his ministry, as indicated by his relationships to those who were powerless, but also in his relationships to those who were seemingly powerful, feared, and loathed. *Jeong* and *han* are intertwined and present not only in his ministry but also on the cross. Our previous chapter's examination of the notion of "mimicry"[19] is critical in our reading of the cross. The cross as a symbol works both to pay homage to patriarchal notions of power and obedience and at the same time to "menace" those concepts.

The rulers of the Roman Empire deployed the cross in order to terrorize people into submission. The fact that early Christianity used the same symbol to mimic and mock the empire attests to the subversive understanding of the cross that was part of the early church movement.[20] Hence, postcolonial notion of mimicry sheds light on our understanding of the cross as a menace when it mimics and so mirrors back a powerful counterinterpretation to the oppressive order and law of the imperial power. The act of execution on the cross by the Roman Empire was by no means a glorious form of punishment. Execution on the cross was always a veiled threat that terrorized the oppressed into staying properly subjected. However, through the power of mimicry, this very sign of abjection becomes a sign of love/*jeong* that is inclusive of the perpetrators. The double-crossing on the cross is this: even as the cross embodies abjection, it works simultaneously against abjection through Jesus' embodiment of *jeong*. While mimicry as a subversive dynamic comes to the front lines, the notion of hybridity becomes crucial in the divine presence on the cross.

The concept of hybridity allows one to perceive a gap, an interstitial space, wherein doctrinal theology might be transformed. One of the key concerns in Moltmann's Christology is the question of God's concern or unconcern for the fate of Jesus on the cross. Moltmann focuses on the Trinitarian dynamism of the cross and thereby claims, "The son suffers and dies on the cross. The Father suffers with him but not in the same way."[21] The theology of the cross must be Trinitarian by implication:

> The grief of the Father here is just as important as the death of the Son. The Fatherlessness of the Son is matched by the Sonlessness of the Father, and if God has constituted himself as the Father of Jesus Christ, then he also suffers the death of his Fatherhood in the death of the Son.[22]

The key emphasis in Moltmann's Christology is that the event of the cross is Trinitarian.[23] He states dramatically, "The content of the doctrine of the Trinity is the real cross of Christ himself."[24] I find myself asking why Moltmann emphasizes God's pathos on the cross to the point of a fusion of identity, but he does not suggest the horror of abjection that is made present on the cross. What I find in my reading of Moltmann is that the cross, despite the suffering of both God and Jesus, is kept untainted. The event of the cross seems tidy—not drenched with the bloody spilling of semiotic eruption. The suffering, utter abjection on the cross, is somehow theologically masked or contained.

Such logic of inner-Trinitarian containment avoids the paradox of "God is dead on the cross yet not dead." The significance of the death of Jesus must take into consideration the "inner-trinitarian tensions and relationships of God and speak of the Father, the Son and the Spirit."[25] In Moltmann's Christology, the death of Jesus on the cross becomes the center of all Christian theology. Rather than "saving" Jesus on the cross why not let Jesus' death become a sign of complete suffering and complete abjection? This seems to be prevented when "the Christ event on the cross is a God event," for this approach functions to contain the utter abjection of the cross.[26] The event on the cross is a "God event," but it is also an abject event. It is not Someone Else on the cross; the cross is full of the abjected other. The cross does not symbolize the death and suffering of one historical figure but rather signifies and points to the abjection of the other as the return of the repressed.

A powerful critique of Moltmann's inner-Trinitarian assertion that God is crucified comes from Asian theologian C. S. Song. Song is insistent that the Father's abandonment of the Son on the cross comes across as merely a "Mutiny within God" as Song further moves from Moltmann's crucified God to his own notion of the Crucified People.[27] I will further examine Song's understanding of the cross in the next chapter. Song's critique of Moltmann is a corrective in that the violence on the cross is not divine violence but human violence. He goes on to insist that the cross is the "suffering of Jesus of Nazareth and it is the suffering of humanity. The cross means human beings rejecting human beings. It is 'human beings abandoning human beings' and not the 'Second person' of the Trinity forsaken by the 'First person' of the Trinity' nor is it about one leaving the other in a lurch."[28]

In previous chapters we have noted that Kristeva and Trinh concur when it comes to the presence of the stranger within the self. Such a complex understanding of the stranger/abject and the "I" within the self no longer sustains the dichotomy of self and other but instead collapses such easy separation. The implication of this convergence of the self and the other in terms of Christology—the convergence of the divine and the human, transcendence and immanence, holy and abject, *han* and *jeong*—would not only question the very assumptions of God-hood but would also radicalize our relational understanding of each in relation to the other. The double gesture on the cross as homage *and* menace to empire works to challenge radically much of the dualistic thinking that is the foundation of Christian theology.

The collapse of dichotomy of self/other and *han/jeong* also reflects what liberation theologians like Leonardo Boff have been saying with regards to Christology. Boff has consistently argued that the cross is a double-edged site: it is at once a symbol of atrocious punishment and also the "mightiest of symbols—the graphic embodiment of Christ's redemption." In the event of the cross, we witness and are reminded that we come into contact with both the logic of love and the logic of violence. Thus it is both abjection/*han*, for it is "the indictment of the wickedness of the persons who caused Jesus' death," and it is the embodiment of *jeong by Jesus*, for it is the "symbol of love stronger than death." The only way of truly opposing suffering and oppression is through love! I do not find Moltmann's emphasis on the solidarity of God on the cross to be enough. Moltmann lets the work of redemption be done within the divine Trinitarian relationality. What has happened to the participation of humanity in redemptive work? Is our part necessary, or has the divine Trinity done all the work already? Does not the work of redemption happen in the process of the historical realm? What happens when the event of the cross becomes divinized? Although Moltmann's Christology brings God into radical solidarity with the Son on the cross, his Christology seems limited by his failure to go far enough to create the interstitial space between *han*/abjection and *jeong*.

It is thus no accident that in Moltmann's theology, incarnation cannot be separated from the cross. Accordingly, the cross of Jesus took place in God and the crucifixion becomes the death of God. This inner-Trinitarian dynamic unravels the traditional contradiction between God and Jesus' suffering and proposes that we understand that "God's being is in suffering and suffering is in God's being itself."[29] If God and Jesus on the cross are as fused as is portrayed by Moltmann, then Jesus represents Otherness within God's self. Jesus would be God's own abjected self. Moltmann offers a reading of the Passion narrative as if "Jesus . . . in his 'Abba' prayer . . . experienced himself as child of the divine Father." This contradiction between his experience of himself and his experience of death is so profound that it has to be understood, according to Moltmann, as the "God forsakenness of the Son of God." In Mark 15:34, Jesus cries out to his Father in utter abandonment, "My God, why hast thou forsaken me?" The Markan account depicts an "eclipse of God in which Jesus died."[30]

But why do theologians thus persist with the assumption that Jesus was in fact abandoned? Did God abandon him? That would imply that God could have saved him from this suffering. The Christian tradition that describes God's silence often depicts it as an "abyss, a sinking into nothingness."[31] Catherine Keller notes, however, "It is only fair that the father should finally be allowed to suffer at the death of his son; that all fathers might at last take up the cross of their own pain rather than pass it on."[32] Moltmann's notion of "being in suffering" has been criticized in particular by Leonardo Boff. To argue that suffering and death are somehow intrinsic to the divine identity and thus an expression of God's essence is to eternalize suffering. If Jesus "takes on suffering for the sake of suffering, because suffering is God . . . then there is no way to overcome suffering." Consequently, Jesus' suffering is only redemptive because it was a result of struggle against suffering.[33] Contrary to Moltmann's understanding of God's being in suffering, Boff persistently maintains that suffering is only redemptive when it is the result of struggle against suffering itself.

For Moltmann, the cross divides and yet fuses the persons in their relationships to each other in the inner-Trinitarian relationship of Moltmann's Christology. For this reason, Moltmann goes on to explain that the "theological dimension of the death of Jesus on the cross is what happens between Jesus and his Father in the spirit of abandonment and surrender."[34] It is such language of "abandonment" and "surrender" that feminist theologian Dorothee Soelle has criticized in Moltmann. Certainly this language of self-abnegation, within the context of those who have been oppressed and victimized, must be challenged for its patriarchal evocative power to legitimate oppressive positions of "surrender" and acceptance of "abandonment." The symbol of the cross is paradoxical as it signifies not only execution but also wholeness and life. Thus, as much as I am critical of Moltmann's inner-Trinitarian frame, I am also not comfortable with Soelle's and other feminist theologians' argument that the cross should not serve as a religious symbol at all but only signifies a political measure of punishment that is confined not only to Jesus but also instigated against all who confront oppressive power. Certainly I agree with feminists that the notion of redemption chosen out of complete obedience and self-giving love continues to justify relationships of domination. But it is also necessary to ask why the cross, with all the suffering it signifies, continues to empower and perform as emancipatory symbol for many who are suffering and oppressed throughout the world.

Within Moltmann's Christology are traces of a radical understanding of love. As Keller observes, the suffering God "emerged as a great trope of the twentieth century, wrested from a hereticized patripassionism."[35] Similar to other liberation theologians, Moltmann contends that God and suffering are no longer contradictions, but instead goes on to argue that "God's being is in suffering and the suffering is in God's being, because God is love."[36] The suffering on the cross is made powerful because it also manifests God's radical expression of love. Central to his theology of the cross is not only the inner-Trinitarian relationship but also a claim that the suffering on the cross expresses radical solidarity and love. Moltmann states,

> God is not only other-worldly but also this-worldly; he is not only
> God, but also man; he is not only rule, authority and law but also the
> event of suffering, liberating love. The death of the Son . . . is the
> beginning of that God event in which the life-giving spirit of love
> emerges from the death of the Son and the grief of the Father.[37]

The paradox then is that even this love of God must be carefully shifted
through oppressive and suffocating forms of love that are often glorified and
foisted upon those who are powerless. Love and suffering are juxtaposed in
what seems a contradiction. The dialectic of the cross must be seen also in light
of the resurrection for Moltmann. In her reading of Moltmann, feminist theologian Rebecca Chopp has noted that this is not to make a choice between
"Jesusology" and "high Christology," but rather, the "historical understanding of Jesus is to be read with what Moltmann calls the eschatological-
theological understanding of Christ."[38] Moltmann himself is critical, despite
his language of "surrender," of Christologies that highlight Jesus' willingness
to die on the cross. Nor does Moltmann accept christological formulas that
emphasize Jesus' death as a "ransom for our sins." Inasmuch as Moltmann
denies such traditional Christologies, he directs us to understand that Jesus did
not passively accept his death upon the cross as fate, but that Jesus cried out
in suffering and with "expressions of profound abandonment by God."[39] Jesus'
cry of "My God!" is both a protest and a recognition.

In my theological language Jesus' protest and recognition symbolize the final
living out of emancipatory *jeong*. Moltmann points out that despite Jesus' very
intimate and close relationship with God during his ministry, the cross "denies,
forgets, and ruptures this fellowship and identification between Jesus and
God."[40] Moltmann's theology of the cross is grounded in the importance of his
understanding of the "sufferings of Christ." Moltmann concedes that the "sufferings of Christ" are not confined to Jesus. On the other hand, the suffering of
Christ has universal dimensions because of the apocalyptic setting. The apocalyptic sufferings of "this present time" are linked to the "sufferings of Christ"
on the cross. Such apocalyptic views pose difficulties for Moltmann as he navi-
gates what he terms the "inclusive" and "exclusive" contours to Christ's sufferings. It is ambivalent when "Jesus' sufferings are not his own personal sufferings,
which he suffers from himself. They are the apocalyptic sufferings which he suffers for the world . . . they are necessary. . . . Consequently he has suffered vicariously what threatens everyone."[41] This theological logic has drawn criticism
from feminist theologians in that it "eternalizes" suffering. Darby Ray counters
that "if the locus of redemption is God's suffering and death—unhinged from
the historical circumstances and choices that brought them on—then suffering
and death can be interpreted as salvific *in themselves*."[42] In addition, such
"timely" apocalypse works effectively to put a closure to the future rather than

seeing the opening for radical transformation. Moltmann's Christology then attempts to embody both exclusive and inclusive aspects of Christ's sufferings, for as he reflects, "Jesus suffers them in solidarity with others, and vicariously for many and proleptically for the whole suffering creation."[43]

Despite the emphasis on the relationality of the Trinity embodied on the cross, what comes across is not a mutual relationship but a unilateral relationship in which the Father takes the initiative. The Son remains passive and remains the abject. Would not the inner-Trinitarian relationality be strengthened if the Father would take on and become as abject as the Son? Here, I want to press Moltmann's claim that God is crucified on the cross. Even as Moltmann makes this assertion, the internal Trinitarian relational language still remains such that the Father and the Son are not fused. What might this mean in terms of Jesus' suffering on the cross? Moltmann excruciatingly attempts to construct liberative relationality between the Father and the Son without noticing that the paradigm itself is dysfunctional. The dysfunction appears in its relational aspect because there does not seem to be concrete mutuality but only a hierarchical relationality in which the Son does not have much to say. One could argue that not only is the Son acted on when he is crucified, but he is again acted on when the Father comes on the scene. *It is my contention that what is transformative and menacing is not the Son who is rescued by his Father but the Son who is the abject.* He is the abject who stares back and mimics and mocks the powers that have rendered him abject. This is what is transgressive and transformative about the cross. In order to extricate a relational Trinity from the grip of this dysfunctional symbolic power of Father-over-Son, we need to see what is lacking and what is not made visible in Moltmann's Trinitarianism. What Moltmann seems to do unintentionally is to domesticate the uncontrollable, uncontainable power of the semiotic rupture on the cross. Too much seems to spill out from the abject on the cross, and thus Moltmann seems to build or at least unsuspectingly sustain the doctrinal dams to stave off the disruption of a semiotic flood.

The event of the cross is then what Taylor has noted as the way of the cross and which I further argue is buoyed and sustained by a particular kind of living. It is a living out of the way of emancipatory praxis of *jeong*.

EMANCIPATORY PRAXIS OF *JEONG*

> Our theological tradition presents some difficulty as far as God in the feminine gender is concerned. There is no woman God, no female trinity: mother, daughter, spirit. . . . We have no female trinity.
> Luce Irigaray, *Sexes and Genealogies*

Feminists have critiqued the limits of traditional christological paradigms wherein oppressive power dynamics are unknowingly sustained. In his emphasis on the solidarity of the Father in the suffering of the Son, Moltmann indeed pushes the limits of this traditional paradigm; however, some paradigms need a considerable push in order to extend their boundaries. A paradigm shift is needed to free the Trinitarian relationship from the remaining traces of oppressive patriarchalism that are found within traditional christological paradigms. It is not only a matter of freeing or finding a way to exonerate the Trinity or strip theology of sexist language; rather, in order for theology to be relevant to communities that struggle against domination we must critique the presence of power and domination on diverse terrains, such as political, social, economical, gender, racial, cultural, and sexual orientation.

A key problem for many feminists is the metaphorical language and conception for the Father-Son relationship. In order to argue for an intimate relationship between the Father and the Son, Jesus' reference to God as "Abba" is often cited. This intimate experience, in conjunction with Jesus' intense sense of abandonment by his Father, lends power to Moltmann's understanding of the cross as an inner-Trinitarian event. This God-forsakenness is what Jesus experienced during his final hours, which could be interpreted as the *han* of Jesus through his experience of abjection. Moltmann acknowledges such endurance and acceptance of his Father's abandonment as Jesus' passion for God's kingdom, but despite his good intentions, Moltmann might here be in danger of sanctioning oppressive concepts of surrender, submission, and obedience. Rather than seeing Jesus' acceptance of his abandonment as his passion for God's kingdom and, by default, his embodiment of *han*, would it not be more liberative, within the conceptual framework of *jeong*, to argue that Jesus' "abandonment" was in fact not *han* but rather his acceptance of the Other through his *jeong* for the Other, sustained by his deep *jeong* for the world? According to Moltmann,

> In the surrender of the Son, the Father surrenders himself too—but not in the same way. The Son suffers his dying in this forsakenness. The Father suffers the death of the Son. He suffers it in the infinite pain of his love for the Son. The death of the Son therefore corresponds to the pain of the Father.[44]

However, the statement that "the sufferings of Christ are already manifested here and now as divine sufferings, and have to be understood as the sufferings of God," avoids addressing the present suffering of those who are powerless, oppressed—the abjects of history. The shift from Christ's sufferings and abandonment to God crucified on the cross is often done in ambivalent ways. Such shifts are too clean, too orderly. Shifting Christ's sufferings to the Crucified God dismisses the redemptive power of Christ's suffering for the abject.

This is not to say that God's role becomes insignificant. If God's being is in suffering because of the incarnation, we must also explore the Godliness of the abject and the abjectness of God's self. If, as Andrew Park argues, *han* is the woundedness experienced by God, then God is not and cannot be removed from *han* and abjection, but rather God is part of both *han* and *jeong*. God is "holy" but paradoxically abject in all abjectness's misery, suffering, and pain.

By stressing the "divine consistency" of the inner life of the Trinity, Moltmann is unable to extricate fully from a patriarchal christological paradigm in order to fully embody incarnational redemptive power. Moltmann's articulation of the relationship between the Father and the Son goes on to maintain that "the self-giving of the Son means that he empties himself of his divine form . . . [and that] self-giving consists in his self-humiliation, and in his 'obedience unto death, even death on the cross.'"[45] He supports his argument further by citing Hebrews: "[Jesus] learnt obedience through what he suffered . . . and he on his side learnt surrender."[46] The language of "surrendering" is effective only when all people practice surrendering, just as the language of fusion of relationships is problematic when it takes place in the context of oppressive relationships. Many feminists are critical of Moltmann's theology precisely at this juncture. Surrendering is not beneficial nor does it make sense for those who have been oppressed and dominated.

What I would like to accentuate in Moltmann's theology, which Moltmann seems to assume but does not highlight, is God's radical presence of love/*jeong* on the cross. The emergence of love/*jeong* within his theology would further radicalize his theology of the cross. I would pursue his reference to Abraham Heschel's concept of "the pathos of God" by arguing that the cross is also an event of God's profound love/*jeong*. The power of the cross is perhaps most liberative when we witness Jesus' utter abjection by the symbolic Father God.[47] Jesus' experience of this abjection and *han* is, I contend, the expression of our primordial separation, our earliest and profoundest experience of *han*.

The *jeong* embodied on the cross is not only the *jeong* of solidarity that ultimately flows from the semiotic divine but also one that powerfully surges from Jesus to the divine and to the suffering creation. Moreover, in light of our conversation in previous chapters on abjection, *han*, and *jeong*, I suggest it is fruitful for a theology of the cross to highlight *jeong* because the cross embodies and continues to function as an embodiment of abjection and love, both *han* and *jeong*.

Moltmann's Christology, precariously if not intentionally, persists in believing that suffering in some way becomes a channel of God's revelation.[48] Consequently, Jesus' ministry becomes secondary, thus implying that the "real action occurs not on earth but in God's being." Jesus' struggle against the oppressive powers could easily be read as an event removed from the human realm and one that has become "primarily a heavenly affair."[49] The executed God's radical solidarity with those who suffer is a doctrinal move away from traditional atonement theory that sees suffering in itself as redemptive. However, language like "suffering is overcome by suffering" needs to be further clarified in order to avoid being read as a patriarchal reification of unsavory power dynamics that we would clearly want to avoid.

Again, as feminists agree, the strength of Moltmann's Christology is that God does not look on helplessly or is unmoved by the sufferings of human beings, but instead dies and suffers with them. This revolutionary transformation of the image of God is "watered down where Moltmann again puts them in a trinitarian pattern of thought."[50]

The most stinging criticism seems to be that levelled by Dorothee Soelle, who claims that despite Moltmann's portrayal of God as the "God of the poor, the peasants and the slaves," his intention is weakened by his less-than-complete departure from the traditional patriarchal theological system. Furthermore, such theology is ultimately "sadistic."[51] However, must we understand the cross only as a symbol of oppressive power? Might we not see the cross as also signifying a risk that one encounters as one lives in the fullness of *jeong*? For as Keller argues,

> There is no deity who causes the suffering or rescues us from it; no divine life-saver. To incarnate intentionally the Wisdom may in fact heighten the risk of crucifixion; but the aim, the lure, is for new creation.[52]

Christological formulations that highlight the cross as a symbol of making right a relationship gone wrong between the divine and the world continue not only to distort concepts of power and love but also deprive the crucifixion of its political power for resistance against suffering and the structures of oppression.

Feminists' critiques disclose that suffering within Christian interpretation has often been a justification of masochism, for "almost all Christian interpretation ignores the distinction between suffering that we can and cannot end."[53] This traditional understanding of suffering accentuates and recommends suffering in light of masochism, when suffering is used to "break our pride, demonstrate our powerlessness, exploit our dependency," and whose intention to bring us back to God does so by making Himself great while we become so small.[54] Every attempt to view suffering as caused directly or indirectly by God is in danger of linking God with sadism. Given the traditional masculinist constructions of the divine and the attending doctrines, it is hardly surprising that sadism has become part of the imagined divine. The symbolic maintains its orderliness and order not only through the repression of the semiotic but through the discipline of punishment and retribution.[55] According to this logic, atonement is only possible as a result of suffering. Most traditional articulations of suffering begin with the notion of punishment from God and thus seek reasons for suffering within this parameter. Consequently, what emerges is the notion of God as the almighty ruler who sends suffering in order to extract justice. Soelle is adamant that within Moltmann's theology of the cross is the Father of Jesus Christ who first acted intentionally, who, in her words, "deliberately slayed his son"—a theology that leads to the ultimate conclusion that it is a form of theological sadism that worships the executioner.[56] Soelle contends, to the contrary, that God is the lover of life, as was Jesus Christ in his ministry and death. Such a God "does not desire suffering of people, not even as a pedagogical device."[57] To such a critique, Moltmann's response is that this would be true only if God is seen as the only active agent and the Son as the passive object. Moltmann insists that Soelle misunderstands his theology of surrender. To him, Jesus is not a "sacrifice" made to meet God's righteousness or "to appease God's wrath." Such agency on the part of God and passivity on Jesus' part would mean that they are in a divided relationship, or, as Moltmann maintains, "They are not present together. They are opposed to one another." Moltmann notes that the traditional expiatory theology has in the past suggested such a position, but he insists that the Father and the Son are in deep relationship with one another. Their relationship is so intimately bound that the Son's suffering becomes the Father's suffering as well.[58]

Thus the cross becomes the center of suffering as a sign of revolt against oppression and suffering. The cross functions as a sign of solidarity with those that are oppressed, disadvantaged, and marginalized. In this, Soelle and Moltmann agree. We are thus called to be in solidarity with those who suffer through the cross, because on the cross Christ was on the side of those who suffer in order to end suffering.

Other feminist theologians, such as Rita Nakashima Brock and Delores Williams, have criticized the traditional atonement theory predominantly because of the issue of power. Traditional atonement reifies what has often been interpreted as an abuse of power in relationships. It sustains the powerful and the powerless in an unequivocal hierarchical relationship. Likewise, from a Korean American feminist standpoint, the patriarchal understanding of the cross reinforces the language of patriarchal power dynamics. Moreover, Schüssler Fiorenza maintains,

> By ritualizing the suffering and death of Jesus and by calling the powerless in society and church to imitate Jesus' perfect obedience and self-sacrifice, Christian ministry and theology do not interrupt but continue to foster the circle of violence engendered by kyriarchal social and ecclesial structures as well as by cultural and political discourse.[59]

Again, while I am in agreement with Schüssler Fiorenza that the cross has been used to perpetuate the domination of women and the powerless, I also wonder to what extent she herself has rendered women, the powerless, and the subaltern voiceless. In the previous quote, one does not get a sense of agency of those who are powerless. Might she not, in this rhetoric, perform the very same gesture that the kyriarchal social structures have done in the past and continue to do so in the present? Might Schüssler Fiorenza render the subaltern and the abject unable to speak with no presence of agency? On the other hand, she contends, "A theology of the cross as self-giving love is even more detrimental than that of obedience because it colludes with the cultural 'feminine' calling to self-sacrificing love for the sake of their families."[60]

Similarly, Korean American sociologist Jung Ha Kim observes that the "sexism preached within the context of the sacred realm of Christianity produces a dangerous atmosphere wherein churched Korean American women may accept the selfless and pain-enduring image as an ideal Christian model for them." Kim goes on to note that the "call for churched women's suffering is often reflective of the image of Christ as 'the suffering servant.'"[61] As such, "the inherent contradiction of the satisfied suffering servant, which resembles a sadomasochistic understanding of the meaning of Jesus' life and death, is justified."[62] By stressing the traditional concepts of suffering and self-denial, Korean women are often dealt two messages: suffering is justified, and oppression is a natural part of reality and, in its consequent spiritualization of suffering, a "Christian virtue."

The ambivalency of the cross itself is pointed out by one of the forerunners of the Minjung movement, Ham Sok Hon, when he comments, "How is the atonement of moral man, who possesses a free will, brought about? . . . It is not the historical man Jesus whom I believe; rather I believe in Christ. He is the eternal Christ, who not only is in Jesus *but who also by nature is in me. Atonement takes place through this Christ only when Jesus and I are no longer separate persons but experience oneness together*."[63] Ham's writing from the perspective of the Korean liberation movement argues for the need to recognize the solidarity between the suffering Christ and the suffering abject. This recognition of Christ suffering with us and of our suffering being reflected in Christ's sufferings is done with the power of *jeong*. Criticizing Moltmann's and other male theologians' valorization of "Christic vulnerability and admission of divine self-limitation" and feminists' wariness of submission and obedience, Sarah Coakley argues that the choice between "dependent vulnerability" and "liberative power and submission"[64] is a false one. Coakley wonders why themes of vulnerability, fragility, and self-emptying have been absent or muted, particularly within white Christian feminist writings, while these themes are explored, embraced, and even woven into the works of nonwhite feminists. Crucial to

Coakley's project is the realization that power and vulnerability are not oppositional; instead the task of Christian feminists is to create a "space" (Third Space?) where "non-coercive divine power manifests itself." According to Coakley, perhaps the mystery and even the backbone of Christianity might be found within this paradox in terms of Christian redemption.[65]

The suffering on the cross by Jesus not only mirrors Korean women's experiences of suffering; it is also in direct solidarity with their own struggle to be freed from such suffering. While the cross and its attending patriarchal misappropriations have drugged many oppressed people, it is my observation that those who are oppressed and repressed are drawn powerfully to the cross because they recognize its subversive power. Here Kristeva's observation of the abject comes to mind. For her the abject is "edged with the sublime" where the subversiveness of the abject is that it alway beckons us as "a deep well of memory."[66] The Korean women are able to see past the imperialist and patriarchal doctrinal veil. Because Jesus was in the fullness of his power, his suffering on the cross exposed not only the *han* and the abjection of the world but simultaneously exposed the radical side of *jeong*/love. His willingness to give up his power into the hands of suffering was possible only because he was already in fullness of *jeong*. This is not to justify or to sublimate suffering, but when *jeong* becomes incarnate within connectedness, within solidarity, it must struggle against powers that cause suffering. We know that many women, children, and people of all races have been and continue to be rendered powerless. When we do not have power, we also cannot willingly give up what we do not have in the first place. Our "willingness" then comes out of domination, fear, and coercion. For this reason, the continuing presence and relevance of traditional atonement theory in churches must seriously be challenged. The cross embodies Jesus' embodiment of *han*/abjection and his radical *jeong* for us. In the strength of those who are weak, Soelle finds the power of the crucified to be alive and work to end suffering. She states that the cross is

> above all a symbol of reality. Love does not "require" the cross, but de facto, it ends up on the cross. De facto Jesus of Nazareth was crucified . . . the cross is no theological invention but the world's answer . . . to attempts at liberation. Only for that reason are we able to recognize ourselves in Jesus' dying on the cross.[67]

Reference to Jesus' intimate relationship with his "Abba" repudiated patriarchy in Jesus' time. However, "the insistence upon the father imagery after Jesus' time has functioned to reinforce patriarchy in church and society with its . . . apparatus of a dominative . . . which trivializes God's immanence."[68] Feminists are critical not only of the dominating model of God's power but also, as Johnson notes, of the linking of the destructive and radical suffering with the "permissive will of God."[69] Given the suffering reality of most women, the emphasis on the powerless suffering of God is more often than not dangerous to women's psyches by firmly embedding already existing feelings of helplessness and powerlessness in the oppressed. The locus of divine involvement in the human experience of suffering is to be found in the cross. The cross becomes the witness of "Wisdom's participation in the suffering of the world and in the eventual overcoming of suffering and evil through the *power of love*."[70] This is what I mean by the power of *jeong* on the cross. It is only through compassion that we might interpret divine suffering as Sophia God's act of love. Johnson insists that "love may yet serve as a crystallization of the relational essence of God's being. . . . [A]s a summation of compassionate love, the symbol of divine suffering appears not as an imperfection but as the highest excellence."[71] Divine compassion, by entering into the suffering, does not mitigate its evil but rather brings consolation and comfort. In what sounds very close to our description of *jeong* in previous chapters, feminist theologian Wendy Farley makes the following observation about suffering on the cross:

> Compassion . . . begins where the sufferer is, in the grief, the shame, the hopelessness. It sees the despair as the most real thing. Compassion is with the sufferer, turned toward or submerged in her experience, seeing it with her eyes. This communion with the sufferer in her pain, as she experiences it, is the presence of love that is a balm to the wounded spirit. This relationship of shared, sympathetic suffering mediates consolation and respect that can empower the sufferer to bear the pain, to resist the humiliation, to overcome the guilt.[72]

Suffering and evil is overcome through a "living communion of love" from within. Overcoming suffering is not done through a unilateral "rescue" from one that has power but rather through communion with the abject. As we have noted earlier, *jeong* is not simply identifiable with compassion, but compassion is a vital part of *jeong*. It is not that suffering is dismissed, or that injustice of *han* is forgotten, but that there comes a point in which one may go beyond *han*. It is at this interstitial space that *jeong* arises between the hearts of the oppressed and the oppressor, in between the harrowing and vulnerable and often tortuous space, the utter abyssal space between the executed and the executioner, victim and the victimizer.

Jeong is what is needed to bring wholeness and healing from abjection and *han*. The practice of *dan* is crucial in dismantling individual and collective experiences of *han*; however, healing can only come through the power of *jeong*. We might be able to wrestle justice out of the unjust, but we cannot extract the more profound changes that only come through love/*jeong*. The practice of *jeong* will be the key that unlocks the grip between the oppressed and the oppressor, between genders, between races, between sexualities. While *jeong* may not bring about the radical dismantling of oppressive systems in a revolutionary upheaval, *jeong* is like the water that flows and over time even reshapes the very rocks it flows over. This notion of love and *jeong* is not "powerlessness" in the face of the "powerful." Rather, the dualistic framework that identifies power with the exercise of dominating power and compassionate love with resignation of power must be critically examined. Instead we must "seek to integrate these two, seeing love as the shape in which divine power appears"[73] especially when the subversive and recreating forces of hybridity and mimicry unfold *jeong's* presence. This "power-with" dynamics is not the antithesis of love; it is love against the power of death. This love manifests through persuasion, care, attention, passion, compassion, vulnerability, solidarity, and mutuality and arises from the interstitial space between the self and the other.[74]

A feminist psychoanalytic understanding of the cross provides a radical inclusivity to this theology. Such inclusivity, similar to *jeong*, acknowledges the presence of *han* and abjection rather than sublimating them. When the Korean experience of *han* and the complex and inclusive depths of *jeong* are read alongside the theology of the cross, what seems to be a very white masculine "high theology" grows within the soil of suffering and love here and now, in our individual and collective bodies and in our worlds.

By attempting to radicalize the cross yet at the same time working within the traditional paradigm, Moltmann's theology of the cross is enmeshed with contradictions posed by the fused yet separated identity of the Son and the Father. For Moltmann, the cross is the event in which both the Father and the Son become fused; yet, at the same time, he argues that it is an event of radical separation so that "on the cross the Father and the Son are so much at one that they present a single surrendering movement." Although Moltmann's theology is psychologically resonant in certain ways, it is imbued with power dynamics that must be deconstructed with feminist psychoanalytic theories. For what is missing in Moltmann's psychological framework of the cross is the maternal semiotic.

Nonetheless, what is problematic in Moltmann contains what is promising. In his inner-Trinitarian relationality, the identity of the Father and the Son are almost completely fused. Such fused relationship, through solidarity, I suggest, can offer a radical way of envisioning God and God's self. Through this double presence, it is my argument that the abject is the stranger/Other within God's self. This shift seeks radical inclusivity: an inclusivity of the other, the abject as interior to our selves. At the same time, this abjection is paradoxical because it is an expulsion that is never a complete expulsion. Inclusion is thus expulsion of one's own life source. In what ways would this then transform Trinitarian, relational Christology? What are the theological challenges if we are to see just how permeable the Three in the Trinity are? Do we then still need the Trinitarian language? And if so, for what purpose? Perhaps we need to go back to the early doctrinal debates to excavate those voices marginalized by the eventual church history. What are the implications of this in terms of how we envision our relationality with ourselves, with the other, and with God with the Son?

Kristeva notes that such abjected elements can never be completely obliterated and made obsolete, but that the abject continues to "haunt the edges of the subject's identity with the threat of disruption or even dissolution."[75] As much as the abject is everything that the subject feels necessary to expel in order to enter into the symbolic, it is also the "symptom of the failure of this ambition."[76] As a compromise between "condemnation and yearning," the abject marks the boundaries and the borders of the self. Transgressing borders, the abject is a witness to society's precarious hold over the fluid and disorderly aspects of individual and collective psyche. As Kristeva brilliantly observes, "abjection is above all ambiguity."[77] Thus, the abject haunts the subject as its inner boundary, which unwillingly gets transgressed so that the abject is "something rejected from which one does not part."[78] The return of the abject is thus a constant reminder that we are fragmented and furthermore that our problem of the abject is not the Other but within ourselves.

More and more, theologians are careful as they articulate the power of the cross. This caution is maintained because of our awareness of the potential to reimbue Christology with the remaining shackles of patriarchalism and imperialism. Moreover, this desire to articulate a liberative theology of the cross becomes urgent precisely because we "know" and have "experienced" the power of the cross in radical liberative ways. Our theological reflections on Christology must grapple with not only abjection as *han* within the individual consciousness but also within the collective consciousness. As a result, we must also examine the attending implications when it comes to our discussions on the doctrine of God. Moreover, a Christology that includes analysis of the abject brings critical attention to the liminal state that hovers on the threshold, the boundary between psychoanalysis, theology, and material history.

The next chapter will further explore the implications of *han*/abjection and love/*jeong* as it is especially drawn through the works of Julia Kristeva. Kristeva's concepts of the abject and love will be linked with *jeong* and Asian American Christologies through their reflections on the meaning of the cross.

5

A Christology of *Jeong*

The cross is not only the expression of God's love for humanity, but also the protest and wrath of God against oppressors.
Andrew Sung Park, *The Wounded Heart of God*

The reconciliatory qualifier also means that Christian liberatory practice even aims to build some kind of community with perceived enemies. . . . Such a love of the enemy can be compatible with both a preferential option for the poorest and a sustained adversarial practice for them.
Mark Lewis Taylor, *Religion, Politics and the Christian Right*

This chapter will present a Christology of *jeong*. In the previous chapter, we explored psychological dimensions of *han* and *jeong* from a feminist perspective before engaging with the Christology of Jürgen Moltmann and then concluding with a feminist critique of his Christology. I would like to frame this chapter with the understanding of the feminist theological task as articulated by Grace Jantzen. Her concept of "double movement" will provide entry into the Christology of *jeong* via Asian American Christologies in conversation with Julia Kristeva's notion of abjection and of love. The latter portion of this chapter, as previously in chapter 2, deals again with psychoanalytic categories because they now can be interpreted as not only political but also theological.

DESTABILIZING THE PATRIARCHAL DIVINITY

Jantzen argues in her recent book that feminists must engage in the radical work of deconstruction. As she explains, "deconstruction is not demolition":

> Religion . . . is utmost in this view, since the masculinist Symbolic of
> the West is undergirded by a concept of God as Divine Father, a God
> who is also Word, and who in his eternal disembodiment, omnipo-
> tence, and omniscience is the epitome of value.[1]

In acknowledging that reality, feminist theologians must do more than
deconstruction in order to "not just re-arrange the same masculinist religious
Symbolic."[2] Kristeva's notion of the abject and abjection is important in analyzing the dynamics of oppression. Abjection is an object as well as a process
by which individual and group identity is formed by the exclusion/expulsion
of anything that threatens the border of that particular identity. It is both
deeply repressed or expelled by the psyche. However, abject elements can
never be completely obliterated and made obsolete, but these abjections
continue to "haunt the edges of the subject's identity with the threat of disruption or even dissolution."[3] What I have stressed is that, even as traditional
Christology has been tidied up and contained, abjection on the cross has been
haunting the edges of doctrinal theology. As much as the abject is everything
that the subject feels necessary to expel in order to enter into the symbolic, it
is also the "symptom of the failure of this ambition."[4] The abject is part of us
that we desperately attempt to repress or expel as we become speaking subjects that are driven to enter into the world of the symbolic. The abject signifies and embodies the semiotic that must be erased/repressed/eradicated as the
subject enters into the symbolic realm of becoming a speaking subject. As a
compromise between "condemnation and yearning," abjection marks the
boundaries and the borders of the self. Transgressing borders, abjection is a
witness to society's precarious hold over the fluid and disorderly aspects of
individual and collective psyches. The abject haunts the subject as its inner
boundary, a boundary that unwillingly gets transgressed so that the abject is
"something rejected from which one does not part."[5] A Christology that
includes analysis of the abject brings critical attention to the liminal state that
hovers on the threshold, the boundaries between psychoanalysis, theology, and
material history.

Julia Kristeva's scholarship on the mother-child relationship takes us into
the psychic disconnection between mother and child. However, Kristeva pro-
claims that the two realms, notably the semiotic (presubjectivity) and the symbolic (formation of the I),[6] should not be divided so decisively, for they are
always intertwined. The symbolic roughly corresponds to Lacan's symbolic
realm, which is associated with the mode of reason and of representation.[7]

The semiotic, on the other hand, is similar to Lacan's "imaginary," for it
refers to the time of undifferentiated union of mother and child.[8] One might
easily fall into the trap of associating and identifying the semiotic with the feminine and the symbolic with the masculine. However, as much as they have

been marginalized within the patriarchal discourse, both realms are ungendered.[9] For example, Kristeva does not feel that the semiotic should have the sole trait of the female/feminine even though her emphasis on pregnancy as the time/site of semiotic presence would make us think otherwise. This is similar to the argument that by accenting *jeong* one would be reifying a patriarchally feminized concept.[10] Here it seems pertinent to note that Jantzen's use of the symbolic is very much informed by both Jacques Lacan and Kristeva's usage. I am here in agreement with Jantzen that deconstruction is a process of "double movement," which starts with a "dismantling of particular structures of thought in order to reveal their underlying but unacknowledged assumptions, and then using that destabilization to create new possibilities which open a passage for thinking otherwise."[11] Many feminist scholars/theologians already do engage in a process of "double-reading," a process of destabilization of the given paradigm and simultaneous construction of new paradigms.

The masculinist predominance of Logos-centered theology has been highly criticized by feminist theologians who argue for the resurrection or perhaps for that matter the "resuscitation" of the repressed abject. Jantzen is supported through her critical reading of Luce Irigaray, in the claim that "women must begin deliberately to project the divine according to our gender, as men have always done according to theirs."[12] It is no longer a question of attempting to find "redeemable" aspects of patriarchal religious projections but rather to expend our energies on the creative and imaginative constructions of the female divine in feminist terms. Simply put, feminists must now fearlessly plunge into the depths of the semiotic, even as repressive patriarchal structures that go even as far as hunting down feminist theologians who proclaim and reimagine the feminine aspect of the Divine in theology and in liturgical practices and accusing them of "heresy."[13]

Feminists have deployed the notion of "Sophia" (Greek: "Wisdom") in various ways. The Divine Wisdom of Scripture lives symbiotically with God.[14] From Jewish Wisdom literature to early Christian writings, the figure of the Divine Wisdom seems to appear. Yet a closer reading shows that a submerged theology of Wisdom or "Sophialogy" permeates the Christian Scriptures.[15] Nonetheless, feminist Schüssler Fiorenza displays a tension within her theory as she continues to privilege the position of the Bible in her theology.[16] Jantzen notes that even if Schüssler Fiorenza's continuous privileging of the Bible is part of her strategy for liberation, she nevertheless continues to fall into the trap of "unintentionally presenting the oppression with a tool of recuperation." By recuperation, Jantzen means that the Bible and feminists' privileging of the Bible is problematic because it inherently embodies structures of domination. Jantzen argues that the "considerable permeation of the

Symbolic" is inherent in the religious discourse and vice versa.[17] Jantzen's critical reading of Schüssler Fiorenza's feminist theology leads her to conclude that such theology falls back on an unspoken yet deep reliance on Scripture and tradition, which is "shot through and through" with the masculinist symbolic.

Schüssler Fiorenza believes that the "Jesus as messenger of Sophia" tradition is theologically significant for feminism because it asserts the unique particularity of Jesus without having to resort to exclusivity and superiority. However, Jantzen suspects Schüssler Fiorenza of a divided commitment to women's liberation and to Christianity. As Jantzen notes, Schüssler Fiorenza often seems too quick to redeem aspects of Christianity that, to Jantzen, do not seem redeemable. Citing Irigaray, Jantzen goes on to note that Schüssler Fiorenza in the end does not "sufficiently challenge, or displace the traditional masculinist religious Symbolic."[18] Schüssler Fiorenza has contributed much from the sociological standpoint; however, at the "level of ontology, she remains, even if critically and uneasily, within a monotheistic and trinitarian doctrinal system that pronounces both the maleness and uniqueness of Christ."[19] Jantzen, from her post-Christian perspective, would no doubt be critical of Schüssler Fiorenza's retrieval of the Christ symbol in her recent book *Miriam's Child/Sophia's Prophet*. My postcolonial Christology is positioned in the interstitial Third Space between post-Christian thinkers like Jantzen and feminist theologians like Schüssler Fiorenza. While I agree with Jantzen's critical view toward a conventional understanding of the cross, I am unwilling to insist that there is absolutely no redemptiveness on the cross, an unwillingness shared by Schüssler Fiorenza.

Jantzen argues that Jesus could indeed be understood to enable the "divine becoming of women through the notion of the incarnation: the idea that Jesus was God made flesh."[20] Jesus' incarnation was only a partial incarnation since maleness is only one of the sexes. Accordingly, "his incarnation leaves room for other incarnations, other trinities, other sexualities. The *masculinist Symbolic which looks above all to salvation from this mortal state is subverted from within*" (italics mine).[21] I would like to suggest that feminist theologians might not only come to grips with and challenge masculinist symbols of the divine but also become courageous enough to plunge into the depths of the semiotic in creative, imaginative constructions of the female divine. If Jesus' incarnation is only partial, then other incarnations are possible.[22] But what exactly is incarnated? What subverts the masculinist symbolic from within? Much of the power that gives credence to the symbolic is the abjection of the semiotic. However, as Kristeva argues, the symbolic is never able to eradicate completely all signs of the semiotic. The semiotic makes its presence even within and despite symbolic efforts to repress it. Poetry, art, music, and liturgical rituals often embody elements of the semiotic that still remain unerased and part of the symbolic. In fact, the symbolic cannot exist without the undercurrent or trace of the semiotic. It is this remnant/trace that has the potential to subvert from within.[23] What we witness on the cross is not just the power and horror of the symbolic to repress and eradicate the abject but what is made visible in the return of the repressed. The semiotic trace, in this case *jeong*, becomes present even alongside *han*, or abjection.[24]

Feminist theology has critiqued not only this repression of the semiotic divine but also its spillover into the theological doctrine of salvation. Here we will highlight the atonement theory derived from Anselm of Canterbury. Since we examined atonement in the previous chapter, I will remind us briefly and simply of his main argument in order to recapitulate feminist criticism, which is most often directed at his emphasis. Anselm focused on sin and claimed that Jesus was innocent and, by his voluntary death, satisfied the debt created by human sin against God. His death therefore paid for our sin, whereby the human relationship to God becomes restored. One of the most problematic aspects of atonement orthodoxy is its reliance on the death of Jesus as "the defining event of the incarnation of God's reconciling work."[25] Also problematic to feminist theologians is the Anselmian focus on the sinlessness of Jesus, who then is understood as the "perfect sacrifice," whose innocent life alone is sufficient to pacify a God who is so thoroughly offended by the bottomless depth of human sin.

As many feminist theologians have pointed out, the attribution of such salvific value to suffering, self-sacrifice, and obedience is too easily distorted into a tool of domination and subjugation.[26] Thus, the "Divine Victim" perpetuates the yoke of victimhood on those who are oppressed. Further, womanist theologian Delores Williams is adamant that Jesus as the Divine Scapegoat raises unsettling questions regarding the Christian tendency to blame "nonmainstream peoples" for all societal ills. Highlighting Anselmian-atonement notions of suffering and redemption in light of surrogacy and scapegoating allows persons in power to legitimate such notions by imagining that God has done likewise.[27] Of the many and diverse feminist and womanist Christologies, I have had to limit the reference to a few scholars who have delved more specifically into Jesus' connection with Sophia. Amongst these scholars, Elizabeth A. Johnson and Rita Nakashima Brock offer the most satisfying Christology for me—a postcolonial feminist Christology of *jeong*. Here, I would like to accentuate Brock's work on a Christology of "erotic power."

Brock suggests another feminist perspective for Christology that comes close to my notion of *jeong*. Reading Brock, Ray suggests that eros, embodied love, "characterized by mutuality, is understood to be the criterion of relationship. . . . Not merely any relationship is reconciling, redemptive, healing, but only those based on . . . mutual respect."[28] Wherein the highest expression of self-sacrific is love. From a feminist standpoint this is problematic. According to Ray, Brock rejects this concept because "it undermines the agency of women and children" compounding their already-existing victimization within a patriarchal culture.[29] Traditional articulations of Christology reflect what is now known as "cosmic child abuse."[30] Traditional Christology is often based in implicit elements of child abuse: Jesus in his human aspect is sacrificed as the one perfect child. Brock is critical of notions of redemption that privilege the powerlessness of humans and our absolute dependence on external sources to redeem us. Satisfaction theories of atonement, according to Brock, assume that original sin could be remedied by the "punishment of one perfect child" by "the perfect father." Such atonement theory is based on the assumption that to make right is to punish. This image of the divine yet abusive father seems embedded in Trinitarian formulas that attempt to absolve God as a father of punitiveness even while he demands satisfaction by the suffering of his "most beloved and only son."[31] Inevitably, "our own suffering has been taken away by someone else's suffering and by a cosmic transaction within the divine life."[32] God's *jeong*, incarnate in Jesus, is also incarnated and made present by the people that come in contact with Jesus. Jesus' living embodiment of *jeong*, his praxis of *jeong*, compels him to take the risk of suffering on the cross as a result of his living out of emancipatory impulses of *jeong*. While rejecting unilateral power, especially in the theological language of redemption, Brock calls instead for a relational, erotic power. Fundamental to her Christology is the assertion that erotic power is "the power of life." For Brock, erotic power is not only love but also a liberating subversive power.

Indeed, Brock's notion of erotic power is in consonance with our working definition of *jeong*. Central to her starting point then is the metaphor of heart. She writes,

> Heart, the center of all vital functions, is the seat of self, of energy, of loving, of compassion, of conscience, of tenderness and of courage.[33]

The root Chinese character that composes the word for *jeong* is heart. It is at the core of understanding the complex contours of multifarious *jeong*. For Brock relational existence is the "heart of our being, our life source, our original grace." Sin is the scission of our "primal interrelatedness." Brock's theological language of sin works well with Kristeva's notion of abjection and Lee's notion of "original *han*." Insofar as abjection and *han* would correlate with Brock's notion of scission and sin, heart and original grace resonate with the power of the maternal semiotic and with *jeong*. I would emphasize, however, that emancipatory *jeong* is distinct from Brock's eros. Brock seems to emphasize the erotic power that comes from and enables mutual relationships. *Jeong*, while composed of similar energies, also exists even with relationships that are not based on mutuality. At the heart of the transgressive power of *jeong* is its presence, its emergence even within the terrain of confrontational and oppositional relationships.

As a complex notion, *jeong* is much more difficult to categorize. *Jeong* manifests itself even between oppressors and the oppressed; its appearance and embodiment is not determined or restricted by differences in culture, gender, race, or social class. Part of its promise is that, from a postcolonial stance, *jeong* knows no boundaries. Because *jeong* moves freely and is embodied across diverse borders and boundaries, life itself becomes more complex. The power of *jeong* is that it is able to wedge itself into the smallest cracks/gaps between the oppressed and the oppressor. The compassion, understanding, affection, and other fluid characteristics of *jeong* ultimately work to render life ironic and to check our tendency to simplify life's ambiguities and complexities. Perhaps one of the reasons for the prevalence of *both/and* philosophy has much to do with this experience of *jeong*. *Jeong* is powerful precisely because it is an emancipative and healing power even in relationships that have been reduced to simple binarism, as is often the case between the oppressor and oppressed. While clear systemic oppressions must be critically analyzed and resisted through active *dan*, *jeong* also recognizes the brokenness and pain of the oppressors. When *jeong* is present in a relationship, a person might appear as an "enemy" because of structural impositions, but in one-to-one relationality, the relation between self and that same enemy could be fraught with compassion, recognition, and even acceptance and eventual forgiveness. Ultimately it is this intimate existential recognition of the self mirrored in the other that leads to transformation of the heart. Because the power of *jeong* is not confined within particular borders, boundaries, divisions, and dichotomies, *jeong* may well overcome *han*/abjection through the redemptive work of love. Similarly Brock uses the metaphor of heart to "turn patriarchy inside out, to reveal its ravaged, faint, fearful, broken heart, and to illuminate the power that heals heart . . . toward a greater experience of the sacred in life."[34] The sacred is life in relationship with itself. Life knows that it is only sustained through the crucial interdependence of one with another.

Brock places the classical Trinitarian theology in the context of parent-child fusion in order to expose atonement Christology's inherent "ghost of the punitive father."[35] In this traditional framework, redemption also reflects the distortion of power in unilateral orientation and the confusion of love with pain, culminating in the person of Jesus as the hero of humanity, the one who had to be sacrificed for our sinfulness. Brock criticizes such christological models, which separate Jesus from any principle of interconnectedness. What is truly christological resides in connectedness, in the reality of erotic power between persons, and not in single individuals. Her understanding of Christology is grounded in the crucial understanding of relationality as the key to justice and love. Christ is possible only within the dynamics of what she creatively terms "Christa/Community." Focus on the individual Jesus is thus shifted to the community of which he was a part. This is illustrated through her version of the Christian christological mythos: "Jesus is like a white cap on a wave . . . it rests on the enormous pushing power of the sea."[36] The sea could perhaps be referred to as Song's metaphor of the "crucified people."

The significance of Jesus of Nazareth resides in the fact that he represented the emergence and disclosure of this erotic power of heart, which he neither reveals nor embodies alone. Instead, Jesus actively participates in this erotic power along with his community. Erotic power as embodied by the Christa/Community generates the divine becoming as men and women create alternative ways of imagining and forming the Imaginary Symbolic. Might not this cohesive force that is practiced, recognized, and nurtured by the Christa/Community be *jeong*?

Brock's chief argument is that a mutual relationship is liberative and has the capacity to embrace and bring about powerful transformations. She notes that relationships create the possibility of a new vision, for in the power of real presence, erotic power—the divine incarnate power—works.[37] A Christology of interconnection and action is based on the recognition of the power of relationality and supported by her reading of the Markan miracle stories. The erotic power present within and in the midst of Christa/Community is the Spirit-Sophia incarnate.[38] Jantzen, similar to Brock, argues that the metaphor of a god of salvation is seen "as the savior who intervenes from outside the calamitous situation to bring about a rescue."[39] Contrary to this, Brock's Christology resonates with Jantzen's argument that what must transpire is for a feminist, life-oriented theology to lead to "the divine source and ground, an imminent divine incarnated within us and between us."[40] I believe Brock's Christa/Community accomplishes this goal through erotic power.

Jantzen claims that many feminist theologians often find themselves in a conundrum when it comes to Jesus. With an idea similar to Brock's concept of the "wave," Jantzen suggests that Jesus could be understood as the one who manifested a passionate struggle for justice, was full of wisdom, and lived in the fullness of compassion. Jantzen proceeds by explaining that the traditional doctrine of atonement would not then be necessary. Instead, citing Irigaray's suggestion, Jantzen goes on to suggest that "Jesus could be seen as an example of incarnation, who in his gendered flesh and blood and in his specific situation showed something of what it means to become divine."[41] This would be a crucial move that begins to "disrupt the masculinist hegemony and open up the gap through which we can move to new horizons, releasing us from the dominance of the phallus."[42] Feminists' move away from the symbolic is, in turn, a move toward a feminist imaginative/semiotic of the divine. It is a staring into the heart of the abject, into ourselves.

Such an imaginative move toward the female divine has been part of discussions by Asian feminist constructive theologies. The emergence of Asian feminist Christology has been and continues to be diverse and creative. Korean theologian Chung Hyun Kyung has suggested that for Korean women, Jesus must be like a female, and especially like a mother who feeds and tends to her children's wellness. Another Korean feminist theologian, Choi Man-Ja, has argued that for *han*-ridden Korean women, Jesus must be like a shaman who unravels the *han* of the people.

An Asian feminist scholar who is engaged with postcolonial theory is Kwok Pui-lan. She has argued that Christian triumphalism and exclusivity has often been rooted in the myth of the uniqueness of Jesus Christ.[43] Postcolonial theory is critical for doing theology because "deconstructing the white and colonial constructs of Christ" to present Christ "as hybrid" creates the space and authority for those who have been marginalized to construct their interpretation of Christology. Kwok thus challenges us to think beyond the limits of our epistemological boundary when thinking about Christ. By calling upon bold postcolonial imagination and the theory of hybridity, Kwok indicates how the identity of Jesus Christ has always been transitive and hybrid.[44] The key christological importance for her is "how is it possible for the formerly colonized, oppressed, subjugated subaltern to transform the symbol of Christ," in a way "that affirms life, dignity, and freedom?"[45] My suggestion for such a transformation is to recognize both abjection/*han* and *jeong*/love on the cross. According to Kwok, the most hybridized concept in Christianity is Jesus/Christ.[46] Her understanding leads her to proclaim that the space between Jesus and Christ is "unsettling," "fluid," and resists "closure," for she declares that this space is the "contact zone" between the divine and the human.[47] Kwok's use of the postcolonial concept of hybridity locates the gap, the opening, the interstice between Jesus and God but, I suggest, also within the politics of doctrinal theology itself. The notion of hybridity pulls wide open the gaps that have been present but nonetheless invisible within and around the politics of doctrinal theology. These gaps are not only openings for women but for all those considered abject to participate in imagining the divine from their own diverse interstices. Such an interstitial gap creates a space wherein the horror and pain of abjection can be fully, glaringly, and fearlessly present and recognized. This presence of abjection/*han* often also brings with it the presence of *jeong*/love. The notion of hybridity then, even within doctrinal theology, creates what might be seen as disorderliness, chaos, complication, and messiness. This hybridity creates yet another exciting threshold to be crossed in our theological constructions.

Christianity has been used to serve the colonization process for the Western world. Without attempting to exonerate this past in the history of Christianity, the colonized have also interpreted and embraced it in rather surprising ways. Christological portrayals have often glorified the suffering and death of Jesus by highlighting his level of endurance, submissiveness, and obedience to the "Lord." Furthermore, to understand Jesus' suffering on the cross, Kwok's response is that we must listen to the voices of those who have been oppressed. We must hear how Jesus' cross has been a source of empowerment for these communities. Thus, she calls attention to not only the criticisms leveled at traditional atonement theories but also the scholars who have creatively and critically articulated the difference a "situated knowledge" can bear on one's perception of a symbol. As much as she is mindful of the damage that traditional atonement theory has done, Kwok reminds us that the suffering of Jesus "must be seen in a nuanced and multi-layered" way in the Asian context.[48] She does not seem categorically to reject atonement theory, as does Brock. Moreover, even as she is in agreement with feminist attempts to reimagine Christology and the image of Jesus, she calls for an organic metaphor for Jesus. Kwok seems less interested in whether the symbol of the cross has abusive undertones and more interested in the subversive ways that the cross has functioned for the oppressed people in Asia. For her, to imagine Jesus as the epiphany of God is to open up possibilities for an "epiphanic Christ," which allows us to "entertain the possibility of encountering God in many other ways: in other human beings, in nature and in the whole universe."[49] Kwok's understanding of the cross reminds us that many Asian theologians, similar to womanist theologians, have to attend seriously to all the ambiguous and complex layers evoked by the cross, especially those in which the cross has functioned to both empower and disempower suffering people. Song asserts that "Jesus is crucified people! To know Jesus is to know crucified people."[50] Jesus on the cross, the crucified people . . . might this just be the return of the repressed . . . the excommunicated, the exterminated abjects of self, memory and history?

What then does the cross mean? I have argued that Jesus' agency on the cross results not only from his confrontative actions but also from his embodied *jeong*. By living the way of *jeong*, Jesus risked the wrath signified by the cross. Feminist theologians do not find anything redemptive about the cross but rather locate any liberative principle in Jesus' teaching and ministry, arguing that the cross signifies oppression and tools of abuse and execution. As much as I disagree with his way of framing the cross through inner-Trinitarian activity, I do find that Moltmann's understanding of the power of the cross, as revealing an irreducibly and divinely felt depth of suffering, comes close to what Jesus would have experienced as he embodied the power of *jeong*. Living the way of *jeong* would have entailed political consequences as well. The political punishment would have been the cross. For Song, the cross signifies human beings rejecting human beings. On the cross, it is not God abandoning Jesus but rather human beings abandoning him. Song develops his Christology further by suggesting that as we witness Jesus' ministry and death we also become identified with him as he did with us. For Song, in Jesus "who is in pain, we are in pain. In the angry Jesus we encounter the angry people. In the suffering Jesus we witness the suffering people. . . . Jesus, in short, is the crucified people."[51] The suffering of Jesus on the cross, then, signifies the *jeong* he embodied in his solidarity with the abject while, at the same time, the cross defies the powers that repress *jeong*.

It has often been the case that Christologies emerging from the boundaries have often been repressed or dismissed. For example, the images of Black Christ, the Corn Mother, Shaman, and Christa are often rejected by masculinist and imperialist religious discourse. What is necessary and vital for the divine becoming of men and women is the opening of an interstitial gap, a fault line, a space, wherein we might subversively dislodge the weight of phallocentric and imperialistic Christologies in order to allow not only the eruption of a semiotic disturbance but the creation of a new hybrid: a feminist symbolic of the divine through our embodied living out of transgressive *jeong*.

HAN/SIN AND *JEONG*/SALVATION

How we theologize "sin" and "salvation" is crucial to how we understand Christology. The emergence of liberation theologies from Latin America, Asia, and Africa, and from marginal groups in North America, have done much to dismantle the conventional focus that sin can only be addressed individually rather than collectively. Thus, redemption must include aspects of the social and ecological transformation. For Latin American liberation theologians like Gustavo Gutiérrez and Jon Sobrino, sin is the rejection of God's kingdom. For this reason, when sin is understood as both personal and social, liberation and our move in the direction of the kingdom of God must include liberation from both individual and structural oppressions.

As diverse as liberation theologies may be, most agree that atonement theory must be critically examined. For liberation theology, the cross of Christ portrays a crucial knowledge not only about humanity but also about God. The cross goes contrary to the conventional expectation of what liberation would entail. The cross as a sign of the abject, of an internalized and grotesque suffering of oppression, also simultaneously discloses a liberating power. Through solidarity in suffering with humanity, God is in solidarity with the Son who suffers, as Moltmann's Christology has illustrated. Taken further, liberation theologians argue that Jesus' solidarity with humanity is disclosed on the cross and subsequently then God is also found to be in profound solidarity with not only the Son but also humanity. This com-passion is God-with-us. Through God's accompaniment, we are empowered to seek and practice love/*jeong* in the face of overwhelming powers and principalities of suffering, oppression, and death. The mimicry present in the symbol of the cross is succinctly stated by liberation theologian Leonardo Boff, as he announces that the cross "is an indictment of the wickedness of the persons who caused Jesus' death," while at the same time it is the "symbol of love stronger than death."[52] According to Boff, this paradoxical ambiguity of the cross must be preserved for its critical and transformative power to exist. The cross of Christ is a living reminder of the evil in the world and of the divine will to radically expose that tragic evil unequivocally. As much as Jesus Christ's saving significance is important in the process of redemption, humanity must also participate through praxis in the concrete historical situation.[53] Boff's Christology seems to embrace the presence and recognizes both *han*/abjection and *jeong* on the cross. His Christology embodies the messiness, horror, and complexity that are at the heart of the cross.

Korean theologian Andrew S. Park delves extensively into the intertwining of sin and the Korean notion of *han*. For Park, sin and *han* itself are the root causes of *han*. Sin produces *han*, and *han* often produces more sin, which produces more *han* in what becomes a vicious cycle. However, "sin is of the oppressor; *han* is of the oppressed."[54] While such easy categorization might be helpful in the praxis of liberation, I disagree with Park regarding this assessment. Sin and *han* are part of both the oppressors and the oppressed. In a violent cycle without *jeong*, *han*, as Park acknowledges, often leads to more sin. Most oppressors have become oppressors because of their experience of *han*. This is not to exonerate oppressors or to blame the victims but to recognize, as we have in the previous discussion of Lee and Kristeva, that *han* is deeply rooted and originates before we are conscious, speaking bodies. These two aspects, sin and *han*, contribute to each other in a cyclical relationship.

Park invokes *han* as an important contribution to theological discourse because Western theology has often been consumed with the state of the sinners and has not given enough attention to the plight of those "who have been sinned against," the victims of the sinners.[55] The feeling amassed by the suffering victims of sin is *han*. Park's contention is that the "collective conscious and unconscious *han* will be resolved only by the understanding . . . compassion . . . confrontation of involved communities."[56] From a psychoanalytic standpoint, Park notes that while *han* embodies the possibility of its structural inheritance from parents, he nonetheless rejects the "biological inheritance of guilt."[57] Salvation must be "relational, dynamic"[58] in order to resolve *han*. Salvation is ultimately about the "intensity of divine presence" in relationship. Furthermore, Park not incidentally cites Rita Nakashima Brock's contention that erotic power is redemptive in relationships. For Park, salvation is a relational event. While not engaged with Kristeva's work, his work nevertheless seems to resonate with Kristeva's notion of "herethics," that is, the ethical and political dimension of the semiotic. An important dimension of "herethics" lies in what Kristeva names as "outlaw love." It is the "mother's love for the child, which is a love for herself but also the willingness to give herself up," which is for Kristeva the basis of new ethics. Herethics is founded in the relationship between the mother and child during pregnancy, when the ambiguity between the subject of the mother and the object/child is most heightened. It is the point that most profoundly shows how the other cannot be separated from the self. Often this inability to separate the self from the other is interpreted as psychosis, but during pregnancy this "psychosis" is accepted by society. This is important to keep in mind because the mother/semiotic is not in relationship with the other that is unreachable or transcendent. The mother/child relationship is not something that the mother has to struggle to recognize, for here the subject-object is of one flesh; the other is within, and the gap with the other is not absolute. This social bond, not force, is what threatens the symbolic order. This mother's love is "narcissism without a properly alien Other."[59]

In light of his discussion of sin and *han*, Park moves toward the cross not as an expression of God's exclusive suffering for humanity, "but also as God's protest against the oppressor."[60] Previous chapters have discussed the cross as the symbol and embodiment of the abject. Similarly, Park shifts *han* to God, who is "fully revealed in the incarnation and crucifixion."[61] Park indicates that sin not only hurts humanity but also God. Sin committed against another human also becomes a wound for God. As God is in solidarity with humanity and thus open to being wounded, Park contends that "God suffers for the Son on the cross not only out of God's love for the Son, but also God's love for humanity. God's love for humanity suffers on the cross. The cross represents God's full participation in the suffering of victims."[62] Moreover, God meets us in suffering. Parks concurs with Moltmann's insistence that the Father's love for the Son is to be one with him on the cross; his theology is thus similar to Moltmann's. Park's examination of the link between divine and human experience of *han* juxtaposed with his portrayal of divine suffering alongside humanity must be more critically and closely examined. As much as Park is cautious in forming a theology of *han* that does not reify sexist dynamics of gendered suffering, he is still, like Moltmann, limited to the traditional doctrinal restrictions that fail to recognize the limitations of the paradigm itself.

As much as Park formulates an alternative understanding of liberative Christology, especially as it relates to the cross, he does not examine critically enough the underside of suffering, which has been predominantly used against women and those who are powerless. Despite his obvious intention not to glorify suffering in and of itself, he does little to do otherwise when it comes to the suffering on the cross. Park's theology must also listen not only to liberation theology but to the liberation theologies emerging specifically from a feminist standpoint. Park is clearly mindful of feminist critiques; nevertheless, I do wish he had delved more closely into the possibility of Brock's erotic power, particularly how Korean women embody this power. Park's understanding of the cross and suffering seems to remain within the parameters of traditional Trinitarian theology, but he offers glimpses of what might be a radical liberative take when he states,

> God's *han*, the wounded heart of God, is exposed on the cross. . . . The cross is the meeting place between God and us. . . . The cross is the place where God experiences human suffering and the place where humans understand God's agony. Sin forces Jesus Christ to be crucified on the cross. Sin forces people to suffer *han*. . . . The incarnation was an expression of the divine *han*, which was fully manifested at the crucifixion.[63]

Park's provocative theology of *han* as the woundedness of God's heart offers a tantalizing glimpse of what might become a full-blown radical theology. However, his reluctance to let the "return of the repressed" present itself on the cross seems similar to Moltmann's unconscious reluctance to recognize the horror of abjection/*han* on the cross as it simultaneously embodies the power of *jeong*. Such reluctance appears to exemplify a systematic problem in christological constructs wherein the Father rescues the Suffering Son. In light of previous chapters' discussions on *han*, abjection, and the cross, the question seems less christological and more about God's inner self.[64]

   A Korean American feminist Christology will have to examine seriously the depth of *han* and its connection to abjection. Suffering through people's experience of *han* and abjection, as I indicated before, must be examined, critiqued, and dismantled from both individual and collective perspectives, from private to structural systems of oppression, from material to mental oppressions; from the symbolic realms to the semiotic depths. Christology has always lain at the heart of our theological dilemma. The cross of Jesus Christ was comforting, empowering, and hope-filled, while simultaneously horrifying, threatening, suffocating, contradictory, and offensive. In reading feminist postcolonial and psychoanalytic studies in light of the already-mentioned feminist Christologies, I have come to realize that the symbol of the cross performs a double gesture and requires a double reading. By arguing that Jesus was abject on the cross and that we need more creative ways of imaging the divine, I hope I have managed to argue persuasively that christological discourse must be moved out of masculinist and imperialist discourse.

In encountering Christology, feminist reflections must question the assumed neutrality of any symbol that functions to reify the masculinist symbolic, specifically the religious symbolic. I have insisted that the language used by conventional Christology, even that of Moltmann and Park, has consistently shied away from radically reenvisioning the cross as the signifier of the abject/semiotic. The cross becomes a resource for opening up the interstitial spaces for the postcolonial and feminist semiotic of the divine through our radical recognition of the abject not merely as Other but as part of our selves. Continuous recycling of conventional Christology, no matter how much we speak of God's solidarity, remains within the masculinist, sanitized, and abstract religious God-talk. The depth of such entrenched fear and perhaps even repulsion is obvious when these Christologies shy away from forging their visions into and over the edge of what might be the feminine, maternal, semiotic abyss.

THE POWERS OF *JEONG* AND THE HORRORS OF *HAN*

> Religion comes to be experienced as a return. In religion, something that we had thought irrevocably forgotten is made present again, a dormant trace is reawakened, a wound re-opened, the repressed returns and what we took to be an *Uberwindung* is no more than a *Verwindung*, a long convalescence that has once again to come to terms with the indelible trace of its sickness.
>
> Gianni Vattimo, "The Trace of the Trace"

In the last chapter and in the earlier section of this one, I have argued that the cross bears a trace of the semiotic long repressed in traditional Christologies. Moreover, this return of the repressed is the return of the abject. As Gianni Vattimo notes in the above quote, "a dormant trace is reawakened, a wound re-opened, the repressed returns."[65] The liberationist claim that, in the passion of Jesus, God is revealed as a suffering God, does not pose a problem in itself. Problematic is the implication that it is in and through God's suffering that salvation occurs.

The problem with this construal of the cross as an inner-Trinitarian struggle is that the suffering of Jesus is dehistoricised by making the event an internal divine affair. The emphasis on the inner-Trinitarian event of the cross often seems to leave out the participation of those who are being redeemed because of this event. However, is it possible nonetheless to read the power of the crucified to be alive and working to end suffering? As Soelle states,

> The cross is neither a symbol expressing the relationship between God the Father and his Son nor a symbol of masochism that needs suffering in order to convince itself of love. It is above all a symbol of reality.[66]

The cross is not redemptive in itself, nor should it stand as a symbol of love alone. For Soelle, love ends up being crucified. The cross then is not a symbol of love but of its risk, the risks taken by a whole lifetime lived on the edge. The cross is a possible risk for those who live in the fullness of *jeong*. It represents the horror of abjection while recognizing the love that simultaneously irrupts on the cross. What is recognized is that the cross works as a symbol of the power and horror of the Law of the Fathers while the long-repressed semiotic makes its emergence. What is significant about the cross, then, is not that Jesus died on it but that because of his living out of *jeong*, he ends up de facto on the cross.

Jeong is what is needed to bring wholeness and healing from abjection and *han*. The practice of *dan* is crucial in dismantling individual and collective experiences of *han*; however, healing can only come through the power of *jeong*. We might be able to wrestle some justice out of the unjust, but we cannot extract the profound transformation of the causes of injustice that come only through love/*jeong*.

JULIA KRISTEVA'S ABJECTION AND LOVE

Feminist psychoanalytic theory on the formation of ego through separation, abjection, melancholy, and love has deep implications for a Korean North American postcolonial Christology of *jeong*. In order to argue that the cross works to perform a double gesture of both the presence of *han*/abjection and *jeong*—or, in postcolonial parlance, homage and menace—it is critical to examine Julia Kristeva's take on abjection and love. Kristeva's concept of abjection will be a fruitful conversation partner, for the idea of abjection resonates with Jae Hoon Lee's "original wound."

Feminists have extensively critiqued Freud's analysis of ego formation, which categorically omits the importance of the mother while giving the father primacy: the "male is the true author of life and his protective powers alone answer to human vulnerability."[67] The cost of entering into the symbolic requires severing the semiotic as abject. In order for this separation, which is never complete, to occur, the inner ego must sever connection with the maternal semiotic.[68]

By not acknowledging the importance of the primary narcissism inherent in the infant-mother relationship, the traditional theory of ego formation works effectively to omit the female. On the whole, such a theory of ego formation, accomplished through painful and disruptive disconnections rather than through the acknowledgment of primal oceanic feelings of the maternal and the connective, can hardly lead to healthy and relational inner selves. As already discussed, the pervasive establishment of the id through separation is not without consequences.

It is my contention that when the establishment of the ego takes place at the cost of abjecting the semiotic, the formation of a "healthy ego," as perceived from the symbolic standpoint, is carried out by its unconscious manifestation of matricidal drives. One's acceptance into the symbolic occurs with the expulsion/repression of the semiotic. The semiotic cannot become part of the symbolic, although as Kristeva indicates, there are cases in which we witness this irruption of the hidden semiotic presence in the symbolic. Disconnection is inherent in the separation process of entering into the symbolic realm. Separation is acquired at the deepest and earliest level through abjection. Ironically, this abjection becomes, to use Lee Jae Hoon's analysis, the cross of our "original wound." This particular process of disconnecting from the semiotic is inherently dangerous not only for female but also for male ego formation. Such early distortions maintained throughout life continue to perpetuate false and damaged selves. Damaged selves evoke not only melancholy (depression) at the unconscious level but work to produce and reproduce our deepest sense of loss, abjection, *han*, and both individual and collective unconscious violence.

In order to work theologically through our sense of abjection/*han*/melancholy, I claim that we must journey back into the depths of the semiotic, maternal oneness, the oceanic feeling of *jeong* that is pre-object and pre-subject. Within the traditional understanding of the Trinity, might we claim that the Spirit, as the incarnate Word, is the presence of the semiotic?

Perhaps this is also why in traditional doctrinal theology the Spirit becomes subordinated to both the Father and the Son. The provocative question then is, "Why did this Divine Sophia, who was sometimes identified with Jesus, get repressed?" What lies behind the tremendous efforts to domesticate and bring under control this Spirit? Did some of the "fathers" worry that this semiotic She might usurp the very seat of the Father? A key insight is offered by Virginia Burrus:

> The Father's secret is his stolen womb. . . . The erasure of the female
> from representation of divine generativity framed exclusively in terms
> of fatherhood and sonship is crucial to a construction of trans-
> cendence. . . . [B]y absenting the maternal womb from theological

discourse, it becomes possible . . . to transform that "first veil" . . .
into the shroud of woman's invisibility—so that there remains only
one sex.[69]

It seems always to come back to the womb. Perhaps, as Burrus implies, the erasure of female generativity spills over into our psychotheological construction
as we erase all traces of the semiotic from the symbolic and as we repress traces
of the semiotic/abject, especially on the cross. Kristeva's works on the importance of the maternal function, which she locates before the subject's entrance
into the symbolic, drive her theory deeper and deeper into the maternal womb.
Kristeva draws from Plato's concept of the "chora" as the space that nourishes
and that is maternal. As a result, Kristeva points back to what is seemingly
obvious but often ignored: that without women, without the maternal body,
there would be no speaking subjects. The negation and identification necessary to human subjectivity are already operating within the maternal function,
even before the subject's entrance into the world of language.

In a related move, Lee Jae Hoon's notion of the "original *han*" is greatly
influenced by Melanie Klein's psychoanalytic theory on early childhood.
Indeed, much of Kristeva's theoretical framework begins with Klein's feminist
psychoanalytic criticisms of the mother-child relationship. Klein's object relation's theory was focused on early childhood, but Lee's notion of "original
wound" and "original *han*" suggests a certain level of agreement with Klein in
her focus on the mother.

Reading Kristeva and Klein together is useful since combining their notions
of "psychic violence provides a structural account of the interweaving between
the unconscious psyche and the socio-political."[70] Kristeva renegotiates Klein's
theory further into the psyche, into the "internal violence of primordial
psychic separation from the mother."[71] Whereas Klein returns to the mother's
breasts, Kristeva returns to the maternal womb. Kristeva's primordial psychic
separation from the mother would very much be reflective of Lee's notion of
"original wound" and "original *han*." Lee's "original *han*" is an important
concept that needs to be examined in order to understand the depth of *han*, as
well as to understand how the cross on a deep psychological level works in our
psyches:

> For abjection . . . is the other face of religious, moral, and ideological
> codes on which rest the sleep of individuals and the breathing spells of
> societies. Such codes are abjection's purification and repression. Nev-
> ertheless, the return of the repressed makes up our "apocalypse," and
> that is why we cannot escape the dramatic convulsions of religious cri-
> sis. . . . Our only difference is our unwillingness to have a face-to-face
> confrontation with the abject. . . . Who, I ask you, would agree to call
> himself abject, subject of or subject to abjection?[72]

If religious codes such as the cross function as both abjection's "purification" and "repression," I am compelled to ask, What then is the abjection that is seemingly needed to be purified and repressed? What is so threatening about abjection that it needs such collaboration from "religious, moral, and ideological" arenas to continually repress it? The abjection on the cross, at one time a signifier of the symbolic, rather than function as a form of repression works to make present the return of the abject/repressed. One might perceive this act to have rendered Jesus a victim. However, on the cross, the depths of both *han* and *jeong* are radically exposed. What is exposed is the profound depth of *han* as abjection while simultaneously disclosing and embodying subterranean *jeong*. Moreover, contrary to Spivak's initial declaration that the subaltern cannot speak for it, the abject as subaltern does and is able to speak through the ruptures of the maternal semiotic power within the symbolic.

Abjection is thus not something to be overcome but that which must be acknowledged and embodied as the stranger/other that is irreparably part of our very selves. Kristeva observes dramatically that "the time of abjection is double: a time of oblivion and thunder, of veiled infinity and the moment when revelation bursts forth."[73] It is the postcolonial mimicry of the cross. It is both submission/victimization and liberation/revolution.[74] As such, the cross embodies both *han* and *jeong*.

The difficulty we have defining and categorizing the notion of *jeong* is due to its elusive semiotic opaqueness. *Jeong*, as a manifestation of semiotic drives, is thus often suppressed, dismissed, or repressed under the rubric of the symbolic/Law of the Fathers. As we have argued previously, if the semiotic akin to the "original *han*" as both destructive yet also comprises of "life energy," the maternal semiotic offers both bondage and creative disruption within the symbolic order. In many respects, such creative disorderliness of the semiotic dimension within the symbolic order frequently occurs within various areas where the issues of boundary and borders are ambiguous. As a result the symbolic can only be subverted from and through the semiotic power.[75] To this end, within the codified terms of liberative praxis, both *dan* and *jeong* must work simultaneously.

The hegemony of the symbolic can be mocked and mimicked through the creative insurgence of the disruptive semiotic. It is excess and surplus of being that "establishes for humans the possibility of creation, communion, newness, pleasure and transgression."[76] Kristeva's focus on the maternal body, as the subversive site of the semiotic from even within the symbolic is key to the feminist Christology of *jeong*. Nonetheless, much to our dismay, as Jantzen points out, "traditional Christianity is however, able to take up the maternal body and with it the semiotic . . . by the 'wiles of theology' make it serve the masculinist symbolic."[77] Even as we imagine and create interstitial sites from which *jeong* might emerge, one must always be aware of how this site can possibly be colonized by the symbolic.

Feminist theological reconstructions of Christology have suggested female divine images that are promising.[78] Kristeva's concept of the semiotic and her understanding of love/Eros confront the traditional dichotomous notions of the separation of subject and object. Equally, as I have reiterated before, the power of *jeong* is that it complicates and blurs the boundary between the self and the other. Kristeva's search to reclaim the maternal semiotic within the symbolic brings us to the deeper ramifications of the maxim "Love your neighbor as yourself." This radical love is experienced during pregnancy by which the distinction of subject-other coexist in and as one. The radicality of Kristeva's take on the semiotic is the resulting notion that the love of self is fused with love of other.[79]

Kristeva argues that the abject shares only one quality with the object, "that of being opposed to I."[80] Thus, abjection is a "twisted braid of affects and thoughts."[81] Likewise all objects are based merely on the "inaugural loss that laid the foundations of its own being. . . . [A]bjection is elaborated through a failure to recognize its kin; nothing is familiar, not even the shadow of a memory."[82] The paradox of the subject formation at the expense of the created other is the very process of initial loss and abjection.[83]

Even prior to any social forms of oppression, the subject has thus already encountered and experienced "original *han*" through the abjection of the maternal and the self. The social being is constituted through the force of expulsion. However, these abjected materials are never fully obliterated, but rather they continue to "haunt the edges of the subject's identity with the threat of disruption or even dissolution."[84] Therefore, "abjection is above all ambiguity."[85] The abject then is something that is rejected from the self but also that which never departs fully.[86] The abject is the unruly that is forcefully jettisoned from the self. Inasmuch as the abject is jettisoned, it is simultaneously experienced as "garbage," the unwelcome waste and filth that "litters" the symbolic.[87] In short, the abject is the "refused refuse," and, as Elizabeth Grosz puts it, the abject is the "place of the genesis and the obliteration of the subject."[88] Kristeva contends that abjection is a form of narcissistic crisis that results from the experience of extreme grieving for the lost object. The maternal is the primary abject and at the same time the tragic loss. However, the disconnection and the ultimate abjection of this semiotic/maternal source is a break that is damaging and accurately accounts for Lee's articulation of the "original wound/*han*." This "original *han*" damages not only the individual psyche but also leaks into one's relations with others. This damage becomes apparent in our cycle of *won-han* and *jeong-han* in both the individual and collective unconscious. For Kristeva, abjection's intimate side is suffering, while horror is "its public feature."[89] Abjection for her is "a crying-out theme of suffering and horror."[90]

For Kristeva, an encounter with the repressed is an encounter with the maternal semiotic. She argues that the abject threatens the social, symbolic order. The symbolic maintains itself and its power by maintaining its borders, even while the abject is a reminder of the fragility of those borders. Thus, Oliver notes that the "symbolic is the order of borders, discrimination and difference."[91] Jesus as abject on the cross confronts the symbolic realm. The cross pays homage to the power of the symbolic while at the same time posing as a menace to its very order.

I suggest that the cross is not the death of the semiotic/*jeong* by the imperial powers, as might be implied by some feminist and political liberation theologians, but it is the cross-ing over into a new form of power. This would then be the power of "herethics": the power of *jeong*. The cross is the interstitial space wherein both homage and mockery are embodied. It is the interstitial/hybrid site where abjection and agency are met. It is the site where the other and the self, while remaining autonomous, also recognize the presence of the both in the self. It is the site where death and life coexist, and where suffering/*han*/abjection, liberation/love and *jeong* challenge one another. The theme of suffering and horror is also present in our understanding of the cross. It comprises what Kristeva terms "sacred horror." She remarks that the osmosis between the spiritual and the substantial takes place in Christ.[92] Such conversion goes beyond any legalistic means to atone for sin as debt and inequity. On conventional Christology, one of the insights of Christianity is to "have gathered in a single move perversion and beauty as the lining and the cloth of one and the same economy."[93] Thus, the cross embodies both the horror of the symbolic violence while at the same time it makes known the presence of the semiotic. The cross embodies *han* and *jeong*, abjection and love. The cross signifies the logic of love that contests the logic of violence as the maternal semiotic confronts patriarchal symbolic law. My position is perhaps best supported by Kwok Pui-lan's hybrid Christology,[94] which reimagines Christ as Christa, women as abject, and the suffering "people" as abject. The abject, and therefore the cross, thus become a threat to the symbolic order of the father(s).[95]

Just as *jeong* and *han* are two different sides of the same heart, Kristeva's abjection and love are both parts of love. For she notes that love is a combination of the sublime and the abject.[96] Love requires two, the self and the other, which allow the subject to cross the boundaries of the self and "be" other.[97] Such love provides identification through difference without abolishing or assimilating differences. Interestingly for Kristeva, love is neither merely semiotic nor merely symbolic. Love is "always and at the same time both."[98] It is both *jeong* and *han*. Kristeva's emphasis on this love is prominent to the extent that she declares love to be the life of the psyche. For that reason, "without love we are living death."[99] The conclusion is that the symbolic, without the subversive trace of the semiotic, is not alive. It is living but with no life. The semiotic is the life source even for the symbolic. Even as the symbolic demands the severing of the semiotic as abject, its source of life comes from the semiotic depths. The cross, read from a semiotic standpoint, functions to relieve psychic wounds of "original *han*." What is interesting is that for Kristeva, religion is most often based on the exclusion of the abject through particular taboos that are in service to the maintenance of the symbolic against any threats from the semiotic.[100] Her observation of religion is that it provides a homogeneous meaning "that covers over the heterogeneous process through which that meaning develops."[101] Yet religious meaning often uses semiotic rather than symbolic elements for overcoming separation. The ultimate separation, between God and humanity in Christianity is overcome through the semiotic irruption within the symbolic/Law of the Father on the cross.

Transference love, as pre-object, brings love into the maternal semiotic womb that opens up ways of reading and seeing the maternal on the cross. Christian identification with the incarnate God works to provide a support for the wounded subject suffering from the primary loss. Such psychoanalytic observations allow us to read "original *han*," "original wound," as abjection and the loss of the maternal semiotic.

The traditional articulations of the cross have not only functioned to reify the patriarchal Anselmian notions of payment for sin, but they have also subversively functioned on the edges by bringing back and making aware the presence of the abject, which has been so compellingly articulated by liberation theologians around the world. The cross, understood from the perspective of the abject, mirrors the suffering and the abjection of ourselves. For many marginalized people, the cross is powerful because of the power of transference love and solidarity. The problem of Christianity is that it replaces the loving and nourishing maternal body with a patriarchal God.

By recognizing this maternal trace, we are better equipped to rediscover the traces of the semiotic presence in our christological reflections. As briefly mentioned before, Kristeva's abjection is overcome through her concept of "herethics," her notion of a love that does not rely on separation. Indeed the mother creates this love. This mother's love does not require the third party "to stand in between both holding apart and bringing together. Her love would be a love outside of the Law."[102] Kristeva imagines this as "Outlaw love." Mother's love is for the child but also love for herself, and the willingness to give herself up is the basis of a new ethics.[103] Let me emphasize that the mimicry and the heresy of the semiotic "herethics" is nowhere so strongly presented as it is during pregnancy when the mother-child relationship is so intertwined.[104]

The love/Eros/ *jeong* of God is incarnated in our lives. The cross signifies the semiotic oneness of the Godself with the neighbors, the created beings. The ironic doubling, or chiasmus, on the cross, unmasks the divine semiotic power wherein God and humanity become interconnected through the *jeong* embodied in the incarnation. The doctrinal symbolic preoccupation with the repression of the semiotic on the cross obscures the divine semiotic participation in suffering. From a postcolonial theoretical perspective, the cross can become the site of the decolonization of the semiotic. As deployed by the symbolic, the cross produces its point of radical departure by jettisoning the maternal divine love. So the suffering on the cross is the return of the repressed/abject.

"Her/ethics" in its "heresy" against the symbolic orthodoxy is really the practice of "Love your neighbor as yourself." Kristeva argues that such obligation to one's self and to the other is only founded in the ambiguity of pregnancy and birth.[105] According to Kristeva, it is during pregnancy that the other cannot be separated from the self.[106] This inability to separate the self from the other is a symptom of psychosis, yet most socially accepted only during pregnancy. Subsequently, Kristeva goes on to say that the symbolic, recognizing the maternal semiotic power, deals with it by repressing it or dismissing it as myth and fantasy.[107] As a result, the other is not an autonomous Other, "out there," but rather is part of who we are. The mother, according to Kristeva, knows there is no transcendent Other. Surely, the other is the "flesh of her flesh and loved."[108] She knows that the Other is not somewhere else but within. Such love threatens to do away with the symbolic order. Oliver notes that Kristeva's concept of love threatens our understanding of psychosis.

I would suggest that the power of the cross constitutes this semiotic rupture within the horror of the symbolic act. On the cross, we witness the breakdown of borders constructed and maintained by the symbolic. On the cross, we witness "herethics" in full force as it contests the repressive power of the symbolic. The cross, read through the semiotic maternal lens, is not only the horror of abjection but also the power of love. It is love that also is inclusive of abjection. The cross is both the power of the symbolic at work in the execution while it is also the irruption of the semiotic as the power of *jeong*. The cross works as a form of revolutionary poetic language in that it functions to reveal both abjection and the outlaw love/*jeong* of the semiotic. It is in this way, therefore, that Kristeva's notion of the abject and the maternal will help concretely to link postcolonial theory and Korean concepts of *jeong* and *han* in my move toward a Christology of *jeong*. Lee's "original *han*" is consonant with Kristeva's notion of abjection and melancholy. Likewise, the postcolonial theory of hybridity and interstitial space can be linked to Kristeva's notions of the ambiguous space between the semiotic and the symbolic/Law of the Fathers.

The postcolonial interstitial space is not to be limited to social, cultural, and political spheres, but should also be inclusive of the interstitial psychic spaces between the semiotic and the symbolic, between abjection and self. When this is read into our postcolonial feminist christological reflections, the cross becomes the Christian event of the return of the repressed. Jesus embodied, or rather, tapped into, the presence of the semiotic. It is no accident then that his awareness of the semiotic allowed for him to recognize and embrace the abject of his context.

My christological claim is that the cross is not a benign story of the Father and the death of His beloved Son, but might it not be the event of a full presence of the repressed/abject? The cross would then represent not an end to life but rather a resurrection, a return of the abject: those who have been repressed, expelled, persecuted, executed, oppressed—all those who have been *han*-ridden. Such presence functions in powerful and subversive ways within the symbolic realm. The cross is double-edged in that as the function of the symbolic/Law of the Fathers, it displays the horrors of its power while simultaneously undermining its powers of horror by the presence of the subversive semiotic. The cross is the semiotic rupture within the orderliness of the symbolic/Law of the Fathers.

The cross becomes double-edged in its power of mimicry as it symbolizes the confrontation between the logic of love and the logic of violence. For Kristeva, Christianity's "fusion with God" is, if anything else, more semiotic than symbolic. For faith to be possible this "semiotic leap" toward the other, the primary identification with the "primitive parental poles close to the maternal container must not be repressed or displaced."[109] More than any other religion, Christianity has "unraveled the Symbolic and physical importance of the paternal function in human life . . . through its insistence on the paternal function," when its desire is actually for a fusion with the semiotic maternal.[110] At the heart of Christianity the symbol that most evokes an attempt at this fusion is the cross.[111] Subsequently, the cross "both reveals and sublimates the repressed/abject . . . the representation of Christ's passion signifies a guilt that is visited upon the son, who is himself put to death."[112] The scandal of the cross is that it embodied the psychic and the physical suffering that "irrigates our lives but even more profoundly in the essential alienation that conditions our access . . . in the mourning that accompanies the dawn of psychic life."[113] Kristeva, writing almost as a theologian, makes a "crowning" Trinitarian move, a tour de force for this theology:

> Christ abandoned, Christ in hell is of course the sign that God shares the conditions of the sinner. . . . The trinity itself, that crown jewel of theological sophistication, evokes, beyond its specific content and by virtue of the very logic of its articulation, the intricate intertwining

of the three aspects of psychic life; the Symbolic, the imaginary and ✓
the real.[114]

In terms of this link with *han* and *jeong* on the cross, it has certainly not been
my intention to "psychologize" the material forms of oppression. The cohe-
siveness of *han* and *jeong* must be examined from both the material forms of its
expressions and also in the individual and collective unconscious. *Han* is thus
experienced through oppression as well as in our earliest psychic experiences
of abjection. Unraveling *han* must thus incorporate not only the practice of
dan but also *jeong*, because it is only through a deliberate focus on *jeong* that
suffering and evil might be overcome.

Jeong has power to unravel *han* through heart and connectedness in the
midst of differences. *Han* is not only caused by political or social oppression.
Han understood as the "original wound" allows me to sustain my contention
that unraveling *han* must go deeper into the individual and collective unconscious. This unraveling requires an entry into the Third Space of hybridity,
and Christ on the cross becomes that entry into the Third Space. Likewise, a
Christology of *jeong* also occupies a Third Space, between Moltmann's insistence on the cross as an inner-Trinitarian relational dynamic, on the one hand,
and the feminist critique that there is absolutely nothing redemptive about the
cross, on the other hand. Asian American Christologies, including a Christology of *jeong*, can contribute to this theological construction. I share the concern of feminists wary of those traditional christological underpinnings that
glorify suffering on the cross, a tradition in part reinscribed by Moltmann.
However, to say that there is no redemption in the suffering on the cross is
also to erase and deny the reality of suffering. A Christology of *jeong* finds itself
positioned beside Taylor's and Song's understanding of the cross as a weapon
of execution and feminist Christologies similar to those of Johnson and Ray
that struggle with acknowledging both the empowering and disempowering
effects of the cross in the Christian tradition.

Conclusion:
Heart of the Cross

We need to recuperate the public and political conception of love. . . . We need to recover today this material and political sense of love, a love as strong as death. . . . Without this love, we are nothing.

Michael Hardt and Antonio Negri, Multitude

Today the fight for life, the fight for Eros, is the *political* fight.

Herbert Marcuse, Eros and Civilization

Relationship is constitutive of who we are and what we can become. . . . Relationship makes us or breaks us.

Eleazar Fernandez, Reimagining the Human

We dream, hope, and live with, by, and through the heart. In a culture that poses heart over and against mind, we must note the importance of the heart metaphor within Judaism as well as in Christianity. The prophets are moved to deliver their prophetic message because their hearts have been moved. God also calls the prophets because God sees, hears, and feels with God's heart the pain and suffering of the people. Yahweh was "a God of tears and compassion, who suffered in his suffering people, who was moved by their sighs and lamentations, who was angered by their meanness of mind."[1] God's relationship with the Israelites is fraught with pathos, passion, eros, heart.[2] Jesus also responded to the prophetic call because his heart was moved. He ministered with heart and even ends up de facto on the cross because of his living out the fullness of his heart. When we live with heart, we cannot remain immune to the other. The other's suffering becomes my suffering, his/her joy my joy in a relationship that is often but not necessarily that of reciprocity. If we do not have heart, we do not have life.

Because the notion of *jeong* defies simple categorical translation into Western categories, I have used the length of the book to shed light on various dimensions of *jeong* while avoiding possible and easy misappropriations of the concept. I hope by now *jeong* is much more tangible, if still no less definable. In this final chapter I would like to present *jeong* more fully than previous chapters, as an alternative postcolonial concept that I believe will provide a tool for theological construction.

Is it still possible to speak of "the cross" as a signifier of redemptive agency while radically taking into account feminist critiques of the traditional interpretations of the cross? While being mindful of these critiques, can we still speak of the power of the cross in any redemptive manner? How shall we then conceive of the engagement of the Korean concepts of *han* and *jeong*? Might *jeong* invite an alternative postcolonial Christology that does not deny the historical *han* present on the cross, while at the same time examining the subversive *jeong*/love that irrupts mimetically on the cross for those who view and are moved by the cross?

I have suggested that from a postcolonial perspective, the cross performs a double gesture. It pays homage to the power of the symbolic that represses and oppresses, while at the same time uses mimicry to make present not only the horror of *han* on the cross but also the transgressive, semiotic *jeong*/love; a transgressive power. The cross intimates the significance of *jeong* but is not immune to the horror of *han*. The cross therefore transgresses doctrinal self-enclosures and instead privileges *jeong* as the divine presence between the divine and the world. The cross is the site of the return of the repressed. The presence of the abject on the cross signifies the horror of the means of domination and expulsion. As the abject has been defined as the refused refuse, it is the refugee of our psyche. It is the return of the abject who brings with its presence the possibility of our own redemption. As a result, the transformative power of the cross is not based on a sterilized view in which *han* is contained either through emphasis on the inner-Trinitarian relationship or through the denial of abject/*han* as some feminists insist, but rather, the transgressive and transformative power of the cross lies in its very complex messiness.

As I have noted earlier, Andrew Park has observed that *han* is "the abysmal experience of pain," while Lee goes further by insisting that on an individual level, *han* "is the original wound."[3] *Han*, from a Korean North American perspective, is not only compounded by classism, sexism, and racism from within but also from the outside. Furthermore, for Korean North Americans, the predominant feeling of *han*, I insist, is intimately bound with our experience of hybridity or, as Fernando Segovia has observed elsewhere, of having two places to stand and no place to stand on. The experience of racism, sexism, and class-ism are all experienced in various complexities within the Korean North Amer-ican immigrant context. These various experiences of *han* can also be articulated as an experience of abjection, as noted by Rey Chow. Our very own ethnicity, whether we are determined to erase it, through thorough assimilation into white culture, or cling to it, in a nostalgic return to some pure originary roots, is often used against us. While ethnicity is bandied about as universal, descriptive, and neutral, it is also used as a boundary marker. Thus the ethnic is both the universal, in which even a white person may claim ethnicity, even while it is heralded as "the local, the foreign, the outside," which mark some ethnics as clearly different and as "Others."[4] This double gesturing of the marker "ethnic" functions to deepen the experience of *han*/abjection within Korean North American contexts. This is nowhere more explicitly pronounced than in the autobiographical literatures of Asian American writers whose sense of claiming their hybrid identities is often not a celebratory and facile process but one that is fraught with ambivalence that is profoundly *han*-ridden. How might we then unravel such complex experiences of both individual *han* ("original wound") and collective *han* (as was illustrated by the films *Joint Security Area* and *Sa-I-Gu*)?

Minjung theologians have argued that the elimination of external causes of *han* through the practice of *dan* is the predominant way of resolving *han*. Not only do we witness here the use of masculine military language as it pertains to the "elimination" of *han*-causing factors, but within this unconscious mas-culine trajectory, it is also highly ironic that the Minjung movement subjugates women—the oppressed among the oppressed.[5]

Elimination of *han* is most often connected with the practice of *dan*. The literal meaning of *dan* is "cutting off."[6] On the personal level, *dan* is the prac-tice of self-denial through which one is to remove oneself from the tempta-tion of being part of the systems of injustice and oppression. The inherent implication of *dan* is its promise of a clean departure from systems of oppres-sion that cause *han*.

It seems fair to say that such a patriarchalized concept is often pitted against what is perceived as the passive and weaker methods toward transformation that have simultaneously been feminized and domesticated. These feminized methods toward unraveling *han* are persistently depicted as "untidy." Yet when we examine Jesus' ministry, we do catch moments of Jesus' angry desire to practice *dan*, especially at the scene of the market economy within the Temple walls. However, Jesus did not practice *dan* in his ministry. Rather, he embod-ied the praxis of *jeong*. His radical living out of *jeong* is found in the way this *jeong* is extended to those who should have been "cut off." Jesus' *jeong* is not limited to those who are victims but also extends to the perpetrators of oppres-sion. His practice of *jeong* is what leads to his suffering and death on the cross, for he risks the wrath of the oppressive symbolic power. Jesus is unwilling to transform the world through *dan* but rather through constant self-evaluation chooses to transform the world through *jeong*. Even as *dan* is a necessary component of liberation, I insist that ultimately *dan* falls short of the fullness of the ongoing, yet never entirely completed work of emancipation. Insisting on the practice of *dan* as the only way toward emancipation from *han*-causing factors is not only disappointing from a feminist standpoint but is also problematic because of what seems to be an inherent lack of critical interrogation along multiple axes of oppression. While *dan* is critical for dismantling oppression, *jeong* transforms relationships, thereby transforming systems of oppression.

Inasmuch as it expresses an integral part of the articulations of relationality, *jeong* also resists definite categorical translations. *Jeong* expresses itself predominantly through poetry, literature, art, and film; it pervades common conversations as well as folk and contemporary songs and is the life energy of relationships. One cannot succinctly define *jeong* without losing the depth of its multiple and shifting contours. Moreover, from what will follow here, one might think that *jeong* is simply identifiable with love. It is not. Nor is it completely identifiable with compassion alone. Koreans understand that *jeong* is often much more powerful than even love. *Jeong* connotes agape, eros, and filial love with compassion, empathy, solidarity, and understanding that emerges between hearts of connectedness in relationality. *Jeong* is a supplement that comes into the interstitial site of relationalism. *Jeong* is rooted in relationalism. As it emerges in between connectedness, it works as a lubricant and as relentless faith that *han* does not have the final word.

Unfolding the Chinese character of *jeong* reveals its multidimensional characteristics. Its multiple shades of meaning are derived mainly from the notions of heart, clarity, vulnerability, and a character that means life when used as a noun and "something arising" when used as a verb.[7] All these components are important in the various experiences of *jeong*.[8] It signifies a genesis of becoming that is intimately linked with connectedness and heart. It connotes an ongoing process of incarnation. *Jeong* emerges within connectedness to blossom hope for unraveling *han* and also in the process of becoming, a new genesis. This resonates with the metaphor of the unleavened bread that rises with yeast when it is used as an analogy for the process of the kingdom of God. For the arising of *jeong* (like the small yeast) within relationality is what generates the power for emancipatory praxis.

Rita Nakashima Brock has noted, "We know best by heart." She notes that when we live within the fullness of our heart, our lives' brokenness becomes whole and healed. Such "fullness of the heart" creates and sustains our sense of relational interconnectedness. A theology of *jeong*, then, is a similar but different reading of a Christology of erotic power as presented by Brock. Fundamental to Brock's Christology is the assertion that erotic power is "the power of life." Accordingly, relational existence is the "heart of our being, our life source, our original grace." Indeed, her notion of erotic power is consonant with our working definition of *jeong*. *Jeong* is the in-between space created by the juxtaposition of *han* and love. Eros emerges even within the paradoxical and ambiguous space between hate and love. In early Western writings, eros comprises both bitterness and sweetness.[9] Similar to eros's embodiment of both bitterness and sweetness, *jeong* creates indeterminacy within the unaccounted-for space between the oppressed and the oppressor, between hate and love, between self and the other, between the semiotic and the symbolic, and between the divine and the world.

Jeong, as well as eros, is rooted in relationality. Because eros has often been understood to demand the loss of the self, the prevalent metaphor for eros has been that of an experience of melting. According to many male scholars, this "melting" is ambiguous. Jean-Paul Sartre describes eros by arguing that it is like a child who sticks his hand into a honey jar. In a tone dripping with disdain, he writes, "It is soft, yielding, and compressible. Its stickiness is a trap, it clings like a leech, it attacks the boundary between it and myself . . . [while] plunging into water gives a different impression; I remain a solid. But to touch stickiness is to risk diluting myself into viscosity."[10] Here, viscosity is an experience that is appealing, repelling, and compelling. Just as *jeong* has often been referred to with much disdain by Korean patriarchal culture as "sticky," so too have the Western counterparts referred to eros as "sticky." However, it is the aspect of "stickiness" that gives *jeong* its staying power. There is an underlying fear, if not male hysteria, in the dissolution of the boundary between the self and the other that is precipitated by the power of eros/*jeong*. Metaphors of eros as melting and sticky from these particular standpoints demonstrate a crisis of contact precisely because, like *jeong*, it is elusive and yet presents itself in the interstitial space within the inner self and also in between connectedness. To those who defy such "stickiness," an influx of eros "becomes a concrete personal threat."[11] It is a threat in a culture that values individualism and separation while devaluing communal interdependence and the interconnectedness of all.

In the same way, Peter Hodgson's use of eros resonates deeply with *jeong*, for he notes that eros names "a kind of love that unites the material energy of life with the distinctive spiritual quality of entering into relationship with another."[12] Just as *jeong* pervades the immanent reality of everyday relationships, which I will argue is also part of divine reality, Hodgson goes on to use the term "primal eros" as the energy of God present in all things, all relationships, to sustain and cherish all that comes into contact. This primal eros that is present in all things, in all that comes into contact, is the presence of *jeong*. Even in the suffering on the cross, even in the presence of the abject, this primal eros/*jeong* is made powerfully present.

Like the eros that Hodgson links with the spirit, *jeong* often functions to trespass given parameters, boundaries, and norms. Contesting both borders and places of difference, *jeong* is present within the gaps and fissures, and in the uncomfortable and often painful interstitial spaces. Because *jeong* moves freely and is embodied across diverse borders and boundaries, life becomes much more complex. The power of *jeong* lies in its ability to wedge itself into the smallest gaps between the oppressed and the oppressor. For as Lee argued, *jeong* and *han* are two sides of the same coin.[13]

Jeong from the Western perspective could be construed to perpetuate either oppression or liberation. Emphasis on *jeong* might project uncertainty of liberation in its immediacy, yet life in the fullness of *jeong* brings healing and a break in the cycle of *han*. Foremost, *jeong* challenges and demands vulnerability from ourselves. By ultimately asking for vulnerability, we are challenged to go beyond ourselves. In fact, I insist that *jeong*'s call for vulnerability challenges us to identify ourselves with those whom we perceive to be the Other. *Jeong* is the divine presence that nudges us not only to perceive but also to accept the often negativized and shadowed parts of ourselves and thus ultimately to awaken to and practice the way of living in the fullness of *jeong*. The presence of *jeong* within and around relationality reveals us to ourselves.

Jeong is also composed of clarity. Perhaps for the Western conceptualization this might pose a problem. Clarity, in the West, has often implied categorization, and neat, straightforward answers. On the other hand, what I propose here is a clarity to recognize complexity and ambiguity—clarity to see *han* and *jeong* intimately linked together. When one's heart is turned into a heart of stone, it is difficult to allow *jeong* into a relationship, but when one's heart becomes a heart of flesh, *jeong* arises within connectedness.

The active calling of *jeong*, through the recognition of the self in the other, is a definite form of collaborative compassion. This collaboration with compassion is not one that seeks to maintain the status quo or to perpetuate oppression. Rather, such collaboration, born out of connectedness, seeks to work towards emancipatory praxis for all. Collaboration for liberation from oppression, as one of many manifestations of *jeong*, is intimately linked with solidarity. A popular saying and sentiment in Korea precisely embodies this collective solidarity that might be uncomfortable for the Western individualistic sensibility: "You die—I die; you live—I live" embodies an extreme sense of *jeong* that emerges within relationality.

There are also multiple uses of *jeong* in derived forms. Most importantly, Koreans refer to two different kinds of *jeong*: *mi-eun jeong* and *go-eun jeong*. The latter emerges within mutual and satisfactory relationships; the former, out of and in spite of relationships full of discontent. These relationships often have mixtures of both *han* and *jeong*. No matter the situation, whether positive or negative, *jeong* makes its presence. Koreans have a saying: "It's better to have *mi-eun jeong* than no *jeong*." Absence of *jeong* implies absence of relationship, and absence of relationship means complete indifference not only to the other but also to the self. While uses of *jeong* permeate Korean ethos, its presence has often not been well defined. *Jeong* has been categorized but certainly not limited/restricted to three types of relationships: *mo-jeong* (between parent and child), *ae-jeong* (between lovers), and *woo-jeong* (between friends).

Although he does not write on *jeong*, John Keenan bases his reading of the Gospel of Mark on what he terms the "dependently co-arisen world," which results from practice of the Buddhist concept of no-self, the practice of emptying one's self. From the Buddhist perspective, the cross is one of the results one might encounter as we live in the fullness of *jeong*. Clearly the notion that *jeong* is too domesticated, as some simplistically argue, is misleading because living by the way of *jeong* often leads to confrontations and other political ramifications. By becoming awakened to the ultimate meaning, Keenan argues that Jesus' very awakening both empties the pretensions of convention "to be absolute and totally reengages one in the dependently co-arisen world . . . for bodhisattva wisdom cannot abide in a non-compassionate silence."[14] Jesus is awakened to no-self through *jeong*. In his journey into the wilderness before beginning his ministry, he chooses no-self in the face of temptations of the self. His awakening to no-self through *jeong* allows him the capacity to have *jeong* for the other even to the point of risking the cross. In the passion narrative he again withdraws, not into the wilderness this time, but into the garden to once again search deep into his heart to reach into the depths of *jeong* for the other so that he might continue to practice the self-emptying even when faced with death. The practice of *jeong* does indeed promise a dependently co-arisen world. In a similar vein, Catherine Keller contends that the "divine and the world form the conditions of each others' becoming."[15] The practice of no-self, or self-emptying, will certainly have negative repercussions to those who have often been rendered as no-self through dominant and oppressive forces, if such practice sanctions oppressive dynamics. However, the practice of self-emptying from a Buddhist perspective is the process toward self-fullness.

Similarly, Park observes that the act of emptying the self, *kenosis*, "means negating the self negated by others. The more one empties one's own self, the more transparent the divine center of the self becomes."[16] Paradoxically, this self-emptying no-self is coming into what he terms as "self-fullness."[17] When *jeong* is present in connectedness, we are able to see clearly the complexity of life so that while we practice self-emptying we simultaneously discover ourselves and others.[18]

Jeong perilously complicates all relationships. Feminists such as Schüssler Fiorenza (*basileia*) and Brock (Christa/Community) have argued that the Jesus movement is inconceivable without Jesus. However, they also note that the movement is inconceivable without Jesus' followers. Throughout Jesus' ministry, not only does he form connectedness with people who are drawn to him, but he is also drawn to people. What we witness in his ministry is a deep awareness and living-out of Jesus' embrace of *jeong*. This is clearly illustrated in his healing and fellowship with the people, but it comes through explicitly in the passion narrative. Here I will examine the biblical passion narrative, drawing especially from the Gospels of Mark and Matthew.

Jesus' awakening to the possible consequence of his living out of *jeong* becomes explicitly clear to the reader in the sharing of the Last Supper. In Matt. 26, Jesus knows one who has been in intimate relationship with him will betray him. In verse 31, Jesus pronounces, "You will all become deserters because of me this night." He is not only aware of his impending death but also knows that the intimate relationships he has had with his disciples will not withstand what is to follow. His entrance into Gethsemane reflects his journey into the wilderness at the beginning of his ministry. Similar to when he entered into the wilderness alone, even as his disciples are present, he is once again alone in Gethsemane. Yet he three times seeks the companionship of his disciples as he faces his impending betrayal.

John Keenan maintains that in Jesus' heartfelt appeal to God, "'If this [cup] cannot pass unless I drink it, your will be done'" (Matt. 26:42) might be interpreted not as God's surrender to God's will that requires a ransom, but rather Jesus' final self-emptying. For the depth of his *jeong* for the world encounters the limitations of his own sense of self with the calling of the no-self. Mark 14:33 informs us that Jesus began to be distressed and agitated. As Keenan's reading of Mark indicates, the passion narrative, especially in Mark, is not "a divine program and that is why Jesus is distraught. If it were simply the unfolding of a preset divine will, there would be no point in praying to avoid suffering and death."[19] Jesus' prayer in Gethsemane does not change the dependently co-arisen events that might be avoided, but rather, the prayer "ushers one into the awareness of the inevitable course that is risked by ultimate self-emptying. This acute awareness has Jesus uttering, 'I am deeply grieved, even to death.'"

In my reading, I encounter here Jesus' struggle of self with no-self and his knowing that the disciples will abandon him as a cause for Jesus' own sense of *han*, which simultaneously is overcome through the power of his profound sense of *jeong*. In Gethsemane, what Jesus encounters is the struggle between his still remaining self and the risk that he will have to accept, as he must choose the ultimate move towards the no-self. The historical place of Jesus' emergence is that of Galilee. Galilee was the region that intensely grappled with the *han* of those colonized by a powerful imperial empire.[20] Accordingly, I would imagine Jesus' experience of not only individual but also collective *han* in his lived experiences. Jesus was a colonized person. He experienced the suffering that comes from colonization. How might he and his community have responded to the empire? How might he have felt toward the colonizer? In his ministry he is often positioned in between the colonizer and the colonized. As such, he must have experienced and known the depth of *han* and yet at the same time must have tasted, witnessed, and received *jeong*. As part of the subaltern, how might Jesus have responded to his position?

It is my contention that he recognized and envisions the Third Space. While fully knowing and having experienced *han*, might he not have opted for the practice of *dan*? Let me emphasize again that while he encounters many situations where his *han* might lean toward *dan*, he instead chooses to practice *jeong*, not only to the *han*-ridden but to those who caused *han*. For Jesus recognized the complexities present in relationships. Unlike other revolutionaries who arose out of such colonized context, Jesus chooses not to practice *dan* but to opt instead for transformation through the power of *jeong* in connectedness. His profound *jeong* for the world empowers him to move toward the no-self. For as Keenan argues, "Jesus is as immersed in the dependently co-arisen events of human history as anyone," so that in Mark the reader must shift back and forth from the perspective of the disciples to Jesus until in verse 33, when the reader must choose. The reader knows by now that suffering and death are inevitable in the dependently co-arisen world of Jesus. Even while Judas, one of his intimate relationships, betrays him, Jesus must empty all self in order that his *jeong* for Judas comes through. For in Matt. 26:50, knowing Judas is the betrayer, Jesus still calls Judas "friend."[21] As Judas comes on the scene with the crowd in verse 47, Jesus renounces the "cutting off," a response of *dan*, to those near him as he says in verse 52, "'Put your sword back into its place; for all who take the sword will perish by the sword.'" Here is an opportunity for Jesus to practice *dan* once again, yet he refuses. Instead, he opts for the praxis of *jeong*.

I want also to emphasize that just as Jesus embodied much *jeong* for those who came into contact with him, there were those within his constellation who practiced *jeong* toward him. The account of the woman with the alabaster jar of oil in the Gospel of Mark is a key example.[22] Mark 14 tells us that while Jesus was at Bethany in the house of Simon the leper, a woman came with an alabaster jar of costly ointment and poured it over his head. Those in the most intimate and immediate relationship with Jesus were angry and scolded her. However, this woman, whose name we do not know, had the perception to recognize Jesus' deep *jeong* and its cost in the near future. It was not the male disciples who were in close relationship with Jesus, but rather a woman who knew the depths of both *han* and *jeong* and who recognized Jesus' embodiment of *jeong*. Her *jeong* enables her to recognize Jesus' *jeong*, and it compels her to anoint him even as she knows intuitively that he will choose *jeong* even in the face of death. Moreover, while the disciples flee and abandon Jesus, the women who had been on the edges of the text come to be with him. As powerless as they might have been, their *jeong* for Jesus overcomes their desire to abandon him as well. For their *jeong* permits them to recognize both Jesus' *han* and *jeong*.

Jesus' teaching to love one's enemies emerges from deep and intimate acknowledgment of *jeong*. The praxis of Jesus' ministry—his encounter with the woman caught in adultery, his associations with outcasts and those who complied with oppression, and his cry "Forgive them for they do not know what they do" while on the cross—demonstrates that Jesus recognized the power of *jeong* to bring wholeness. By catching glimpses of our own multifarious image within the hearts of others, we begin to allow space for *jeong* to come into existence even in oppressive relationships. Jesus' openness to others and his option to practice *jeong* rather than *dan* reminds me of Korean *Pansori* singers. *Pansori* is the voice that emerges from the heart of *han* and *jeong*. *Han* and *jeong* are difficult to conceptualize, but for Koreans, *Pansori* comes closest to expressing the semiotic depths of both *han* and *jeong*. Jesus is like the *Pansori* singer who sings by pulling *jeong* through the depths of *han*.

Pansori is a traditional Korean way of singing that embodies both *han* and *jeong* and is similar to the African American blues.[23] In Korea, the voice of *Pansori* is recognized as the most profound and effective way by which *han* is articulated. The singer of *Pansori* must therefore have experienced and embodied *han* to the fullest while knowing *jeong* as well. The singer must incarnate the complex intertwining of *han* and *jeong* through her voice. A recent film, *SOPYONJE*, illustrates this traditional Korean singing. In *SOPYONJE*, a character that caused much *han* to another character in the process of teaching her to be a *Pansori* singer tells her, "You must have forgiven me for I do not hear any strands of *won-han* in your voice . . . for if you made me your enemy/oppressor, *won-han* would be buried in your voice. But you do not have that. If *dongpyonje* is filled with old unresolved *han*, *sopyonje* has much of *jeong-han*."[24] However, he informs her to dig deep and to reach for self-emptying so that her voice embodies neither *dongpyonje* nor *sopyonje*. Instead what remains is sutra-enlightenment/nirvana, for that is the only way to unravel *han*. Andrew Park has argued that the unraveling of *han* is through transcendence, for transcendence occurs through compassionate confrontation. This is true. Yet the process of self-emptying must also be present, as it also empties out *han* in order to form a sense of attachment in detachment. That is the only way of unraveling *han*.

One of the countercriticisms I anticipated is the argument that because *jeong* works powerfully to blur the boundary between the oppressed and the oppressor, praxis of liberation would be hindered. My response has been that it is through this transgression of the erected boundary between the oppressed and the oppressor that transformation of *han* might well take place.[25]

Similar to typical critiques of eros as mere seducer and betrayer of the self, especially for women and those victimized through self-abnegation and what Levinas refers to as the potential "hemorrhaging" of the self for the other, I do not doubt that appropriation of *jeong* as an important aspect of future theological constructs will be confronted with similar criticisms.[26] While a patriarchal critique of *jeong* continues to insist that it is too grasping, possessing, or knowing, *jeong* never collapses the space between the I and the other. For *jeong* does not practice the elements of possessing, grasping, or knowing which are, as Emmanuel Levinas argues for eros, synonyms of power. Rather, *jeong* fosters and is fostered within relationships, not by assimilation; it is precisely for this reason that *jeong* works powerfully to create a deep bond between the self and the other. *Jeong* creates an interstitial space from which one might practice "relational autonomy."

Feminist appropriation of *jeong* must be fully on guard against the debilitating aspects of *jeong*. Patriarchal domestication of *jeong* has justified unhealthy and disempowering relational fusions. Feminist appropriation of the power of *jeong* then must be balanced by its power to recognize the self within the other while maintaining the distinction of identity. Feminist appropriation of *jeong* is not oblivious to the necessity of *dan* in the "undoing" of *han*. Rather, appropriation of *jeong* in light of *dan* is to renegotiate and open up the gap, the interstitial space, from which radical subversive resistance can emerge creatively and where one might embody what I have termed the "hermeneutics of complexity."

Contrary to patriarchal essentialized misappropriations of *jeong* as a passive and feminine form of relationality, I suggest here that women's embodiment of *jeong* is dynamic, empowering, subversive, disruptive, sly, insurgent, and most often oriented toward sustaining life. While avoiding essentialized and feminized concepts of *jeong*, I am arguing here for a politicized appropriation of *jeong* as a possible alternative for the unraveling of the causes of *han*. Emergence of *jeong*'s presence occurs where the boundaries of the self and the Other touch, often conflictually. Its presence within postcolonial theological reflections, I maintain, will help to imbue our theological constructs with heart. For in the end, we are always moved through and by the heart.

Johnson observes that there is a danger to women when we speak of the powerless suffering of God in our christological reflections. However, she also insists on "the pathological tendency in the present culture of First World

countries to deny suffering and death in human experience. . . . [I]n this context speech about redemptive suffering and the power of suffering God is gen-
uinely counter-cultural, and of benefit to women who know their own
experience as a full cup of anguish."[27] As I have noted in chapter 5, feminist
theology is wary of overstressing the notion of love, which has traditionally
been seen as agape and self-giving love. These forms of love often fail to promote mutuality and self-affirmation and thus reinforce self-abnegation and
powerlessness. Johnson maintains that

> we seek an understanding that does not divide power and compas-
> sionate love in a dualistic framework that identifies love with a resig-
> nation of power and the exercise of power with a denial of love. Rather,
> we seek to integrate these two, seeing love as the shape in which divine
> power appears.[28]

My reading of Christology from my location within the Third Space of postcoloniality has allowed me to agree with Johnson. What we need are new forms
of understanding the power of the cross and how they might work to subvert
in radical ways our modes of solidarity, relationality, emancipation, and love.

By examining the Korean concept of *jeong*, we come into contact with an
all-pervasive concept that has been the life force of Korean people, who have
experienced much *han*. If *han* has been a predominant experience of Korean
people for generations, then the familiarity of *jeong* is also indicative of the
presence of a life force that counters and resists the corrosiveness of *han*. By
linking it with the concept of *jeong*, our Christology can shift away from salvation through sacrificial suffering and can become a salvation based on relational power of *jeong*. This Christology of *jeong*, informed deeply by liberation
theologies, feminist theologies, and postcolonial theory, arises from and
between connected relationality of life. The cross in the Christology of *jeong*
signifies both the horror of *han* and the power of *jeong* in a profound move
toward freedom and wholeness.

Notes

Introduction

1. I first began exploring the concept of *jeong* as a way of doing theological reflection in 1991 while writing a paper for my Feminist Theology course at Princeton Theological Seminary. It then was developed for my dissertation proposal. At this time there was no way to spell the word in English. After trying various ways, I settled on the present spelling as the closest approximation of how the word is pronounced in Korean. The first theological articulation of this concept was presented at the American Academy of Religion in 1996. Then an even more fully developed version was presented at the American Academy of Religion in 2002, followed by numerous lectures both here in the United States and in Korea. Brief articles on this concept were also published. For the most recent article on *jeong*, see Catherine Keller, Michael Nausner, and Mayra Rivera, eds., *Postcolonial Theologies: Divinity and Empire* (St. Louis: Chalice Press, 2004).

2. Julia Kristeva, *Powers of Horror: An Essay on Abjection* (New York: Columbia University Press, 1982), 4.

3. Cf. Noelle McAfee, "Abject Strangers: Toward an Ethics of Respect," and Norma Claire Moruzzi, "National Abjects: Julia Kristeva on the Process of Political Self-Identification," both in *Ethics, Politics and Difference in Julia Kristeva's Writing*, ed. Kelly Oliver (New York: Routledge, 1993), 116–149.

4. Elizabeth Grosz, *Sexual Subversions: Three French Feminists* (Boston: Allen & Unwin, 1989), 71.

5. Habermas has argued that a dual relationship exists between theory and praxis. Claims to theological validity must then be verified and affirmed through a process of praxis. See Jürgen Habermas, *Theory and Practice*, trans. John Viertel (Boston: Beacon Press, 1973), 2.

6. Anselm Min, "From Autobiography to Fellowship of Other: Reflections on Doing Ethnic Theology Today," in *Journeys at the Margin: Toward an Autobiographical Theology in American-Asian Perspective*, ed. Peter C. Phan and Jung Young Lee (Collegeville, MN: Liturgical Press, 1999).

7. For the importance of autobiography in theological reflections, see Min, *Journeys at the Margin*.

129

8. For further theopolitical analysis see Mark Lewis Taylor, *Religion, Politics and the Christian Right: Post 9/11 Powers and American Empire* (Minneapolis: Fortress Press, 2005).

9. Edward Said, *Out of Place: A Memoir* (New York: Alfred Knopf, 1999), 6.

10. I would like to bring to our attention that not only is this identity struggle experienced by Korean Americans but also in Korea itself there are a very large number of people of mixed racial heritage who have been under the oppression of Korea's strong sense of patriarchalized homogeneity. Their *han* is interlaced with the racism of Korean people but also with Japanese colonialism, imperialism, Western economic neocolonialism, and the consequences of the American military presence. One of the most critically acclaimed recent films from Korea that delves into this situation is *Address Unknown*.

11. Julia Kristeva, *Strangers to Ourselves*, trans. Leon S. Roudiez (New York: Columbia University Press, 1991), 15.

12. Mikhail Bakhtin, "Discourse in the Novel," in *The Dialogic Imagination*, ed. Michael Holquist, trans. Caryl Emerson and Michael Holquist (Austin: University of Texas Press, 1981), 360.

13. Walter D. Mignolo, *Local Histories/Global Designs: Coloniality, Subaltern Knowledges, and Border Thinking* (Princeton, NJ: Princeton University Press, 2000), 252–53.

14. For an excellent discussion of the biblical concepts of "foreigner" and "stranger," see Kristeva, *Strangers to Ourselves*, 42–93. She traces the "foreigner/stranger" concept in the Hebrew Scriptures to Pauline and Augustinian texts.

15. Kristeva, *Strangers To Ourselves*, 28.

16. Ibid., 14.

17. Jacques Derrida, *Negotiations: Interventions and Interviews 1971–2001* (Stanford, CA: Stanford University Press, 2002), 13–14.

18. Moustafa Bayoumi and Andrew Rubin, eds., *The Edward Said Reader* (New York: Vintage Books, 2000), 371.

19. Gauri Viswanathan, ed., *Power, Politics and Culture: Interviews with Edward W. Said* (New York: Pantheon, 2001), 236.

20. For a critical analysis of citizenship and identity, refer to Kwame Anthony Appiah, *Ethics of Identity* (Princeton, NJ: Princeton University Press, 2005).

21. For an excellent critical reflection on the question of how orientalism has functioned in places like Korea, and how Korean identity is different from Korean American identity, see Nam Soon Kang, "Who/What is Asian? A Postcolonial Reading of Orientalism and Neo-Orientalism," in *Postcolonial Theologies*, ed. Keller, Nausner, and Rivera, 100–117.

22. Paragraph quoted on p. xviii.

23. Rita Nakashima Brock, "Interstitial Integrity: Reflections Toward an Asian American Woman's Theology," in *Christian Theology Today: Contemporary North American Perspectives* (Louisville, KY: Westminster John Knox Press, 1998), 183–95. See also Jung Young Lee, *Marginality: The Key to Multicultural Theology* (Minneapolis: Fortress Press, 1995).

24. With the emergence of postcolonial theory as a viable alternative, we also witness the emergence of various contestations of postcolonial theory. The most heated debates from within postcolonial theory have much to do with the "intrusion" of French "high" theory, notably related to Jacques Derrida, Jacques Lacan, and Michel Foucault.

25. Aamir Mufti and Ella Shohat, "Introduction," in *Dangerous Liaisons: Gender, Nation, and Postcolonial Perspectives*, ed. Anne McClintock, Aamir Mufti, and Ella Shohat (Minneapolis: University of Minnesota Press, 1997), 2.

26. Catherine Keller, *God and Power: Counter-Apocalyptic Journeys* (Minneapolis: Fortress Press, 2005), 99.

27. Andrew Sung Park, *The Wounded Heart of God: The Asian Concept of Han and the Christian Doctrine of Sin* (Nashville: Abingdon Press, 1993), 120. Park seeks to illustrate this thick and rich part of predominantly women's relational experience by offering brief stories and vignettes highlighting different elements of *jeong*.

28. Rita Nakashima Brock, *Journeys by Heart: A Christology of Erotic Power* (New York: Crossroad, 1988). Her concept of "erotic power" in connection with what she terms the "Christa/Community" comes very close to mirroring *jeong*.

29. An examination of *jeong* in its Chinese written characters reveals that *jeong* is made of three words: heart, clarity, and vulnerability. I note here that "vulnerability" is the one most open to double-edgedness.

30. Catherine Keller, *From a Broken Web: Separation, Sexism, and Self* (Boston: Beacon Press, 1986), 17–28, 156–63. Keller describes "Eros," using Alfred Whitehead's words, as "the divine element in the universe" or as "the name for that unlimited desire, the desire that drives beyond the fixed bounds of all separations."

31. Cf. Gayatri Chakravorty Spivak, "The Politics of Translation," in *Destabilizing Theory: Contemporary Feminist Debates*, ed. Michele Barrett and Anne Phillips (Stanford, CA: Stanford University Press, 1992), 177–200.

32. Cf. Diana Fuss, *Essentially Speaking: Feminism, Nature and Difference* (New York: Routledge, 1989).

33. Cf. William D. Hart, *Edward Said and the Religious Effects of Culture* (Cambridge: Cambridge University Press, 2000).

34. Grosz, *Sexual Subversions*, 43.

35. Jung Ha Kim, *Bridge-Makers and Cross-Bearers: Korean American Women and the Church* (Atlanta: Scholars Press, 1997), 77–85. For further constructive reflections on Korean American faith experiences, see Su Yon Pak, Unzu Lee, Jung Ha Kim, and Myung Ji Cho, *Singing the Lord's Song in a New Land: Korean American Practices of Faith* (Louisville, KY: Westminster John Knox Press, 2005).

36. Here I include Bhabha's notion of "margin of interrogation" that opens up space for a "subversive slippage" of identity and authority.

37. R. Radhakrishnan, *Diasporic Mediations: Between Home and Location* (Minneapolis: University of Minnesota Press, 1996).

38. Kim, *Bridge-Makers and Cross-Bearers*, 82.

39. Dorothee Soelle, *Suffering* (Philadelphia: Fortress Press, 1975), 32. She further notes that "explanation of suffering that looks away from the victim and identifies itself with a righteousness that is supposed to stand behind the suffering has already taken a step in the direction of theological sadism, which wants to understand God as the torturer."

Chapter 1: Identity Out of Place

1. Gayatri Chakravorty Spivak, "Postmarked Calcutta, India," in *The Post-Colonial Critic: Interviews, Strategies, Dialogues*, ed. Sarah Harasym (New York: Routledge, 1990), 93.

2. The Western psychoanalytic stand posits the emergence of the subject with the simultaneous emergence of the other/object. The crucial implication of this, which will be further discussed in a later chapter, is that the formation of subject is inevitably linked with the formation of the other/abject/object. Thus, without the abject/other/object, there is no self/subject. Contrary to this, the East Asian notion of the no-self in much of Taoist and Buddhist traditions points to this very conflated and contested area. The practice of no-self perhaps better meets the needs of postmodern deconstruction and critique of the split between the self and the other.

3. Aamir Mufti and Ella Shohat, "Introduction," *Dangerous Liaisons: Gender, Nation, and Postcolonial Perspectives*, ed. Aamir Mufti and Ella Shohat (Minneapolis: University of Minnesota Press, 1997), 8.

4. R. Radhakrishnan, *Diasporic Mediations: Between Home and Location* (Minneapolis: University of Minnesota Press, 1996), xxiii.

5. Julia Kristeva, *Strangers to Ourselves*, trans. Leon S. Roudiez (New York: Columbia University Press, 1991), 29.

6. Not only are children being nurtured and birthed within the union of diverse backgrounds, but more and more, children from different racial ethnic and sexual orientation are now being adopted into families that are radically different from their birth place/origins. Another noticeable shift is in the foods we consume. Culinary repertories are now very hybrid. The culture's hybridity is found within the emergences of "fusion" cuisines. For a critical examination of "food colonialism" and "culinary imperialism" as it pertains to the construction of ethnic identities and the commodification of "ethnic" foods, refer to Uma Narayan, "Eating Cultures: Incorporation, Identity, and Indian Food," in *Dislocating Cultures: Identities, Traditions, and Third World Feminism* (New York: Routledge, 1997).

7. For further examination of the complex terrain of identities, see also Henry W. Leathem Rietz, "My Father Is Japanese, But I Have My Mother's Last Name," in *Asian Americans and Christian Ministry*, ed. Inn Sook Lee and Timothy D. Son (Seoul: Voice Publishing House, 1999), 49–59.

8. Radhakrishnan, *Diasporic Mediations*, xxvii.

9. Ibid., 173.

10. In order to highlight the importance of contextual theology as being not in direct opposition to or a retreat into various forms of metanarratives, Segovia examines the complexities within particular diasporic experiences. Although he makes direct observations based on his analysis of Hispanic American communities, I strongly believe them to be relevant to the various Korean American immigrant experiences. See Fernando Segovia, "Toward Intercultural Criticism: A Reading Strategy from the Diaspora," in *Reading from This Place: Social Location and Biblical Interpretation in Global Perspective*, ed. Fernando Segovia and Mary Ann Tolbert, vol. 2 (Minneapolis: Fortress Press, 1995), 303–30.

11. For an excellent discussion of Korean American immigrant hermeneutics, see Chan-Hie Kim, "Reading the Cornelius Story from an Asian Immigrant Perspective," in *Reading from This Place: Social Location and Biblical Interpretation in the United States*, ed. Fernando F. Segovia and Mary Ann Tolbert, vol. 1 (Minneapolis: Fortress Press, 1995), 165–74.

12. Stuart Hall, "Who Needs Identity?" in *Questions of Cultural Identity*, ed. Stuart Hall and Paul du Gay (London: Sage Publications, 1996), 3.

13. Jacques Derrida, *Of Grammatology*, trans. Gayatri Chakravorty Spivak (Baltimore: The Johns Hopkins University Press, 1998), 65–66.

14. Cf. Julia Kristeva's "Woman Can Never Be Defined," in *New French Feminisms*, ed. Elaine Marks and Isabelle de Courtivron (New York: Schocken Books, 1981), 137–41.

15. Uma Narayan, "Essence of Culture and a Sense of History: A Feminist Critique of Cultural Essentialism," in *Decentering the Center: Philosophy for a Multicultural, Postcolonial, and Feminist World*, ed. Uma Narayan and Sandra Harding (Bloomington: Indiana University Press, 2000), 82.

16. Luce Irigaray, *This Sex Which Is Not One*, trans. Catherine Porter (Ithaca, NY: Cornell University Press, 1985), 78.

17. Cf. Luce Irigaray, *Speculum of the Other Woman*, trans. Gillian C. Gills (Ithaca, NY: Cornell University Press, 1985) and *Sexes and Genealogies*, trans. Gillian C. Gills (New York: Columbia University Press, 1993). For a critical reading of Irigaray also refer to Naomi Schor, "This Essentialism Which Is Not One: Coming to Grips with Irigaray," in *Engaging with Irigaray*, ed. Carolyn Burke, Naomi Schor, and Margaret Whitford (New York: Columbia University Press, 1994), 57–78.

18. Cf. Lorraine Code, "How To Think Globally: Stretching the Limits of Imagination," in Narayan and Harding, *Decentering the Center*, 67–79.

19. Ellen T. Armour, *Deconstruction, Feminist Theology and the Problem of Difference: Subverting the Race/Gender Divide* (Chicago: University of Chicago, 1999), 184. Armour offers an excellent critique and challenge to the limits of white feminism and feminist theology, which she argues continue to be centered around the erasure of race.

20. Susan Bordo, "Feminism, Postmodernism and Gender-Scepticism," in *Feminism/Postmodernism*, ed. Linda J. Nicholson (New York: Routledge, 1990), 136.

21. Ibid., 136.

22. Ibid.

23. For excellent essays on the convergence of feminism and epistemology, refer to *Feminist Epistemologies*, ed. Linda Alcoff and Elizabeth Potter (New York: Routledge, 1993).

24. Bordo, "Feminism," 140.

25. Ibid., 142.

26. For an interesting discussion on the relationship between writing, femininity, and feminism, refer to Julia Kristeva's interview "Talking about Polylogue," in *French Feminist Thought: A Reader*, ed. Toril Moi (Cambridge: Blackwell Publishers, 1987), 110–17.

27. Cf. Naomi Schor, "This Essentialism Which Is Not One: Coming to Grips with Irigaray," in *The Essential Difference*, ed. Naomi Schor and Elizabeth Weed (Bloomington: Indiana University Press, 1994), 40–62.

28. Catherine Keller, "Seeking and Sucking," in *Horizons in Feminist Theology: Identity, Tradition and Norms*, ed. Rebecca S. Chopp and Sheila Greeve Davaney (Minneapolis: Fortress Press, 1997), 55–70.

29. Diana Fuss, *Essentially Speaking: Feminism, Nature and Difference* (New York: Routledge, 1989), 118.

30. See Kristeva, *Strangers to Ourselves*. Cf. also Noelle McAfee, "Abject Strangers: Towards an Ethics of Respect," in *Ethics, Politics and Difference in Julia Kristeva's Writing*, ed. Kelly Oliver (New York: Routledge, 1993), 116–34.

31. Serene Jones, *Feminist Theory and Christian Theology: Cartographies of Grace* (Minneapolis: Fortress Press, 2000), 44.

32. Gayatri Chakravorty Spivak, "Criticism, Feminism, and the Institution," in Harasym, *The Post-Colonial Critic*, 11–12.

33. For an excellent discussion on antiessentialist debate, despite the focus on Julia Kristeva, see Tina Chanter's "Kristeva's Politics of Change: Tracking Essentialism with the Help of a Sex/Gender Map," in Oliver, *Ethics, Politics, and Difference*, 171–95.

34. Pnina Werbner, "Essentialising Essentialism, Essentialising Silence: Ambivalence and Multiplicity in the Constructions of Racism and Ethnicity," in *Debating Cultural Hybridity: Multi-Cultural Identities and the Politics of Anti-Racism*, ed. Pnina Werbner and Tariq Modood (London: Zed Books, 1997), 226.

35. Kristeva, *Strangers to Ourselves*, 38.

36. Kelly Oliver, *Reading Kristeva: Unraveling the Double-Bind* (Indianapolis: Indiana University Press, 1993), 153.

37. Ibid., 149.

38. Julia Kristeva, "Women's Time," in *The Kristeva Reader*, ed. Toril Moi (New York: Columbia University Press, 1989), 187–213.

39. Trinh Minh-ha, *When The Moon Waxes Red: Representation, Gender and Cultural Politics* (New York: Routledge, 1991), 194.

40. Sang Hyun Lee, "How Shall We Sing the Lord's Song in a Strange Land?" *Journal of Asian and Asian American Theology* 1 (Summer, 1996): 77–81.

41. Sang Hyun Lee, "Pilgrimage and Home in the Wilderness of Marginality: Symbols and Context in Asian American Theology," in *Asian Americans and Christian Ministry*, ed. Inn Sook Lee and Timothy D. Son (Seoul: Voice Publishing House, 1999), 75–88.

42. R. A. Saugiartha, *Asian Biblical Hermeneutics and Postcolonialism: Contesting the Interpretations* (Maryknoll, NY: Orbis Books, 1998), 109.

43. Ibid., 92.

44. Trinh Minh-ha, *Woman, Native, Other: Writing Postcoloniality and Feminism* (Bloomington: Indiana University Press, 1989), 6–20.

45. Trinh Minh-ha, *Cinema Interval* (New York: Routledge, 1999), 182–85.

46. Rita Nakashima Brock, "Interstitial Integrity: Reflections toward an Asian American Woman's Theology," in *Introduction to Christian Theology Today: Contemporary North American Perspectives*, ed. Roger A. Badham (Louisville, KY: Westminster John Knox Press, 1998), 183–95.

47. Radhakrishnan, *Diasporic Mediations*, xvi.

48. Rey Chow, *Ethics after Idealism: Theory-Culture-Ethnicity-Reading* (Bloomington: Indiana University Press, 1998).

49. Ella Shohat, "Notes On the Postcolonial," *Social Text* 31, no. 32 (1992): 101.

50. Ibid.

51. Ibid., 102.

52. David Tracy, *Plurality and Ambiguity: Hermeneutics, Religion, Hope* (Chicago: University of Chicago Press, 1987), 18.

53. Radhakrishnan, *Diasporic Mediations*, 32.

54. Cf. Lorraine Code, *What Can She Know? Feminist Theory and the Construction of Knowledge* (Ithaca, NY: Cornell University Press, 1991). Code critically examines the politics of epistemology from a feminist standpoint, which consequently also spills over into politics of difference and identity.

55. Cf. Elaine K. Chang, "Run through the Borders: Feminism, Postmodernism, and Runaway Subjectivity," in *Border Theory: The Limits of Cultural Politics*, ed.

Scott Michaelson and David E. Johnson (Minneapolis: University of Minnesota Press, 1997). Cf. Alfred J. Lopez, ed., *Postcolonial Whiteness: A Critical Reader on Race and Empire* (New York: State University Press of New York, 2005).

56. Kristeva, *Strangers to Ourselves*, 117.

57. Seyla Benhabib, "Feminism and Postmodernism," in *Feminist Contentions: A Philosophical Exchange* (New York: Routledge, 1995), 19. Also see Seyla Benhabib, *Situating the Self: Gender, Community, and Postmodernism in Contemporary Ethics* (New York: Routledge, 1992). Cf. Seyla Benhabib, ed., *Democracy and Difference: Contesting the Boundaries of the Political* (Princeton, NJ: Princeton University Press, 1996).

58. Benhabib, *Democracy and Difference*, 30.

59. Ibid., 20.

60. Cf. Gayatri Chakravorty Spivak, in Harasym, *The Post-Colonial Critic*.

61. There are many fine scholarly works in conversation and in critique within and about the feminist movement, particularly in the North American context. The following two scholars offer extensive analysis of the ensuing dynamics due to differences among women. Paula Giddings, *When and Where I Enter: The Impact of Black Women on Race and Sex in America* (New York: William Morrow, 1984). See also Patricia Hill Collins, *Black Feminist Thought: Knowledge, Consciousness, and the Politics of Empowerment* (Boston: Unwin Hyman, 1990).

62. Teresa de Lauretis, "Feminist Studies/Critical Studies: Issues, Terms, and Contexts," in *Feminist Studies/Critical Studies*, ed. Teresa de Lauretis (Bloomington: Indiana University Press, 1986), 9.

63. Ibid., 126.

64. Susan Stanford Friedman, *Mappings: Feminism and the Cultural Geographies of Encounter* (Princeton, NJ: Princeton University Press, 1998), 20–35.

65. For an excellent discussion on the intersection of feminism, postcolonialism, and postmodernism, see Musa W. Dube, "Postcoloniality, Feminist Spaces, and Religion," in *Postcolonialism, Feminism and Religious Discourse*, ed. Laura E. Donaldson and Kwok Pui-lan (New York: Routledge, 2002), 100–120.

66. Spivak, who observes that the prevalent tokenism—whether that is on gender, race, or sexuality—often works simultaneously with "ghettoization," voiced one important complexity.

67. Nancy Frazer and Linda Nicholson, "Social Criticism without Philosophy: An Encounter Between Feminism and Postmodernism," in *Universal Abandon? The Politics of Postmodernism*, ed. Andrew Ross (Minneapolis: University of Minnesota Press, 1988), 102.

68. Chandra Talpade Mohanty, "Cartographies of Struggle: Third World Women and the Politics of Feminism," in *Third World Women and the Politics of Feminism*, ed. Chandra Talpade Mohanty (Bloomington: Indiana University Press, 1991), 13. See also Donna Haraway, *Simians, Cyborgs and Women: The Reinvention of Nature* (New York: Routledge, 1991) and Adrienne Rich, "Notes toward a Politics of Location," in *Blood, Bread, and Poetry: Selected Prose, 1979–85* (New York: Norton, 1986).

69. For a critical discussion on the often-damaging relationship between women of color and white women, especially in the scholarly arena, see Kwok Pui-lan, "Unbinding Our Feet: Saving Brown Women and Feminist Religious Discourse," in Donaldson and Pui-lan, *Postcolonialism*, 62–81.

70. Iris Marion Young, *Justice and the Politics of Difference* (Princeton, NJ: Princeton University Press, 1990), 156–71.

71. Judith Butler, "Contingent Foundations: Feminism and the Question of 'Postmodernism,'" in *The Postmodern Turn: New Perspectives on Social Theory*, ed. Steven Seidman (Cambridge: Cambridge University Press, 1994), 166.

72. Judith Butler, *Gender Trouble: Feminism and the Subversion of Identity* (New York: Routledge, 1990), 18.

73. Butler, "Contingent Foundations," 166.

74. Audre Lorde, *Sister Outsider: Essays and Speeches* (Berkeley, CA: Crossing Press, 1984).

75. Friedman, *Mappings*, 104.

76. Ibid., 103.

77. Ibid., 75.

78. Trinh Minh-ha, "Not You/Like You: Postcolonial Women and the Interlocking Questions of Identity and Difference," in Mufti and Shohat, *Dangerous Liaisons*, 415.

79. Trinh, *Cinema Interval*, 61.

80. Ibid., 62.

81. Trinh Minh-ha, "All-owning Spectatorship," in *Feminism and the Politics of Difference*, ed. Sneja Gunew and Anna Yeatman (Boulder, CO: Westview Books, 1993), 157–76.

82. bell hooks, *Yearning: Race, Gender, and Cultural Politics* (Boston: South End Press, 1990), 21.

83. Trinh Minh-ha, *Woman Native Other: Writing Postcoloniality and Feminism* (Bloomington: Indiana University Press, 1989), 82.

84. Tensions between white, middle-class feminists and women-of-color feminists have been well articulated within the past decade. Feminists doing postcolonial studies have also noted similar criticisms. Musa Dube, in *Postcolonial Feminist Interpretation of the Bible* (St. Louis, MO: Chalice Press, 2000), 112, argues that "while Western middle-class women hardly acknowledged that while they were discursively colonized patriarchal objects, they were also race-privileged colonizing subjects, thus collapsing the category of a woman into a monolithic entity. . . . [E]arly feminists over-looked the imperialist social position they occupied."

85. Radhakrishnan, *Diasporic Mediations*, 72.

86. Ibid., 148.

87. Friedman, *Mappings*, 103 and 227.

88. For an excellent discussion of this dilemma, see Julia Kristeva's "Women's Time," in Moi, *Kristeva Reader*, 187–213.

Chapter 2: *Han* and *Jeong*

1. Cf. David Kwang-sun Suh, "Liberating Spirituality in the Korean Minjung Tradition: Shamanism and Minjung Liberation," in *Asian Christian Spirituality: Reclaiming Traditions*, ed. Virginia Fabella, Peter K. H. Lee, and David Kwang-sun Suh (New York: Orbis Books, 1992), 31–43.

2. Jae Hoon Lee, *The Exploration of the Inner Wounds—Han* (Atlanta: Scholars Press, 1994), 6.

3. Ibid.

4. Andrew Sung Park, *Racial Conflict and Healing: An Asian-American Theological Perspective* (Maryknoll, NY: Orbis Books, 1996), 23–25.

5. Andrew Sung Park, *The Wounded Heart of God: The Asian Concept of Han and the Christian Doctrine of Sin* (Nashville: Abingdon Press, 1993), 10.

6. Ibid., 20.

7. Ibid., 15.

8. Ibid., 50.

9. Ibid., 15.

10. Lee, *The Exploration of Inner Wounds*, 15.

11. Cf. Janice Doane and Devon Hodges, *From Klein to Kristeva: Psychoanalytic Feminism and the Search for the "Good Enough" Mother* (Ann Arbor: University of Michigan Press, 1995.)

12. Lee, *The Exploration of Inner Wounds*, 20.

13. Ibid.

14. Ibid., 24.

15. Ibid., 26.

16. Ibid.

17. Ibid.

18. Ibid., 48.

19. I would press further that on a theoretical level Koreans might resist homosexuality: yet on a relational level, we find that the complexity and fluidity embodied by *jeong* allows for overcoming even homophobia. Moreover, *jeong* fosters intimate same-sex relationships, despite the protest that traditionally Koreans are just very affectionate. I believe that on a deeper level, the Korean embodiment of *jeong* allows for unconscious acceptance and understanding of sexuality on a continuum rather than in a dichotomous way, i.e., hetero- over homosexuality. This theme is seen in a new avant-garde film from Korea, *Bungee Jumping*, which explores the issue of sexuality, though not explicitly, because the director understands that for Koreans love is not about heterosexuality but about a continuum of sexualities. In *Bungee Jumping*, a heterosexual couple's love ends with the death of the woman. The man cannot forget his deep love for the dead woman despite his new marriage and his daughter. After many years, while he is teaching in a high school, he encounters odd incidents in one of his students: reoccurrences. Through the Asian concept of reincarnation, the director explores human *jeong* and love beyond just homosexuality. The tragic conclusion leaves no doubt how such relationships would have been met in a patriarchal, homophobic culture, either in closed-up closets or in vehement denials.

20. Julia Kristeva, *Black Sun: Depression and Melancholia* (New York: Columbia University Press, 1989), 4.

21. Lee, *The Exploration of Inner Wounds*, 36.

22. Ibid., 37.

23. Ibid.

24. A person whose *han* has turned to full-fledged *won-han* often experiences a psychological disorder with feelings of annihilation and an overwhelming sense of threat. I would further argue that oppressed people who turn to terrorism suffer under extreme *won-han* that has gone to the next extreme—a paranoiac stage of *hu-han*.

25. Lee, *The Exploration of Inner Wounds*, 36.

26. Ibid., 93.

27. Ibid.

28. Ibid., 94.

29. Ibid., 144.
30. An interesting aspect of Minjung theologians' study of *han* is its prevalence among women. Women, as the "Minjung of Minjung," experience deep scars caused by *han*. I wonder to what extent there is a link between the fact that many "ghosts" are female, that women experience much "*shin-byung*" phenomena, and that traditional ways of unraveling *han*, shamanism, have been performed by female shamans.
31. Lee, *The Exploration of Inner Wounds*, 151.
32. Ibid., 152.
33. Ibid., 48.
34. Ibid., 145.
35. As a feminist, I must caution against the dangers of celebrating biological essentialism. Again, as I recognize the fine line we tread between constructivism and essentialism, my position obviously is somewhere in the interstitial space between both sites. Ibid., 152–53.
36. The Korean film industry has undergone much change in recent years; in particular, the ease of government censorship can be drastically experienced when viewing emerging avant-garde Korean films, which surprisingly are welcomed with critical acclaim from both overseas and domestic viewers. Emerging out of extremely talented young Korean directors and filmmakers, an explosion of critically acclaimed films into the international arena can be traced to the late 1990s.
37. Chung Hyun Kyung, "*Han-Pu-Ri*: Doing Theology from Korean Women's Perspective," in *Frontiers in Asian Christian Theology: Emerging Trends*, ed. R. S. Sugirtharajah (New York: Orbis Books, 1994), 52–62.
38. Refer also to Choi Man Ja, "Feminine Images of God in Korean Traditional Religion," in Sugirtharajah, *Frontiers in Asian Christian Theology*, 80–89.
39. David Suh, "Theology of Reunification," in Sugirtharajah, *Frontiers in Asian Christian Theology*, 198.
40. Ibid.
41. Excerpt from "Minjoek Tong-il eh Gil," *Voice of the People* (1971). Translation mine.
42. Gayatri Chakravorty Spivak, "The Politics of Translation," in *Destabilizing Theory: Contemporary Feminist Debates*, ed. Michele Barrett and Anne Phillips (Stanford, CA: Stanford University Press, 1992), 177–200.
43. Trinh T. Minh-ha, *Cinema Interval* (New York: Routledge, 1999), 61–62.
44. *Joint Security Area* (Gondong Geongbi Guyeok), dir. Park Chan-Wook, perf. Byung-Heon Lee, Yeong-Ae Lee, Tae-Woo Kim, and Ha-Kyun Shin, Korea, 2000.
45. Spivak, "Politics as Translation," 177–200.
46. Suh, "Theology of Reunification," 197.
47. Ibid., 198.
48. Ibid., 199.
49. Homi Bhabha, *The Location of Culture* (New York: Routledge, 1994), 86.
50. Here I include Bhabha's notion on "margin of interrogation" that opens up space for a "subversive slippage" of identity and authority.
51. Bhabha, *The Location of Culture*, 4.
52. Regina Freer, "Black-Korean Conflict," in *The Lost Angeles Riots: Lessons for the Urban Future*, ed. Mark Baldassare (Boulder, CO: Westview Press, 1994), 180.
53. Ibid., 192.
54. David Leiwei Li, *Imagining The Nation: Asian American Literature and Cultural Consent* (Stanford, CA: Stanford University Press, 1998), 10.

55. Nancy Abelmann and John Lie, *Blue Dreams: Korean Americans and the Los Angeles Riots* (Cambridge, MA: Harvard University Press, 1995), 153–54.

56. For an excellent critical reflection that seriously accounts for the ambivalence of the riots in terms of racial/class/ethnicity, refer to a one-woman performance and also the text version by Anna Deavere Smith, *Twilight: Los Angeles, 1992* (New York: Doubleday, 1994).

57. Howard Winant, *The New Politics of Race: Globalism, Difference, Justice* (Minneapolis: University of Minnesota Press, 2004), 205–7. This is an excellent analysis on how and why race still remains. Winant examines the complexity of the origins and the nature of racial politics that still continue to pervade identity, social structures, and political processes.

58. Park, *Racial Conflict*, 26.

59. Rey Chow, *The Protestant Ethnic and The Spirit of Capitalism* (New York: Columbia University Press, 2002), 148.

Chapter 3: Postcolonial Theory and Korean American Theology

1. Henry Giroux, cultural critic, remarks that identity politics enabled many formerly silenced and displaced groups to emerge from the margins of power and dominant culture to reassert and reclaim suppressed identities and experiences; yet in the process they often substituted one master narrative for another and moreover went on to suppress differences within their own "liberative" narratives. In his writing, Giroux urges those who are involved in resistance to construct a notion of border identity that challenges any essentialized notion of subjectivity while simultaneously demonstrating that the self "as a historical and cultural formation is shaped in complex related and multiple ways through its interaction with numerous and diverse communities." Henry A. Giroux, "Living Dangerously: Identity Politics and the New Cultural Racism," in *Between Borders: Pedagogy and the Politics of Cultural Studies*, ed. Henry A. Giroux and Peter McLaren (New York: Routledge, 1994), 38.

2. Michael Omi and Howard Winant, *Racial Formation in the United States: From the 1960s to the 1990s* (New York: Routledge, 1994), 12.

3. Ibid., 56.

4. Ibid., 65–66.

5. Ibid., 70.

6. Charles W. Mills, *The Racial Contract* (Ithaca, NY: Cornell University Press, 1997), 126.

7. Giroux, "Living Dangerously," 40.

8. Ibid., 50.

9. Gayatri Spivak, *In Other Worlds: Essays in Cultural Politics* (New York: Routledge, 1988), 202.

10. R. Radhakrishnan, *Diasporic Mediations: Between Home and Location* (Minneapolis: University of Minnesota Press, 1996), 166.

11. Lisa Lowe, *Immigrant Acts: On Asian American Cultural Politics* (Durham, NC: Duke University Press, 1996), 64.

12. For an interesting mathematical take on "borders/limits" see *Border Theory: The Limits of Cultural Politics*, ed. Scott Michaelsen and David E. Johnson (Minneapolis: University of Minnesota Press, 1997). Patricia Seed here notes, "Boundary values are mathematical solutions in the form of differential equations that must satisfy two distinct requirements. First, the equation must describe how a quantity behaves in a region . . . second, condition defines its complexity. The boundary value must also either describe the future behavior

of a function or characterize the influence from the outside region . . . on a mathematical boundary value-describes the inside while simultaneously characterizing the influences from the outside," 5.

13. Lowe, *Immigrant Acts*, 66–67.
14. Gayatri Spivak, "Subaltern Studies: Deconstructing Historiography," in *In Other Worlds*, 211.
15. Spivak's postcolonial theory seems much more complex and layered than the others due to her acknowledgment that not all Western influence should be considered negative. She does not see colonial history as an uninterrupted narrative of oppression and exploitation. Thus, she insists on the paradox of "enabling violence" or "enabling violation." See Spivak, "Bonding in Difference: Interview with Alfred Arteaga," in *The Spivak Reader*, ed. Donna Landry and Gerald MacLean (New York: Routledge, 1996), 19.
16. Cf. Lowe, *Immigrant Acts*, 82. Stuart Hall, "Cultural Identity and Diaspora," in *Identity: Community, Culture, Difference*, ed. Jonathan Rutherford (London: Lawrence and Wishart, 1990), 226.
17. Lowe, *Immigrant Acts*, 82.
18. Susan Stanford Friedman, *Mappings: Feminism and the Cultural Geographies of Encounter* (Princeton, NJ: Princeton University Press, 1998), 63–66.
19. Ibid., 89–91.
20. Homi Bhabha, *The Location of Culture* (New York: Routledge, 1994), 7.
21. Ibid., 114.
22. Ibid.
23. Ibid., 86.
24. Ibid.
25. Anne McClintock, *Imperial Leather: Race, Gender and Sexuality in the Colonial Contest* (New York: Routledge, 1995), 63.
26. Ibid., 64.
27. Ibid., 63.
28. Ibid., 64. McClintock also notes that Bhabha effectively "re-inscribes mimicry as a male strategy" without acknowledging its gendered specificity. As a result, the "Man" in "Of Mimicry and Man" both conceals and reveals his implicit reification of gender power so that "masculinity becomes the invisible norm of postcolonial discourse."
29. Bhabha, *The Location of Culture*, 90.
30. Mimicry often seems to be at its most acute awareness in writings and films/art and in avant-garde performances. Traditional mask-dance performance in Korea is often used to mimic, ridicule, transgress, mock, and accent the fissures and fractures between the rich and the poor. In avant-garde writings and films, we often witness transgression and mimicry of the status quo (gender, class, race, sexuality) that is less homage and more of a critical menace. One area of art/performance that interests me is the tradition of the jester/comic/comedienne. During my visit to one of the better-known comedy clubs in New York City, I witnessed firsthand the power of mimicry in performance. The comedienne performs as a catalyst while the audience also performs through its response. The comedienne uses the power of mimicry to ridicule, transgress, brutally portray, induce acute discomfort, evoke outrage and outrageously offend, leaving people somewhere between hilarity and tears. Through the power of mimicry then, the thrill of recognition and the pain of disavowal pull us.

31. Bhabha, *The Location of Culture*, 88.

32. Ibid., 121.

33. See Homi Bhabha, "Signs Taken for Wonders: Questions of Ambivalence and Authority under a Tree Outside Delhi, May 1817," in *"Race," Writing, and Difference*, ed. Henry Louis Gates Jr. (Chicago: University of Chicago Press, 1985), 163–84.

34. Bhabha, *The Location of Culture*, 120.

35. Ibid., 185.

36. Ibid., 2.

37. Ibid., 207.

38. Ibid., 1.

39. Martin Heidegger, *Poetry, Language, Thought* (New York: Perennial, 2001), 141–60 in Bhabha, *The Location of Culture*, 207.

40. Bhabha, *The Location of Culture*, 37.

41. Amritjit Singh and Peter Schmidt, "On the Borders Between U.S. Studies and Postcolonial Theory," in *Postcolonial Theory and the United States: Race, Ethnicity, and Literature*, ed. Amritjit Singh and Peter Schmidt (Jackson: University Press of Mississippi, 2000), 23.

42. Bhabha, *The Location of Culture*, 185.

43. Ibid., 114.

44. Trinh Minh-ha, *When the Moon Waxes Red: Representation, Gender and Cultural Politics* (New York: Routledge, 1991).

45. Ibid., 159.

46. Trinh Minh-ha, *Woman, Native, Other: Writing Postcoloniality and Feminism* (Bloomington: Indiana University Press, 1989), 89.

47. Ibid.

48. Trinh, *When the Moon Waxes Red*, 17.

49. Ibid., 108.

50. Trinh Minh-ha, *Cinema Interval* (New York: Routledge, 1999), 27.

51. Trinh Minh-ha, *Framer Framed* (New York: Routledge, 1992), 141.

52. Trinh, *Cinema Interval*, 10–49.

53. Trinh, *Woman, Native, Other*, 28.

54. Julia Kristeva not only reflects on the speaking subject-in-process, but recently her works have focused on the encounter between that subject with internal and external forms of otherness. This particular work stretches the scope from the personal to the political, which seems to resonate with Trinh Minh-ha's observation that the self is multiple from within as much as it is induced from the outer spheres. Refer to Julia Kristeva, *Strangers to Ourselves*.

55. Although this essay is in response to *Dictee*, Kim articulates the problem of identity politics from a Korean American perspective. Elaine Kim, "Poised on the In-between: A Korean American's Reflections on Theresa Hak-Kyung Cha's *Dictee*," in *Writing Self/Writing Nation: Essays on Theresa Hak-Kyung Cha's Dictee*, ed. Elaine H. Kim and Norma Alarcon (Berkeley, CA: Third Women Press, 1994), 1–30.

56. Radhakrishnan, *Diasporic Mediations*, 161.

57. Homi Bhabha, "The World in the Home," in McClintock et al., *Dangerous Liaisons: Gender, Nation, and Postcolonial Perspectives* (Minneapolis: University of Minnesota Press, 1997), 445–54.

58. Homi Bhabha, "Culture's In-Between," in *The Question of Cultural Identity*, ed. Stuart Hall and Paul du Gay (London: Sage Publications, 1996), 58.

59. Bhabha, *The Location of Culture*, 120.

60. Fumitaka Matsuoka, *Out of Silence: Emerging Themes in Asian American Churches* (Cleveland: United Church Press, 1995), 59.

61. Ibid., 62.

62. Jung Young Lee, *Marginality: The Key to Multicultural Theology* (Minneapolis: Fortress Press, 1995), 31.

63. Ibid., 46.

64. Cf. Peter C. Phan, *Christianity with an Asian Face: Asian American Theology in the Making* (New York: Orbis Books, 2003).

65. Lee, *Marginality*, 50.

66. Ibid., 53.

67. Ibid., 60.

68. Ibid., 61.

69. Ibid., 67.

70. Ibid., 70.

71. Anselm Kyongsuk Min, "The Political Economy of Marginality: Comments on Jung Young Lee," *Journal of Asian and Asian American Theology* 1, no.1 (Summer 1998): 84. For further critique of the need to "transcend" particularity and difference within theological reflections, see his most recent and excellent book, *The Solidarity of Others in a Divided World: A Postmodern Theology After Postmodernism* (London: T. & T. Clark, 2004).

72. Ibid., 86.

73. Min, "Political Economy," 91.

74. For discussions on "the postcolonial," see Stuart Hall, "When Was 'The Post-colonial'? Thinking at the Limit," *The Post-colonial Question: Common Skies/Divided Horizons*, ed. Iain Chambers and Lidia Curtis (New York: Routledge, 1996), 242–60.

75. Peter van der Veer, "'The Enigma of Arrival': Hybridity and Authenticity in the Global Space," *Debating Cultural Hybridity: Multi-Cultural Identities and the Politics of Anti-racism*, ed. Pnina Werbner and Tariq Modood (London: Zed Books, 1997), 105.

76. Aijaz Ahmad, *In Theory* (New York: Verso, 1992). See also *Debating Cultural Hybridity*, ed. Werbner and Modood.

77. Bart Moore-Gilbert, *The Postcolonial Theory: Contexts, Practices, Politics* (New York: Verso, 1997), 12–20.

78. Pnina Werbner, "The Dialectics of Cultural Hybridity," in Werbner and Modood, *Debating Cultural Hybridity*, 19. Cf. Chandra Talpade Mohanty, "Feminist Encounters: Locating the Politics of Experience," in *Destabilizing Theory: Contemporary Feminist Debates*, ed. Michele Barrett and Anne Phillips (Stanford, CA: Stanford University Press, 1992), 74–92.

79. Said further notes in a similar vein, in a metaphorical sense to theory, that the "exile for the intellectual in this metaphysical sense is restlessness, movement, constantly being unsettled, and unsettling others. You cannot go back to some earlier and perhaps more stable condition of being at home; and, alas, you can never fully arrive, be at one with your new home or situation." See Edward Said, "Intellectual Exile: Expatriates and Marginals," in *The Edward Said Reader*, ed. Moustafa Bayoumi and Andrew Rubin (New York: Vintage Books, 2000), 368–81.

80. Robert J. Young, *Postcolonialism: An Historical Introduction* (Oxford: Blackwell, 2001).

81. Moore-Gilbert, *The Postcolonial Theory*, 168.

82. For more on the politics of rewriting and unwriting, refer to Jacques Derrida, *Dissemination*, trans. Barbara Johnson (Chicago: University of Chicago Press, 1981).

83. Pnina Werbner, "Essentialising Essentialism, Essentialising Silence: Ambivalence and Multiplicity in the Constructions of Racism and Ethnicity," in *Debating Cultural Hybridity*, ed. Werbner and Modood, 249.

84. Bhabha, *The Location of Culture*, 19.

85. Ibid., 22.

86. Ibid., 25.

87. Ibid.

Chapter 4: The Crucified God

1. Anthony W. Bartlett, *Cross-Purposes: The Violent Grammar of Christian Atonement* (Philadelphia: Trinity Press International, 2001), 2.

2. Ibid., 258.

3. Ibid., 262.

4. Mark Lewis Taylor, *The Executed God: The Way of the Cross in Lockdown America* (Minneapolis: Fortress Press, 2001), xiii.

5. Ibid., 2.

6. Ibid., 3.

7. Ibid., 2.

8. Ibid., 6.

9. Ibid., 7.

10. Ibid., 14.

11. Ibid., 15.

12. Ibid., 71.

13. Ibid., 85.

14. Ibid., 108.

15. Herbert Marcuse, *Eros and Civilization: A Philosophical Inquiry into Freud* (Boston: Beacon Press, 1966), 70, 71.

16. Ibid., 71.

17. Taylor, *The Executed God*, 118.

18. Ibid., 158.

19. Homi Bhabha, *The Location of Culture* (New York: Routledge, 1994), 86.

20. See also Richard Horsley, *Jesus and Empire: The Kingdom of God and the New World Disorder* (Minneapolis: Fortress Press, 2003).

21. Jürgen Moltmann, *The Crucified God: The Cross of Christ as the Foundation and Criticism of Christian Theology* (Minneapolis: Fortress Press, 1993), 203.

22. Ibid., 243.

23. In his theology of the cross, despite its emphasis that the event is Trinitarian, Moltmann does not dwell much on the power of the Spirit. This is surprising since it is my contention that the Spirit works as the semiotic power that becomes present in Jesus. Moltmann does, however, examine the role and power of the Spirit in his later works on pneumatology.

24. Ibid., 246.

25. Ibid., 204.

26. Ibid., 205.

27. C. S. Song, *Jesus: The Crucified People* (New York: Crossroad, 1990), 98.

28. Song, *Jesus*, 98–99.

29. Geiko Muller-Fahrenholz, *The Kingdom and The Power: The Theology of Jürgen Moltmann* (Minneapolis: Fortress Press, 2001), 72.

30. Jürgen Moltmann, *The Way of Jesus Christ: Christology in Messianic Dimensions* (San Francisco: Harper, 1990), 166.

31. Ibid., 167.

32. Catherine Keller, *Face of the Deep: A Theology of Becoming* (London: Routledge, 2003), 226.

33. Darby Kathleen Ray, *Deceiving the Devil: Atonement, Abuse, and Ransom* (Cleveland: Pilgrim Press, 1998), 93.

34. Moltmann, *The Crucified God*, 207.

35. Keller, *Face of the Deep*, 226.

36. Moltmann, *The Crucified God*, 227.

37. Ibid., 252.

38. Rebecca S. Chopp, *The Praxis of Suffering: An Interpretation of Liberation and Political Theologies* (New York: Orbis Books, 1986), 107.

39. Ibid., 108.

40. Ibid.

41. Moltmann, *The Way of Jesus Christ*, 153–55.

42. Ray, *Deceiving the Devil*, 88.

43. Moltmann, *The Way of Jesus Christ*, 152.

44. Ibid., 173.

45. Ibid.

46. Ibid., 173–176.

47. For an excellent and inspiring reading of this from a deconstructivist perspective, see the concluding chapter, "A Passion for God," in John Caputo's *The Prayers and Tears of Jacques Derrida: Religion without Religion* (Bloomington: Indiana University Press, 1997), 331–39.

48. Ibid., 116.

49. Ray, *Deceiving the Devil*, 88.

50. Muller-Fahrenholz, *The Kingdom*, 78.

51. Dorothee Soelle, *Suffering* (Philadelphia: Fortress Press, 1975), 32. She further notes that "explanation of suffering that looks away from the victim and identifies itself with a righteousness that is supposed to stand behind the suffering has already taken a step in the direction of theological sadism, which wants to understand God as the torturer."

52. Keller, *Face of the Deep*, 220.

53. Soelle, *Suffering*, 19.

54. Ibid.

55. For more, refer to works of Michel Foucault, especially *Discipline and Punish: The Birth of the Prison*, trans. Alan Sheridan (New York: Vintage Books, 1995).

56. Soelle, *Suffering*, 28.

57. Ibid.,108.

58. Moltmann, *The Way of Jesus Christ*, 176.

59. Elisabeth Schüssler Fiorenza, *Jesus: Miriam's Child, Sophia's Prophet: Critical Issues in Feminist Christology* (New York: Continuum, 1994), 106.

60. Ibid., 102.

61. Jung Ha Kim, *Bridge-Makers and Cross-Bearers: Korean American Women and the Church* (Atlanta: Scholars Press, 1997), 82.

62. Ibid.

63. Ham Sok Hon, "Kicked by God," trans. Douglas V. Steere (Pendleton, PA: The Wilder Quaker Fellowship, 1969). http://www2.gol.com/users/quakers/Kicked_by_god.htm (accessed March 6, 2006).

64. As this book was published after the manuscript was written, I was not able to do full justice to the text but simply note her critical and important work on the complexity of power and "submission." Cf. Sarah Coakley, *Powers and Submissions: Spirituality, Philosophy and Gender* (Oxford: Blackwell, 2002).

65. Ibid., 4–5.

66. Julia Kristeva, *Powers of Horror: An Essay on Abjection*, trans. Leon S. Roudiez (New York: Columbia University Press, 1982), 11.

67. Soelle, *Suffering*, 164.

68. Catherine Keller, "Pneumatic Nudges: The Theology of Moltmann," in *The Future of Theology: Essays in Honor of Jürgen Moltmann*, ed. Miroslav Volf, Carmen Krieg, and Thomas Kucharz (Grand Rapids, MI: Wm. B. Eerdmans, 1996), 149.

69. Elizabeth A. Johnson, *She Who Is: The Mystery of God in Feminist Theological Discourse* (New York: Crossroad, 1994), 253.

70. Ibid., 263.

71. Ibid., 265.

72. Wendy Farley, *Tragic Vision and Divine Compassion: A Contemporary Theodicy* (Louisville, KY: Westminster/John Knox Press, 1990), 81.

73. Johnson, *She Who Is*, 269.

74. For a critical postcolonial reading of Sophia as "figure of the multiple others that haunt not only theological systems, but social ones as well," see Mayra Rivera, "God at the Crossroads: A Postcolonial Reading of Sophia," in *Postcolonial Theologies: Divinity and Empire*, ed. Catherine Keller, Michael Nausner, and Mayra Rivera (St. Louis, MO: Chalice Press, 2004), 186–203.

75. Anne McClintock, *Imperial Leather: Race, Gender and Sexuality in the Colonial Context* (New York: Routledge, 1995), 71.

76. Ibid.

77. Kristeva, *Powers of Horror*, 4.

78. Ibid., 9.

Chapter 5: A Christology of *Jeong*

1. Grace M. Jantzen, *Becoming Divine: Towards a Feminist Philosophy of Religion* (Bloomington: Indiana University Press, 1999), 3.

2. Ibid.

3. Anne McClintock, *Imperial Leather: Race, Gender and Sexuality in the Colonial Context* (New York: Routledge, 1995), 71.

4. Ibid.

5. Julia Kristeva, *Powers of Horror: An Essays on Abjection*, trans. Leon S. Roudiez (New York: Columbia University Press, 1982), 9. The Oedipus complex attempts to account for the emergence of the speaking subject. This psychic process has been traditionally understood as divided into two stages: presubjectivity and the period following that allows entrance to the symbolic at the cost of abjecting and/or repressing the semiotic.

6. This symbolic realm is that of self-awareness, all that is differentiated and of the fully conscious subjectivity.

7. Much of Kristeva's concept of the symbolic/Law of the Fathers comes from Jacques Lacan. Her acceptance of his articulation of this idea is problematic to many feminists. Foremost is his acceptance of the dominance of the phallus as the ultimate and given symbol to which women must enter. Ironically, women, when we do enter, must enter by becoming like men. Thus, women do not and cannot, according to Lacan, speak as women. Kristeva's acceptance of this is

problematic because she also argues in *The Revolution of Poetic Language* that women cannot really speak as women. For an excellent overview of Lacanian thought, in addition to Kristeva's point of alignment and departure from Lacan, refer to Jantzen, *Becoming Divine*.

8. It is often understood as the inverse of the symbolic realm, for it is marked by chaos, irrationalism, and emotionalism. Such qualities have traditionally been marginalized and repressed into the unconscious.

9. A. K. M. Adam, ed., *Handbook of Postmodern Biblical Interpretation* (St. Louis: Chalice Press, 2000), 144–50.

10. As much as my call for *jeong* could be critiqued as essentialist, so too is Kristeva often accused of essentialising women with what has been critiqued as her identification of semiotics with the maternal body.

11. Jantzen, *Becoming Divine*, 4.

12. Jantzen, *Becoming Divine*, 15.

13. Re-imagining Revival, St. Paul, MN, April 16–19, 1998.

14. Elisabeth Schüssler Fiorenza, *Jesus: Miriam's Child, Sophia's Prophet: Critical Issues in Feminist Christology* (New York: Continuum, 1994), 133.

15. Ibid., 139.

16. Jantzen, *Becoming Divine*, 107.

17. Ibid.

18. Ibid., 16.

19. Ibid.

20. Ibid.

21. Ibid., 17.

22. For a critical postcolonial reading of the incarnation as divine economy see Marion Grau, "Divine Commerce: A Postcolonial Christology for Times of Neocolonial Empire," in *Postcolonial Theologies: Divinity and Empire*, ed. Catherine Keller, Michael Nausner, and Mayra Rivera (St. Louis, MO: Chalice Press, 2004), 164–84.

23. Cf. Joy Morny, Kathleen O'Grady, and Judith L. Poxon, eds., *Religion in French Feminist Thought: Critical Perspectives* (New York: Routledge, 2003).

24. For a similar but not identifiable reconfiguration of my Christology from a womanist perspective, see JoAnne Marie Terrell, *Power in the Blood? The Cross in the African American Experience* (New York: Orbis Books, 1998).

25. Darby Kathleen Ray, *Deceiving the Devil: Atonement, Abuse, and Ransom* (Cleveland: Pilgrim Press, 1998), 56.

26. Again, see more in Sarah Coakley's nuanced interpretations of power and submission through her analysis of *kenosis* in *Powers and Submissions: Spirituality, Philosophy, and Gender* (Oxford: Blackwell, 2002).

27. Delores S. Williams, *Sisters in the Wilderness: The Challenge of Womanist God-Talk* (New York: Orbis Books, 1993), 143–70.

28. Ray, *Deceiving the Devil*, 105.

29. Ibid.

30. Joanne Carlson Brown and Rebecca Parker, "For God So Loved the World?" in *Christianity, Patriarchy and Abuse: A Feminist Critique*, ed. Joanne Carlson Brown and Carole Bohn (New York: Pilgrim Press, 1989), 1–30.

31. J. Denny Weaver, *The Nonviolent Atonement* (Grand Rapids: Wm. B. Eerdmans Publishing Co., 2001), 138–43.

32. Rita Nakashima Brock, *Journeys by Heart: A Christology of Erotic Power* (New York: Crossroad, 1988), 55–56.

33. Ibid., xiv.

34. Ibid., xv.
35. Ibid., 60.
36. Ibid., 105.
37. Ibid., 67.
38. Ibid., 103.
39. Jantzen, *Becoming Divine*, 160.
40. Ibid., 161.
41. Ibid., 163.
42. Ibid., 182. Moreover, Jantzen's concept of the "chiasmus" is interesting to point out here in light of our earlier discussion of the cross in Christology. The chiasmus is a figure taken from the Greek letter *X*, which shows a "crossing-over." Jantzen cites Derrida, noting that chiasm is "the figure of the double-gesture, the intersection." It is the dominant sign both always and already situated. Yet, also paradoxically, it is intersected by its own "undoing," which *opens a gap* for thinking differently. For that reason, this notion of the chiasmus can work in conjunction with the postcolonial mimicry in our understanding of the cross as a subversive form of projection and imagination.
43. See also Kwok Pui-lan and Laura E. Donaldson, eds., *Postcolonialism, Feminism, and Religious Discourse* (New York: Routledge, 2002).
44. Kwok Pui-lan, *Postcolonial Imagination and Feminist Theology* (Louisville, KY: Westminster John Knox Press, 2005).
45. Ibid., 168.
46. For an excellent discussion, from an entirely different angle, on the historical development that led from the earthly Jesus of Nazareth to the divine Christ of orthodox Christian faith, refer to John Hick, *The Metaphor of God Incarnate: Christology in a Pluralistic Age* (Louisville, KY: Westminster/John Knox Press, 1993).
47. Kwok, *Postcolonial Imagination*, 168–85.
48. Kwok Pui-lan, *Introducing Asian Feminist Theology* (Cleveland: Pilgrim Press, 2000), 80.
49. Ibid., 93.
50. C. S. Song, *Jesus: The Crucified People* (New York: Crossroad, 1990), 215.
51. Ibid., 52–53.
52. Leonardo Boff, *Passion of Christ, Passion of the World* (New York: Orbis Books, 1987), 72.
53. Leonardo Boff, *Jesus Christ Liberator* (New York: Orbis Books, 1978), 25–26.
54. Andrew Sung Park, *The Wounded Heart of God: The Asian Concept of Han and the Christian Doctrine of Sin* (Nashville: Abingdon Press, 1993), 69.
55. Ibid., 72.
56. Ibid., 74.
57. Ibid., 77.
58. Ibid., 101.
59. Kelly Oliver, *Reading Kristeva: Unraveling the Double-Bind* (Bloomington: Indiana University Press, 1993), 67–68.
60. Park, *The Wounded Heart of God*, 112.
61. Ibid., 118.
62. Ibid., 121.
63. Ibid.
64. Edward F. Edinger, *The New God-Image: A Study of Jung's Key Letters Concerning the Evolution of the Western God-Image*, (Wilmette, IL: Chiron Publications, 1996). Refer especially to chapters 5 and 6.

65. Gianni Vattimo, "The Trace of the Trace," in *Religion: Cultural Memory in the Present*, ed. Jacques Derrida and Gianni Vattimo (Stanford, CA: Stanford University Press, 1998), 79.

66. Dorothee Soelle, *Suffering* (Philadelphia: Fortress Press, 1975), 164.

67. Catherine Keller, *From A Broken Web: Separation, Sexism, and Self* (Boston: Beacon Press, 1986), 94.

68. According to object-relations theory regarding the formation of the id, the mother, erased from the process, comes to pose a primal threat to the smooth becoming of a healthy ego as it attempts to become an integral part of the symbolic/Law of the Fathers, for the abject/semiotic continues to haunt at the edges of the psyche.

69. Virginia Burrus, *"Begotten, Not Made": Conceiving Manhood in Late Antiquity* (Stanford, CA: Stanford University Press, 2000), 158, 189.

70. Jan Campbell, *Arguing with the Phallus: Feminist, Queer and Postcolonial Theory* (London: Zed Books, 2000), 30.

71. Ibid.

72. Kristeva, *Powers of Horror*, 209.

73. Ibid., 9.

74. This doubleness is like Jantzen's reference to the chiasmus performing a double gesture, embodying both homage and menace.

75. The irrepressible semiotic "jouissance" is the power that disrupts and transgresses the symbolic order.

76. Martha J. Reineke, *Sacrificed Lives: Kristeva on Women and Violence* (Bloomington: Indiana University Press, 1997), 24.

77. Jantzen, *Becoming Divine*, 198.

78. Marcella Althaus-Reid, *Indecent Theology: Theological Perversions in Sex, Gender and Politics* (London: Routledge, 2000), 119. Marcella Althaus-Reid's articulation of the "Indecent Jesus" seems to point to the necessity of recognizing and bringing into the christological framework that which is abject, indecent, "perverted." By articulating the need for a Bi/Christ, Althaus-Reid seeks an "imprecise Christology," for she argues that the precision of traditional Christology is problematized by its adherence and reliance to an either/or symbolism as well as political economy. Imprecision, on the other hand, brings forth that which has been repressed as indecent and decentered. She goes on to argue that as the Bi/Christ category is "unsettled. . . . Bi/Christology walks like a nomad in lands of opposition and exclusive identities. . . ." For her, not only has the reliance on either/or cleaned Christology of sexuality and indecency, but also love. Her insistence on highlighting indecency is closely tied to abjection and indeed *jeong*. For she asks, "Why either/or? Why choose between agapian or erotic love?"

79. Julia Kristeva, "Stabat Mater," in *The Kristeva Reader*, ed. Toril Moi (New York: Columbia University Press, 1986), 160–86. Again, what is questionable about Kristeva's own work is the emphasis on pregnancy. Perhaps a wider and more promising take on this might be found through emphasis not on the biological pregnancy of the female but on birthing creativity in different ways. We are not only reduced to biological generativity but to creativity.

80. Kristeva, *Powers of Horror*, 1.

81. Ibid., 15.

82. Ibid., 5.

83. Anne McClintock makes a very interesting analysis of Kristeva's abjection as it is rendered in various forms and processes: differentiations such as abject objects,

states, and zones, and the appointed agents, psychic processes, and political processes of abjection, to name several. Refer to McClintock's *Imperial Leather.*

84. Ibid., 71.
85. Kristeva, *Powers of Horror*, 9.
86. In reading Kristeva's notion of the abject, McClintock illustrates that abjection is "that liminal state that hovers on the threshold of body and body politics— and thus on the boundary between psychoanalysis and history." As the never-departed part of the self, the abject lives on the edges of our inner consciousness always to return unexpectedly and unsuspectedly.
87. Martha Reineke, *Sacrificed Lives: Kristeva on Women and Violence* (Bloomington: Indiana University Press, 1997), 22.
88. Elizabeth Grosz, *Sexual Subversions: Three French Feminists* (London: Allen and Unwin, 1989), 71–76.
89. Kristeva, *Powers of Horror*, 140.
90. Ibid.
91. Oliver, *Reading Kristeva*, 56.
92. Kristeva, *Powers of Horror*, 119.
93. Ibid., 125.
94. Chung Hyun Kyung, *The Struggle to Be the Sun Again: Introducing Asian Women's Theology* (New York: Orbis Books, 1990), 63. See also Chung Hyun Kyung, "Who Is Jesus Christ for Asian Women?" *Asian Faces of Jesus*, ed. R. S. Sugirtharajah (New York: Orbis Books, 1999), 223–46. Liberation theologians like Boff have argued for the subversive nature of the cross by insisting that it is both a sign of the imperial power but also that of profound solidarity. Similarly, Korean feminist theologian Chung writes, "Many Asian women portray Jesus with the image of the mother. They see Jesus as a compassionate one, who feels the suffering of humanity deeply, suffers and weeps with them. . . . Jesus felt the pain of all humanity like a compassionate mother. . . . We may call Jesus the 'woman Messiah'" (*The Struggle to Be the Sun Again*, 63).
95. Song, *Jesus: The Crucified People*, 226. In addition, Song notes that in the figure of the Christa, the Christ symbol becomes female. His argument is similar to other versions of Christology "from-below" in that Jesus on the cross is the suffering "crucified people."
96. Julia Kristeva, *Tales of Love*, trans. Leon S. Roudiez (New York: Columbia University Press, 1987), 368.
97. Ibid., 4.
98. Oliver, *Reading Kristeva*, 122.
99. Kristeva, *Tales of Love*, 15.
100. Julia Kristeva, *In the Beginning Was Love: Psychoanalysis and Faith*, trans. Arthur Goldhammer (New York: Columbia University Press, 1987), 39–41.
101. Oliver, *Reading Kristeva*, 126.
102. Ibid., 65.
103. Kristeva, *Tales of Love*, 262.
104. Oliver, *Reading Kristeva*, 66. Is it then so far-fetched to imagine this pregnancy and birth in the dynamism of Jesus' birth as the Semiotic/Spirit/Sophia incarnate? The Word becoming flesh that dwelt among us?
105. As I pointed out earlier, Kristeva appears to come dangerously close to biological essentialism.
106. For a different yet similar take on the same mandate to love the neighbor as one's self, see Emmanuel Levinas, *Totality and Affinity: An Essay on Exteriority*

(Pittsburgh: Duquesne University Press, 1969) and *Otherwise than Being or Beyond Essence*, trans. Alphonso Lingis (The Hague: Nijhoff, 1981).

107. Oliver, *Reading Kristeva*, 67.
108. Ibid., 68.
109. Kristeva, In *the Beginning Was Love*, 25.
110. Ibid., 40.
111. Many feminist theologians articulating Sophia Christology, I suggest, are attempting precisely this task of recognizing a "fusion" that is embedded in the feminine divine. Theologians like Elizabeth A. Johnson explicitly name Jesus-Sophia as "She Who Is." Nonfeminist conservative faith groups that experience extreme difficulty in accepting any feminine dimension to the Divine have received the emergence of Sophia Christology with mounting hysteria.
112. Kristeva, *In the Beginning Was Love*, 41.
113. Ibid., 40.
114. Ibid., 41.

Conclusion: Heart of the Cross

1. John D. Caputo, *The Prayers and Tears of Jacques Derrida: Religion without Religions* (Bloomington: Indiana University Press, 1997), 336.
2. The Hebrew notion of *hesed* resonates with the complexity of relational *jeong*, which is also somewhat identifiable with *pathos*.
3. *Han* as a concept is much more complex and has layers, such as *won-han, jeong-han*, and *hu-han*, which will not discussed here. Furthermore, at a certain depth experience of *han*, a creative energy can be channeled. It is my suggestion that this is where *jeong* exists simultaneously with *han*. For excellent artistic embodiments of *han* and *jeong* refer to four recent films: *The Way Home, Joint Security Area, Sopyonje*, and *301/302*.
4. Rey Chow, *The Protestant Ethnic and the Spirit of Capitalism* (New York: Columbia University Press, 2002), 28.
5. In turn, women's reliance on traditional shamanistic rituals as a form of unraveling *han* has been regarded with suspicion and disdain in addition to falling under the penetrating gaze of patriarchal disciplinary measures. It is also important to keep in mind that the influence of Western Christianity and imperialism also have to do with the demonization of traditional shamanic practices that embodied the semiotic.
6. Jae Hoon Lee, *The Exploration of Inner Wounds—Han* (Atlanta: Scholars Press, 1994), 153.
7. The three characters representing heart, clarity, and vulnerability were not difficult to decipher. However, I am deeply indebted to Buddhist scholar, mentor, and colleague Dr. Hyun Choi for this particular deconstructive insight to life and "something arising." Her persistence in tracing as far as possible the origin of the words in their underived forms added this crucial component to my study.
8. There are multiple contours to the concept of *jeong* for Koreans. *Minjung Essence Korean-English Dictionary* only makes notation of three derivatives of *jeong*: (1) *ae-jeong*, which comes very close to the idea of affection that emerges out of relationship with one's spouse/partner, between parent and child, and between people in an intimate relationship (not necessarily sexual); (2) *ihn-jeong*, which means compassion, sympathy, or, as I maintain, a recognition of one's humanity in the face of the Other; and (3) *gahm-jeong*, which means feelings or intuition within a relationship.

9. Anne Carson, *Eros the Bittersweet* (Princeton, NJ: Princeton University Press, 1998), 3–16.

10. Jean-Paul Sartre, *Being and Nothingness* (New York: H. E. Barnes, 1956), 606–7.

11. Carson, *Eros*, 45.

12. Peter Hodgson, *Winds of the Spirit: A Constructive Christian Theology* (Louisville, KY: Westminster John Knox Press, 1994), 97.

13. Lee, *The Exploration of Inner Wounds*, 71–75.

14. John P. Keenan, *The Gospel of Mark: A Mahayana Reading* (New York: Orbis Books, 1995), 187.

15. Catherine Keller, *Face of the Deep: A Theology of Becoming* (London: Routledge, 2003), 227.

16. Andrew Sung Park, *The Wounded Heart of God: The Asian Concept of Han and the Christian Doctrine of Sin* (Nashville: Abingdon Press, 1993), 139.

17. Ibid., 140.

18. Again, for more feminist reconfigurations of *kenosis*, refer to Sarah Coakley, *Powers and Submissions: Spirituality, Philosophy and Gender* (Oxford: Blackwell Publishers, 2002).

19. John P. Keenan, *The Meaning of Christ: A Mahayana Theology* (New York: Orbis Books, 1993), 353.

20. Richard A. Horsley, *Jesus and Empire: The Kingdom of God and the New World Disorder* (Minneapolis, MN: Fortress, 2003), 15–54.

21. While Mark and Matthew do not do this, Matthew in chapter 27 portrays what I understand as possible cause of *han* in Judas's own life.

22. The significance of this account from Mark 14:3–10 is the basis of Elisabeth Schüssler Fiorenza's *In Memory of Her: A Feminist Theological Reconstruction of Christian Origins* (New York: Crossroad, 1983).

23. Angela Y. Davis, *Blues Legacies and Black Feminism: Gertrude "Ma" Rainey, Bessie Smith and Billie Holiday* (New York: Pantheon Books, 1998).

24. *SOPYONJE*, 1992.

25. Feminist Iris Marion Young further examines the debate regarding group identity, in this case that of the oppressed or the oppressor, and how, why, and when such collective identities come into power. By comparing the different ways that "difference" is used either to serve individual or collective needs, Young calls for what she calls an "unassimilated Otherness" that resonates with Whitehead's related entity. See Iris Marion Young, *Justice and the Politics of Difference* (Princeton, NJ: Princeton University Press, 1990).

26. A future trajectory for further research on *jeong* might be to enter into deeper conversation with Emmanuel Levinas's understanding of the self and other, especially on the mandate to "love your neighbor as your self" as another possible paradigm approach to theological anthropology.

27. Elizabeth A. Johnson, *She Who Is: The Mystery of God in Feminist Theological Discourse* (New York: Crossroad, 1994), 254.

28. Ibid., 269.

Index

Abelmann, N., 139 n.54
abjection (the abject), xiv, xxii–xxiii, xxv,
 xxvi, 19, 47, 54–55, 72, 74, 76–77,
 82–83, 87, 90, 91, 92, 96, 99, 101,
 105, 108, 113, 115, 119, 132 n.2,
 148–49 n.83, 149 n.86
 on cross, 109
 as narcissistic crisis, 110
Adam, A. K. M., 146 n.9
Address Unknown (film), 130 n.10
African Americans, 55, 126
 and Asians, 42–44, 46
agape, 120, 128
Ahmad, A., 66, 69, 142 n.76
Alcoff, L., 133 n.23
alterity, 8, 55
Althaus-Reid, M., 148 n.78
ambiguity, xv, 53
ambivalence, 15, 60, 62, 141 n.33
American dream, myth of, 41, 45, 47
Anselm. *See* atonement: Anselmic
antiessentialism, xxiv, 7, 134 n.33
 See also essentialism
Anzaldua, G., 32
apocalypse, 108
Appiah, K. A., 130 n.20
Armour, E. T., 5, 133 n.19
assimilation, 53, 59
atonement, xiii, xxii, 86–87, 97, 100, 111
 Anselmic, 72, 73, 95, 112

expiatory, x, xxv, 75, 84–85, 96
 nonviolent, 146 n.31
authenticity, 60, 142 n.75
authority, 53, 54, 57, 59, 131 n.36, 138
 n.49, 141 n.33
autobiography, xv, 129 n.7

"bad mother's breast." *See* negative
 mother complex
Bakhtin, M., xviii, 130 n.12
bamboo, empty. *See jook sing*
Bartlett, A. W., 71, 143 n.1
bell hooks, 17, 65, 136 n.82
belongingness, xviii
Benhabib, S., 13, 135 nn.57–58
"beyond," 16
Bhabha, H., 9, 39–40, 53,
 55–56, 59, 69, 131
 n.36, 138 nn.48–50,
 140 nn.20, 28–29; 141
 nn.31–34, 40, 42, 57–58;
 142 n.59, 143 nn.19, 84,
Bi/Christ, 148 n.78
bilanguaging. *See* language
binarity, 17, 64, 69
birthing creativity, 148 n.79
Black Christ, 101
body. *See* maternal body
Boff, L., 78–79, 102, 147
 nn.52–53

153